D1524285

Tropical Forests and the Human Spirit

Tropical Forests and the Human Spirit

Journeys to the Brink of Hope

Roger D. Stone and Claudia D'Andrea

UNIVERSITY OF CALIFORNIA PRESS

Berkeley   Los Angeles   London

University of California Press
Berkeley and Los Angeles, California

University of California Press, Ltd.
London, England

© 2001 by the Regents of the University of California

Library of Congress Cataloging-in-Publication Data

Stone, Roger D.
    Tropical forests and the human spirit : journeys to the
brink of hope / Roger D. Stone and Claudia D'Andrea.
        p. cm.
    Includes bibliographical references (p.).
    ISBN 0-520-21799-3 (cloth : alk. paper) —
ISBN 0-520-23089-2 (pbk. : alk. paper)
        1. Community forests—Tropics—Management.
    2. Forest management—Tropics—Citizen participation.
    3. Forest conservation—Tropics—Citizen participation.
    I. D'Andrea, Claudia, 1966–. II. Title.

    SD669 .S76 2001
    333.75'16'0913—dc21
                                            2001027613

Manufactured in the United States of America

10 09 08 07 06 05 04 03 02 01
10 9 8 7 6 5 4 3 2 1

The paper used in this publication is both acid-free and
totally chlorine-free (TCF). It meets the minimum requirements of ANSI/NISO Z39.48–1992 (R 1997) (*Permanence of
Paper*).

CONTENTS

ILLUSTRATIONS

MAPS

FIGURE

ACKNOWLEDGMENTS

Foremost, we would like to express deep thanks to the John D. and Catherine T. MacArthur Foundation, and especially to Dan Martin of what is now called its Program on Global Security and Sustainability. Without three years of MacArthur support to underwrite the time and extensive travel required to produce this book, it simply could not have been done. Participation in the activities of the World Commission on Forests and Sustainable Development, in many lands, was itself highly instructive and put us in touch with many very well informed experts on forests. The same is true of our close relationship with the International Union for the Conservation of Nature and Natural Resources, and especially its Working Group on Community Involvement in Forest Management, of the Asia Forest Network that Mark Poffenberger has for many years guided with great energy and skill, and of the "Forests Vision" gatherings at the Council on Foreign Relations that we have been privileged to attend.

The hundreds of people in many lands from whose knowledge we drew, often during the course of travels far off the beaten track, are listed in the book's chapters and chapter notes. Their friendship and generosity, and the lengths to which they often went to help us try to understand, are most greatly appreciated. None merit our respect and gratitude more fully than the community forest managers we met along the way. Were it not for their remarkable abilities, there would be no point to this book. And finally, we express our thanks to editor Howard Boyer, whose enthusiasm and quietly thoughtful guidance has been inspiring throughout.

INTRODUCTION

Three hundred and fifty million people living in or near forests depend heavily on them for income, food, fuel, medicines, and even spiritual well-being. Most of these people live in poor tropical or subtropical countries, as do most of the 2 *billion* people who rely less directly but hardly less importantly on the many goods and services that forests provide. Throughout history the world's powerful have often ignored the needs of these weaker elements of society, regarding forests as a commodity to be harvested rather than as a resource to be protected. Millennia ago the forests surrounding the Mediterranean were thus stripped. Economies and societies suffered, but no lessons were learned. During the past two centuries, especially after World War II, the world's tropical forests have undergone an equally systematic and devastating attack. Fully two-thirds of all the forests in South and Southeast Asia have vanished; some countries, such as the Philippines and Thailand, have virtually none left. Many African nations that once exported timber now import it and have formerly forested areas that have become desert. Central America and large portions of the South American continent have been ravaged.

Forty recent years of intensive government-mandated logging have caused a good part of the damage. So have myriad projects to convert once forested lands into plantation monocultures. In areas with rising populations, roads built by ranchers, loggers, and miners give home-steading migrant farm families access to forestland. Aid lenders and do-nors long encouraged commercial forestry. For many years nongovern-mental conservation organizations struggled to establish regulatory regimes that would protect wildlife and biological diversity and wildlife in some forests while ignoring the interests of local people. "We as-sumed that all community use was *over*use," admitted one high-ranking conservationist at a recent United Nations meeting. Almost everywhere in the tropical Southern Hemisphere, from the dawn of colonialism to this day, the state has ignored forest peoples' traditional ownership and user rights, typically claiming possession of all forestland and unilater-ally deciding what use to make of it. "Without significant change of direction," reports one analyst, "in fifty years much remaining tropical forest is likely to have been converted to other land uses or substantially degraded except in some large, very remote frontier areas of the western and northern Amazon, the Central Congo Basin, and some well-managed national parks and other reserves."[1]

Some people remain undisturbed. If we continue to do our forest business as we have, it is argued in some quarters, the world will grow its way out of the problem as the combination of economic expansion, industrialization, and urbanization leads to the restoration of healthy forests. In some areas, such as western Europe and the United States, forests are in fact returning as less and less land is needed for agriculture and forests naturally regenerate. The same transition is likely to occur in some other parts of the world, including Taiwan and certain of the fast-industrializing tropical nations of Southeast Asia. Long-departed wildlife species will reoccupy these newly reforested lands, as have the wild turkey, the black bear, the coyote, and the cougar in the eastern United States.

Some people depend on forest destruction. As long as there are trees to harvest, the $400 billion wood products industry and associated work-ers are beneficiaries. Profitable mining and oil exploration companies often must open the forest to do their work. So must those who cannot, in parts of the world where soils are good enough, grow sufficient food or raise livestock without cutting trees for farmland or mixed cropping systems. When they prove to be sustainable, the larger-scale farming activities that result from forest clearing can represent dramatic economic gains. The bountiful U.S. midwest, abnormally blessed with twelve feet of rich topsoil that had never been exploited before settlers arrived in the eighteenth and nineteenth centuries, is a case in point.

For most people in most places, however, tropical deforestation's consequences range from negative to catastrophic in political and economic, as well as in strictly ecological, senses. If stripping the tropical forests benefits a privileged few, this book argues, the rest of us are paying a terrible environmental, economic, and social price for allowing them to be so recklessly assaulted, diminished, and destroyed. It is not only that standing forests sequester carbon, which is released into the atmosphere when the forests are cut and becomes a major factor in the atmospheric carbon buildup that results in global warming. It is not only that forests in the tropics hold a very high portion of all the world's species of plants and animals (most of which have not even been discovered by science, let alone studied for their possible benefits to human health and well-being), at a time when the world is experiencing species losses at a rate not equaled since the dinosaurs died sixty-five million years ago.

It is also that the role of these forests as a regulator of the earth's landscape has been grossly underappreciated. What humans ruthlessly shoved aside during this past century of mindless deforestation was what had once been treasured: the forests' ability to stabilize regular freshwater supplies, inhibit floods and erosion, provide nutrients and other services for agriculture, and maintain fisheries in rivers, in estuaries, and along coastlines. There is no way to exaggerate their importance to the people who depend on them. Accelerating forest losses will condemn the rural poor in many lands to a future that is no brighter than what awaits those who are today barely surviving in such ravaged landscapes as those of denuded islands like Madagascar and Haiti. All people and most plant and animal species will have to suffer the adversities and sacrifices resulting from faster rates of global warming and the attrition of our priceless biological diversity if the forests continue to die. It is simply not tolerable to accept the loss of the amount of tropical forest that could vanish by the middle of the coming century if we continue to do forest business as usual.

In recent years has come a rising interest in arresting the attrition through actions by national governments and the international community, revisions in the policies of conservation organizations and aid donors, setting limits or bans on commercial logging in virgin forest areas, and creating rules or incentives to encourage "sustainable forest management." While some seek to monitor and control the trade in hardwoods from the tropics, where the most aggressive assaults on the forests are concentrated, others favor diplomatic steps in the direction of a global convention to regulate forest use. Some aid donors and wildlife organizations are advocating the sequestration of large blocks of forest in order to save them from the axe and the bulldozer. Others experiment with market-based approaches that make it attractive for some companies or countries to spare forests in exchange for the right to emit more greenhouse gases elsewhere or the exclusive "bio-prospecting" rights to canvass them in search of commercially viable resources. International institutions are testing ways for forested nations to stop cutting down their trees and instead receive compensation for the ecological services their forests provide. Still others feel that cracking down on corruption in business and government circles is the key.

Looking across this broad terrain, one often senses failure. Neither governments nor their bureaucracies have been able to stem the tide of forest loss. International institutions from the United Nations's Food and Agriculture Organization (FAO) to the World Bank show increasing sensitivity and concern, but the numbers indicate the inadequacy of their efforts. After two weeks of intense debate culminating in an all-night effort to achieve consensus, delegates to the fourth session of the

United Nations's Intergovernmental Forum on Forests in early 2000 unanimously agreed to "consider (within five years) with a view to recommending the parameters of a mandate for developing a legal framework on all types of forests"—whatever that means. International environmental organizations have learned the folly of pursuing the goal of designating strict nature reserves, but they have still to learn much about adapting their ideas to the needs of local people. The predatory habits of many in the forest industry remain a powerful negative force, and victories in the struggle to bring it to heel will be hard won.

All the remedies that have been suggested have some merit, but it is the thesis of this book that *no single one of them is more important, or holds more promise, than the relatively simple act of allocating responsibility for managing and protecting forests to the local groups and communities that depend upon their healthy survival rather than on their destruction.* Community forestry, as the practice has become generically known, occurs in many different forms of interaction among local leaders, government officials, and representatives of national and international aid and environmental protection agencies. Although transferring power, in whatever form, to local hands is no panacea, it has more than anecdotally won its spurs as an effective management technique that strengthens local economies, leads to enhanced social cohesion, lowers rates of forest-damaging shifting cultivation, narrows the gender gap—*and* increases the ability of forests to provide their multiple benefits to people and the landscape. It has become fashionable for national governments and international institutions to say that their policies encourage local participation; our view is that the world has barely begun to achieve the vast potential that the concept offers.

While doing the research for this book the authors saw many remarkable examples of how proficient even the poorest and most needy local people can be in bringing about the stabilization and recovery of formerly destitute forest regions. One striking example came from northern Thailand's Golden Triangle, a turbulent area where a number of forest and watershed protection efforts are succeeding despite strong crosscurrents involving local and international corruption, the drug trade, and trans-Mekong timber traffic with Laos and Burma. At the edge of a village called Khun Sa Nai, which is north and west of Chiang Mai and is occupied by Hmong tribespeople, what was a fully bared hillside a decade ago has enjoyed a remarkable comeback thanks to policies allocating power to local people. Healthy large trees once again dominate this microwatershed, and clean fresh water flows into almost every house. The local economy has greatly improved as well, as the village headman noted to our small visiting delegation.

In older times, before the watershed had begun to recover, farmers were forced to range farther and farther afield and spend more time away from their families. Now, we learned, many of the villagers were farming near home and owned trucks to carry their produce to market. Lychee and vegetables were growing within the village. All children attended a primary school in the village, and many went on to a high school an hour's drive away on the main road. Houses were being built and enlarged. The only complaint we heard was about fluctuating commodity prices. "It's amazing how fast a forest can recover if you give it a chance," said Thai forester Lert Chuntanaparb. Clearly this was also a recovering society.

Equally striking are the accomplishments of the Dumagats, an indigenous people inhabiting a remote corner of central Luzon in the Philippines. They make much of their living by gathering rattan, a fiber used for basket weaving, from the forest. Small in physique, the Dumagats live in tiny and primitive settlements. Two to eight families form a community; each sleeps on the bare ground under a thatched roof that barely covers all occupants. Cooking is done outdoors over an open fire. A Dumagat man typically owns no more than the ragged clothes he wears, a transistor radio, a knife for rattan cutting, and an old automotive inner tube that he uses to float rattan strands downstream to a roadside pickup point. Traditionally fishing and hunting gave the Dumagats most of their food, but with the advance of logging game became ever harder to find. One skilled Dumagat hunter-gatherer said that early in 1993 he was still able to trap an ample supply of deer, but he admitted that conditions for hunting and rattan collection were becoming ever more difficult.[2]

Some twenty Dumagat leaders were gathered to discuss the detailed management plan that, if approved by government officials, would help them recover title to their ancestral lands and trigger the disbursement of government cash to carry out the program. The meeting took place on stony ground under a bridge that crossed a semidry riverbed. Most of the participants in the meeting were men, but several women formed an outer circle and watched the proceedings intently. Large sheets of white paper were taped onto bridge abutments. Facilitators used marker pens to note Dumagat comments about how the land and its benefits were to be managed and shared, what rules would govern its use and how these would be enforced, how mapping and monitoring would be accomplished, how to plan to maintain the fertility of the land by rotating crops, planting nutrient-fixing shrubs, and giving only careful access to goats. These were nomadic people not accustomed to this sort of process, but they were faithfully showing up at these planning meetings, which lasted a full day. At the end of this day the facilitators returned elated from the bridge, confident that the Dumagats would complete the management and land-use plan for the region by the deadline they had imposed upon themselves.

We gained similar insights in other lands. In India, where the contemporary model of community forestry first took hold late in the 1970s, we learned how district forest officials had found that they would be able to do their work far more effectively by sharing responsibility with local villagers rather than by trying vainly to force those barely surviving people away from almost totally vanished forest resources. Even in such politically dysfunctional lands as Laos and Cambodia, there are heartening examples of local communities assuming the responsibility of protecting forests. In many parts of West Africa, close observers told us, the restoration of traditional, locally based forms of managing forests and rural resources has far better prospects than do either the continuance of colonialist, top-down systems of forest governance or the more recent efforts of well-meaning nongovernmental agencies to superimpose their own methods over many centuries of successful communal practice. A positive aspect of life in rural Africa, we heard, is that in many areas colonialism lasted such a short time that it never really took hold, while traditional practices somehow survived. We saw how well the indigenous people in such regions, and their counterparts in Mexico and Central America and in many parts of the South American continent, could do the job if given half a chance.

If community forestry fulfills its promise, the result will not be a series of idyllic islands of pristine or regenerated forest, sealed off from the nearby people and interspersed with areas of otherwise devastated landscape battered by excessive human use. More likely it will be a mosaic in which forests and people quite freely interact, with local villagers taking the leadership in establishing the sustainable limits of forest use and then learning to live within them. Indigenous peoples ranging from the Kayapó in the Brazilian Amazon to the much-studied villagers of Kissidougou, a province in the West African nation of Guinea, have quite aggressively manipulated the forest and the landscape to meet their own needs while retaining enough forest to enable it to continue providing the critically important ecological services of which it is capable. In some areas individual smallholders have also brought greater stability to rural landscapes through their use of trees as part of the farming systems they have created. The way such people manage the landscape and share the use of the commons is hardly tragic.

In part I we review the dismal history of forest use and misuse and examine the causes and consequences of this careless behavior. Part II offers examples, from various parts of the tropical world, of the accomplishments of local communities after they have been at least somewhat empowered to manage these resources. Special emphasis is given to India, the cradle of modern community forestry, and to Indonesia, a country of great cultural and biological diversity and importance with which Claudia D'Andrea is especially familiar. In part III we suggest steps that national governments and international institutions might take to enliven their stated commitment to local participation—and to accelerate what is already an encouraging trend. In the final chapter we assess the stakes, which are far higher than most people believe, stressing the benefits that a healthier forest future offers in terms of regional and global security as well as in the quality of life for hundreds of millions of rural people. We suggest that policies that affect forests should be made not by foresters or middle-ranking bureaucrats with open palms but by those at the highest levels, whether in governments or institutions, who seek to bring orderly progress to the management of the forests within their nations and on the planet. The wisest course that such people can take, we conclude, is to open their own hands and those of their nations more freely, in large measure delegating the control and management of national forest properties to local people like the Hmong of Khun Sa Nai or the Dumagats of central Luzon.

This book was a collaborative effort in which the authors commented on and edited each other's work. The responsibility for authorship was divided: chapters 4 and 5, on India and Indonesia, were written by Claudia D'Andrea; the balance of the text was written by Roger Stone.

PART I

The Dismal Record

CHAPTER 1

Forest Use and Misuse

Images of forest destruction assault us. No television documentary on the rainforest is complete without the obligatory shot of a lone man, deep in the jungle, attacking a giant hardwood tree with a snarling chain-saw. The tree at last succumbs. Creaking and groaning, carrying down with it a supporting cast of smaller trees and vines, it crashes to the forest floor. Then there is silence and the fluttering of leaves. Another classic shot is that of machines like giant fingernail cutters that snip the trunks of plantation trees off at the roots and hoist the logs skyward to be picked up by trucks or helicopters for transport to the sawmill. Strik-ing clips from *Broken Treaty at Battle Mountain*, a powerful documentary about land disputes in the western United States, show two large bull-dozers, connected by a heavy chain, clattering in formation across wooded terrain and ruthlessly leveling everything along the way. A fa-miliar sight is that of developers clear-cutting and burning little remnant patches of suburban forest, building shopping centers or housing sub-divisions, then adorning them with smatterings of juniper bushes or other shrubbery. These acts are often said to represent economic and cultural progress—the advance of civilization.

Forests once covered half the earth. Eight thousand years ago, they thickly mantled North America and Russia, greened the Mediterranean coastline, and spread across much of what is now barren desert in the Middle East and parts of Asia (maps 1 and 2). About half of this forest cover was located within today's industrial nations. Boreal forests, part of a biome known as the "taiga," extended from the northern regions of North America through Russia and Scandinavia and constituted about one-third of all the world's forests. Today, some 13 percent of the planet's temperate zone, mostly in Europe and the United States, is forested. In the tropics, forests are concentrated within a globe-circling equatorial belt across Africa, Asia, and Latin America. They occupy high portions of the total land surface in large countries such as Brazil, Indonesia, and Congo. All of these forests are in a state of decline as a result of steady increases in the intensity of human activity. Deforestation has reached a rate of 15 million hectares a year and has transformed yesterday's tropical hardwoods into timber and fuelwood and converted the tropical forestland to farmland, cattle ranches, towns, and cities. Overall forest cover is down to 3.4 billion hectares, or barely more than a quarter of the earth's surface—a figure that includes cut-over wooded scrublands that have lost much of their initial quality and value.

The forests of most western European countries have had a long history of relatively effective management, and they support highly developed forest industries. Even so, the modern world imposes multiple stresses on them and on the forests of North America, eastern Europe, and Russia as well. Temperate and boreal forests, although not reduced in size and even on the increase in some regions, are being degraded. Logging has already severely affected some of these areas, and it now invades even the least accessible of them. In Russia a combination of poor management and the violation of regulations in recent decades will destroy the nation's mature forests by the mid-twenty-first century if the cutting continues at present rates. The effects of air pollutants such as sulfur dioxide, nitrogen oxide, and ozone, pests and diseases, forest fires, poor harvesting and silvicultural practices, fires, and climate variations all contribute to the weakening health of temperate and boreal forests. In the United States the sadness of experiencing a dead or dying forest has become all too familiar to hikers in the mixed-species woodlands of the Northeast.

In tropical and subtropical regions, on which this book heavily concentrates, the record is even worse. South and Southeast Asia have experienced dramatically severe forest losses, totaling about two-thirds of all original forest cover. Once thickly forested parts of Thailand, Indonesia, and the Philippines have been reduced to fire-prone scrubland and grassland. Upland watersheds in Nepal, Bhutan, China, India, and Pakistan have been badly degraded as a result of deforestation. Although tropical rainforests that are little damaged still cover 100 million hectares of western and central Africa, deforestation has led to desertification in many of this region's drier areas, with severe implications for local people. So much of the once-abundant tropical forest in Nigeria has vanished that, during the 1980s, the country astonishingly became a net importer of timber. The 967 million hectares of tropical forests in Latin America and the Caribbean account for more than half of all the world's closed (relatively undisturbed) tropical forests, and at least 75 percent of the enormous Amazonian forest remains intact. But even here, the spread of human settlements and the harvesting of forest resources are causing accelerating rates of forest loss and attrition of plant and animal species.

Four-fifths of all forests that existed after the last ice age, according to a recent World Resources Institute analysis, "have been cleared or substantially altered by human activity."[1] At the 1992 Earth Summit in Rio de Janeiro the world pledged to undertake a "rational and holistic approach to the sustainable and environmentally sound development of forests."[2] Yet some 100 million additional hectares of forest disappeared between the Rio gathering and mid 2000. Almost all of this lost forest was located in tropical or subtropical regions where human population growth is also heavily concentrated. Without major changes in how we regard and manage our forests, states one recent estimate, "by around 2010 only about a tenth of the world's original forest cover will be left in anything like its original state."[3]

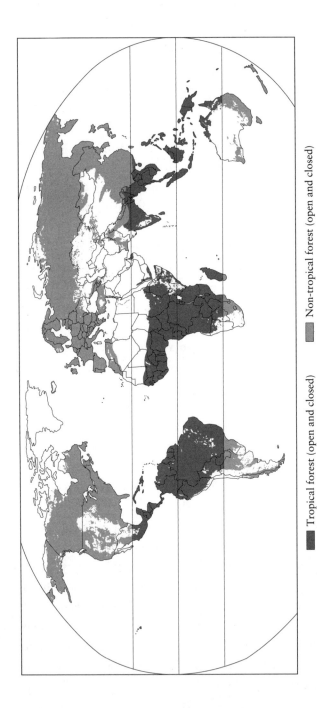

■ Tropical forest (open and closed)   ■ Non-tropical forest (open and closed)

Map 1. Forest ecosystems 8,000 years ago. Adapted from World Commission on Forests and Sustainable Development, *Our Forests, Our Future* (Cambridge: Cambridge University Press, 1999), 8.

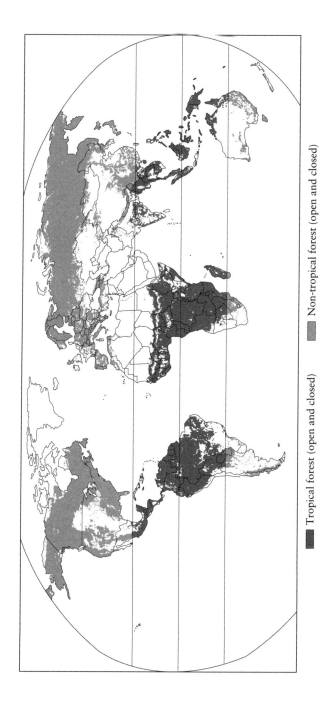

Map 2. Forest ecosystems today. Adapted from World Commission on Forests and Sustainable Development, *Our Forests, Our Future* (Cambridge: Cambridge University Press, 1999), 9.

■ Tropical forest (open and closed)　　■ Non-tropical forest (open and closed)

Before there were countries, local people controlled forest resources and for the most part used them with care to satisfy their own needs. When the earliest nation-states formed and seized command of these large territories, rulers quickly began to see them not as living resources to be prized and protected but as assets to be harvested for profit or security, or as nuisances that impeded agriculture or urbanization. They instituted laws and practices that barred villagers from ownership and traditional user rights, deprived them of management authority, and encouraged deforestation.

History offers many examples of how the abuse of forestland for the food and fuelwood on which most ancient societies heavily depended led to the demise of a culture. The powerful Bronze Age civilizations of the Fertile Crescent, where the Tigris and the Euphrates once flowed through heavily wooded hillsides, declined rapidly after these forests had been bared. Siltation and salinization did grievous harm to irrigated farming systems and disrupted food production. In those places, as in many other early societies, there was no generally used alternative to wood as an energy and construction resource and as the means of maintaining both naval power and commercial shipping. To Aristotle's dismay the power of ancient Athens withered when her supplies of trees and wood dwindled. This pattern was repeated in ancient Egypt, ancient Rome, and England starting in the seventeenth century.

Starting in the sixteenth century colonial powers turned to the forest resources of their newly occupied territories after depleting their own. The chopping in the Philippines began shortly after Spain established its first permanent settlement in 1565. In Java the Dutch quickly wrested control of the island's extensive teak forests away from local users after they took power early in the seventeenth century. Teak was in fact the principal reason why the Dutch were there, as political ecologist Nancy Lee Peluso explains: "The strength of their navy had made the Dutch the most powerful traders in the world, and Amsterdam was the Singapore of seventeenth-century Europe. The dense, durable teak was among the finest species in the world for ships' timber, and the tall, straight trees made majestic masts for the most formidable battleships."[4] After exhausting their supplies of suitable domestic timber, the British did likewise in the seventeenth century, stripping New England to get spars for naval vessels.[5] To found a sugar industry, Portugal denuded Madeira, an island named for its abundance of timber. The British followed suit in Barbados.

Postcolonial rulers treated the forest as the colonialists had, as we shall see in later chapters of this book. They practiced what became widely known as "scientific" tree harvesting: withholding for themselves the best lands and most valuable forests, keeping trees that could be profitably sold abroad out of the hands of local users. Peluso emphasizes that from colonial times forward "the forests' major enemy was the state itself" and notes that forest laws imposed by the Dutch were still in effect in Indonesia in the 1990s. "Forest police" remained deployed throughout the land, their principal mission being to keep local communities' hands away from forest resources.[6]

DECLINE IN AMAZONIA

The Amazon Basin is the most biologically diverse place on earth: it is home to 10 percent of the globe's plant and animal species. This mighty 6,700-kilometer river system stretches from the Andes to the Atlantic. It dumps 255,000 cubic meters of water per second into the Atlantic, and the sediment it discharges turns the water brown 150 kilometers away from land. The Amazon Basin offers a striking example of how humans have used, then misused, a priceless forest resource. Since the beginning of the basin's recorded history, observers have advanced sharply divergent ideas about the role of humans there. Some have found this remarkable ecosystem to be terrifyingly implacable, an area that fostered the dread that Europeans often associated with uncleared forest, where indigenous "savages" could do no better than eke out a precarious living as hunters and gatherers. In a much-cited book published in 1971, the anthropologist Betty J. Meggers terms the region a barely habitable "counterfeit paradise," ironic in its juxtaposition of tall trees with soil severely lacking in nutrients.[7] The basin has also often been seen as a cornucopia of exploitable natural treasure, whose human "conquest" could bring alive the El Dorado legend. The more some visitors suffered in the region, the more they treasured the notion of Amazonian abundance. Some proposed to clear-cut the forest to plant grains to feed the world on soils that they assumed were highly fertile if they could support such magnificent trees.[8]

Recent scholarship illuminates flaws in all these perceptions. Those who study the region's history increasingly find Amazonia to be neither a green hell nor a breadbasket. Rather, they see it as a zone of surprising variety and resilience that, when closely examined, bears the stamp of human manipulation and domination to a far greater extent than previously supposed. These findings are being assembled from new archaeological and anthropological discoveries about prehistoric Amazonia, from the work of historians and cultural geographers, and from social scientists' investigations of contemporary Amazonia. Human intervention in the region has been manifested in a richness of prehistoric art, in a colorful and diverse folklore, and in a lively contemporary literature.

This latest research suggests that before the Europeans arrived during the sixteenth century Amazonians in many parts of the basin practiced agriculture, adjusting the ecosystem to accommodate their basic needs. They grew maize and manioc. They planted Brazil nut and cashew trees where it suited them and where soils offered the greatest promise, as the archaeologist and anthropologist Anna Roosevelt learned. Roosevelt found Indian mounds, war clubs, life-size terra cotta human figures, and many examples of ancient pottery that show considerable sophistication; all date from before the conquest of the region. Aboriginal Amazonians were quite able, Roosevelt reported, to manipulate their surroundings. The Kayapó and other forest-dwelling indigenous groups devised elaborate systems of cultivation that are still in use today. Throughout the basin, not just in small portions of it, pre-

conquest Amazonians built fairly large towns and made impressive ar-
tifacts that have been discovered only very recently.[9] Geographer William Denevan has estimated the human population of the region before
the conquest to have been perhaps 5 million—a human density regained
in the Amazon Basin only in the mid-twentieth century after a precipitous plunge during the era of European occupation and colonization.[10]
"This is not the primeval forest that it looks like," says Roosevelt. "It is
manmade. For more than 10,000 years before Europeans came to the
Amazon, Indians worked this land. They built large settlements and
controlled this environment. They lived a healthy and fastidious life.
Then the Europeans came, and Amazonia fell apart."[11]

The massive war clubs these people wielded when first contacted
make it plain that strife was not unknown in prehistoric Amazonia. The
European conquest took the region on a sharp turn for the worse,
launching successive waves of conflict, degradation, and torpor that have
persisted over more than four centuries of mostly disheartening history.
Europeans arriving during the sixteenth and seventeenth centuries
founded missions and trading posts. When they tried to enslave the
natives, many of these formerly settled farmers melted into the forest
and adopted the "primitive" hunter-gatherer lifestyle for which they are
most widely known today. Foreign diseases felled most of those who
remained closer to the European outposts. The introduction of African
slaves led to further turmoil in Amazonia. It culminated in the *cabanagem*
of 1835–36, a basin-wide revolt that cost the general populace some
30,000 lives.

The El Dorado dream briefly beckoned for a few high-living Amazonian traders (some of European descent, some of mixed ancestry)
during the late nineteenth century, when wild rubber harvested by badly
oppressed tappers dominated a burgeoning world market. Competition
from rubber plantations in Asia swept past in the early twentieth century
and the South American rubber boom collapsed. Amazonia again faced
top-down development pressures when Henry Ford tried without success to establish rubber plantations in the 1920s and again in the 1930s.

During World War II the United States sought vainly to exploit Amazonian resources to support the war effort. The generals and planners who governed Brazil during the 1960s launched a series of ill-advised, capital-intensive programs to transform the region into ranches and farmland. They saw the "opening" of the vast Amazon forest as the key to future prosperity, subsidized its conversion for cattle ranching, and convinced aid donors to help finance road construction projects and colonization schemes. Inefficient hydropower dams, such as the Balbina near Manaus in the central Amazon, flooded large areas of forest but delivered little energy. Such projects exceeded the government's frail administrative capabilities and the basin's ecological limits. Prospectors scoured riverbanks, poisoned Amazonian streams with mercury, and dug deep pits to exploit rich lodes of Amazonian gold. Discoveries of vast deposits of iron ore, bauxite, and other minerals led to large-scale extraction and refining programs, some with sharply negative environmental side effects.

Some people have been able to cope with this encroachment. Ranchers have been successfully running cattle on Marajó island, at the mouth of the Amazon, ever since English, Irish, and Dutch settlements were founded there during the seventeenth century. *Caboclos*—mestizo Amazonians—have developed a viable nature-based culture on the basis of the region's natural resources and the rich supply of nutrients that wash from the Andes down onto the alluvial *várzea* during the annual flood season. Descendants of Confederate refugees from the American Civil War and of migrants who fled severe droughts in the arid Brazilian northeast, not to speak of the prosperous Japanese-Brazilian farmers working in small communities near Belém, are well established in Amazonia. So is an urban bourgeoisie that is still forming the social core of fast-spreading Amazonian cities such as Belém, Manaus, and Santarém. Far more frequent, however, are the tales of woe that have become ever more widespread as forest loss has accelerated. Over the past three decades millions of poor migrants have gravitated toward the Amazonian promise of gold or free land, leaving crowded urban centers or over-farmed fields elsewhere in Brazil. Few of them have succeeded in establishing viable farms or ranches on the poor soil that previously supported the former Amazonian forest, and few of the gold prospectors, called *garimpeiros*, have become rich.

So it has been across the forested tropics, in Asia as well as in South America. During the latter half of the twentieth century, when fully half of all tropical deforestation took place, key nations frequently let loggers exploit the forests without much thought as to what would happen after loggers had exhausted their resource. Brazil eliminated the possibility of forest regeneration by allocating the newly bare lands for development. The political leaders of Indonesia, seeking to relieve population pressure on the island of Java and increase Javanese political and cultural leverage on other islands, made the same choice. Their method, which was supported by the World Bank, was to ship Javanese homesteaders out to clear heavily forested areas in Kalimantan and elsewhere in the archipelago and establish small farms.

FORESTS AND THE LANDSCAPE

It is odd that we should have mistreated our forests so abusively, for they are indisputably of fundamental importance to life on earth and to the essential workings of the biosphere. In their natural state, not disrupted by human incursions, forests stabilize and restore the landscape. Especially in upland watershed areas, the binding action of tree roots slows soil erosion, reducing sedimentation and protecting rivers and fishery resources. Coastal mangroves guard the land against erosion while providing breeding grounds for many species of fish and shellfish on which humans heavily depend. Standing forests serve in such fundamental ways to create conditions for environmentally sound development, and their decline often leads to unproductive landscapes.

Many hazards loom after a region is clear-cut. Without trees to anchor it, the ground becomes less stable. Flooding is one frequent consequence. Water from storms washes loose soil into streams and rivers, and water that was once clear and clean becomes laden with mud. The soil-laden water moves downstream into estuaries and coastal waters, and the resulting siltation snarls hydropower facilities, renders waterways unnavigable, and damages or destroys marine life and fisheries. The subaquatic vegetation that feeds many species is blocked from the sunlight and withers. Floodwaters carry toxic substances (from chemically fertilized farms, oil exploration, and mining projects) into heavily populated areas, where they become a threat to animal health. In the 1980s, in the Philippines, a river carried sediments from adjacent logging roads into Bacuit Bay, killing much of the coral. The consequences for the local fishery and for tourism were disastrous.[12]

During the summer of 1998 devastating floods ravaged China's Yangtze basin, home to 400 million people. Although officials blamed seasonal rains for the heavy damage and the loss of some 3,800 lives, they also admitted that the loss of some 85 percent of the basin's original forests had greatly amplified the disaster. All logging in relevant watersheds was subsequently prohibited.[13] If forest losses can result in flooding, watershed disruption from deforestation in drier areas can have the opposite effect. It can cause the supplies of water that irrigate croplands—the water on which billions of rural people in developing countries depend—to become less regular or, in some instances, to disappear altogether.

Other problems occur in the tropics not just because trees are cut but also as a consequence of how the land is used after they are gone: agriculture and cattle ranching, or the extraction of resources, can leave the landscape far less capable of functioning in a way that is ecologically beneficial. In all forests nourishing elements such as calcium, magnesium, potassium, and nitrogen are essential to the workings of the ecosystem. They cycle between the earth, the biomass, and the atmosphere. In temperate regions trees take up these nutrients from the topsoil, which is often well endowed with them. In the tropics the trees themselves usually store almost all nutrients, leaving deficient soils under a thin leafy veneer at the surface. Deforestation shatters this fragile system, seriously reducing the productive capacity of the land and allowing it to sustain only limited livestock and crop production without substantial additions of artificial fertilizer. Few farmers in developing countries can afford such chemicals. If they are applied, they eventually filter into surrounding waterways and pollute them. The poor soils suffer further damage when heavy equipment is used to clear forests in the tropics, especially when the cleared land is beset by severe, nutrient-robbing rains.

If forest decline continues unabated, it is likely that the expansion of the earth's desert areas will accelerate in countries with dry climates and fragile soils. Landslides and rockslides occur more frequently when storms occur in mountainous regions that have been stripped of their trees. Deforested land is more susceptible to damage from earthquakes. The major fires that afflicted several rainforest regions in 1997 and 1998 were the result of deforestation coupled with weather distortions that were provoked by El Niño. The smoke from the fires closed airports, schools, and entire communities in Indonesia and affected urban conditions in neighboring countries.[14]

Although analysts tend not to attribute a single cause for these unprecedentedly ferocious fires, there is no doubt that deforestation was a principal factor. Many of the areas that burned began as moist tropical forest, which in its natural state is too wet to burst into flames. Deforestation enabled the sun to penetrate the canopy and dry up the remaining forest. In 1997 and 1998 forest fires reached unprecedented intensity in Brazil, where, according to the nongovernmental organization Environmental Defense, "the increased burning is impairing the ability of up to half the entire Amazon rainforest to remain green during the tropical dry season. . . . The end of the Amazon forest may be much closer than anyone has ventured to guess."[15] Fires in Mexico and Central America sent smoke adrift across many parts of the southern United States, raising awareness of what had seemed a remote issue to most American citizens.

FORESTS AND THE PLANET

Forests, then, are critical factors in maintaining the stability of land-scapes. In two other important senses, deforestation's anticipated consequences involve the fate of all life on earth. For one thing, there is a close relationship between forests and the planet's currently fast-rising temperature. Certain gases reaching the atmosphere from earth as a result of human activity, principally carbon dioxide, trap heat that would otherwise disperse into outer space. Instead this heat is reflected back to earth. The consequence of this so-called greenhouse effect is global warming. Higher emission rates lead to accelerated warming; a reduction in emission rates would slow the warming. The scientific research that supports this finding is amply validated. The rising global temperature might not seem like much from year to year, but if the warming trend continues at the upper end of present forecasts, the climate transformation could bring disaster to most of the planet. While increases in greenhouse gases and the earth's temperature would make some land more productive, the likely consequences for most areas include severe storms and droughts, the extinction of many species, major disruptions in food supplies, spreading disease and pestilence, and a rise in sea level that would be sufficient to cause the inundation of some low-lying countries. One-third of all forests will experience greater stress as a result of climate change, affecting their health and regenerative capacity.

Greenhouse gas emissions from the consumption of fossil fuels by motor vehicles and industrial sites are far and away the biggest contributors to the atmospheric buildup. Forests play a key supporting role in the drama of greenhouse gas emissions, either as emitters of carbon dioxide when fires occur, or, when they remain intact and growing, as storehouses for carbon, lessening the rate of the greenhouse gas buildup. Boreal forests absorb about one-sixth of all global carbon emissions, and the influence of tropical forests is even greater because they contain more biomass per unit of area. When the carbon that trees sequester is released from the earth's surface through burning, it builds up in the atmosphere and contributes to the greenhouse effect. Fires occur naturally because of lightning, especially in the boreal forest zone, but far more often people cause them. Fire is often employed by migrant farmers, shifting cultivators, and agribusiness operators to clear forested land for agriculture and ranching. In sum, at least 20 percent of all greenhouse gas emissions can be attributed to forest burning. Moreover, the occurrence of forest burning is growing, thus lessening the forest's ability to provide its prime environmental service of sequestering carbon.[16]

The other great global benefit provided by the forests is protection for the planet's biological diversity. Estimates of the number of species of plants and animals on Earth vary from 5 million to 100 million or more. Only about 1.5 million of these have been described by scientists, let alone assessed for their potential to contribute to human health and well-being as foods and medicines. Tropical rainforests cover only 6 percent of the earth's land area, yet they harbor at least half, and possibly 90 percent, of all species, many that have very localized habitats and are highly vulnerable to deforestation. Other forest types such as dryland and temperate forests, although less rich in terms of numbers of species, contain plants and animals that are vitally important to the functioning of ecosystems and to meeting local subsistence, health, and economic needs. Each year brings new evidence of how wild species help people. A recent example is the painkiller ABT-594, developed at Abbott Laboratories from poison on the skin of *Epibpedobates tricolor*, a frog found in Ecuador. It appears, say Abbott researchers, that ABT-594 could be two hundred times as effective as morphine, but without negative side effects. Although some such medicines can more easily be synthesized in the lab than harvested from the wild, and pharmaceutical companies have yet to reap great profits from "bio-prospecting" ventures, the field still holds great promise and appeal. "Seventy percent of the cures for cancer now being studied involve plants that grow exclusively in tropical forests," reports one authoritative source.[17]

The term *genetic resources* refers to the economic, scientific and social values of the genetic variation found among and between species. The world's forests, especially those of the tropics, are natural laboratories for the selection of genetic material on a scale that cannot be matched in any conceivable research station. In an era of increasing pressure on resources and significantly changing global environmental conditions, they represent one of humanity's most effective ways of guarding itself against an uncertain future. Genetic diversity buffers ecosystems from disruption brought about by pests, diseases, and climate change, and it provides the building blocks for selection and breeding to adapt plants and animals to a range of environments and end uses. At a time when humans have been deliberately narrowing the gene pool to increase timber and agricultural yields, diversity lowers the risk of grave losses.

We are in the midst of an unprecedented crisis. If the current trend toward extinction continues, one-quarter of the world's species may disappear in less than half a century. Ecologist Walter Reid, then at the World Resources Institute, estimated that by the year 2020, up to 14 percent of the tropical forest species of Asia, Africa, and South America may vanish unless deforestation rates drop substantially.[18] If the rate doubles, Asian tropical forests could lose close to half their remaining species in the same period. Even more ominous are signs that extinction rates are accelerating. "The current reduction of diversity," biologist Edward O. Wilson wrote in 1988,

> seems destined to approach that of the great natural catastrophes at the end of the Paleozoic and Mesozoic eras—in other words, the most extreme in the last 65 million years. In at least one important respect, the modern episode exceeds anything in the geological past. In earlier mass extinctions, which some scientists believe were caused by large meteorite strikes, most of the plants survived even though animal diversity was severely reduced. Now, for the first time, plant diversity is declining sharply.[19]

Present rates of species extinction are between 100 and 1000 times the natural rates, and much of the reason is human-induced forest decline.

FORESTS AND POOR PEOPLE

If tropical forests are essential to the general stability of our landscape and climate, protecting the priceless biological diversity that is one of the planet's richest assets, so too do they play a more direct part in satisfying immediate human needs—especially those of the poorest and weakest elements of society. Fifty million people live within the world's tropical forests. These forest dwellers, many with indigenous or tribal ethnic backgrounds, depend almost wholly on what the forest provides. From its plants and trees come food, fuel, clothing, medicine, building materials, and marketable goods to sell elsewhere and improve village economies. Meat from the forest's animals provides protein. For many forest-dwelling indigenous people forests also have aesthetic and spiritual importance. There are exceptions, but traditional knowledge acquired over centuries of interaction with forests and trees, combined with other values, normally ensures their protection and sustainability. Put the other way, the survival of these forest-dwelling people and their cultures and the survival of the forest usually go hand in hand.

Perhaps 300 to 400 million people inhabit rural areas adjacent to tropical forests. High percentages of all the workers in these towns and villages make their living from the forest's natural resources. Shrubs and farm trees producing fruits, fodder, fuelwood, and medicines are important sources of income and subsistence. In India some 275 million landless people and small farmers benefit from gathering resources they find within the adjoining forest. In one lowland village in the Philippines researchers found that 73 percent of households surveyed collected forest products for supplementary and emergency income, with more than half depending on rattan collection. Others who depend in part on the forest are the rubber tappers of the Brazilian Amazon, Central Americans who gather chicle and palm fronds, those who harvest wild mushrooms and fruits in southeast Asia, and Liberia's wild game hunters, who supply 80 percent of the meat for the nation's rural population.

Shifting cultivators on the forest margins do not necessarily value the forest itself, but their survival depends on the land underneath the trees as a resource for food production for subsistence and sometimes for commercial sales in local markets. The trees themselves supply fruits, nuts, and other important foodstuffs. Seasonal harvesting of forest products is critically important to most shifting cultivator households. This is especially so when families need income to buy food during the "hungry" period between harvests. In Sierra Leone, researchers found that "fuelwood selling provided the first cash income from forestland cleared by shifting cultivators for rice production. Subsequently fuelwood collection for the market was concentrated during the off peak agriculture period, providing cash income in a period when food supplies were at their lowest."[20]

Millions of small-scale agroforesters the world over use large forest trees to protect cultivated crops from erosion and the sun's glare. Tree shelterbelts slow wind velocity and lower the temperature, conserving moisture and increasing crop yields. Forests shade and feed domestic livestock. Greater food security and the enhancement of agricultural productivity are but two of the basic services that forests and trees extend to these rural populations. They also create rural employment opportunities, generate rural income, and provide fuel, fodder, medicines, and construction materials.

In 1860, 80 percent of all energy was generated by burning wood. Today that figure has dwindled to only 5 percent. What these figures disguise is that 2 billion people in developing countries still rely on fuelwood as their principal source of energy. Fuelwood accounts for 58 percent of all energy use in Africa, 15 percent in Latin America, and 11 percent in Asia. The importance of fuelwood is hard for those living in advanced societies to understand. Fuelwood and charcoal enable rural people to cook, and cooking enables them to digest grains and other foods (for example, millet in the Sahel) that when uncooked provide little nutrient value. Many rural people have learned to burn cow dung or agricultural residues such as chick pea stalks instead of fuelwood; still, rural well-being in many parts of the world will indefinitely continue to depend heavily on access to fuelwood from forests and scrublands and farm trees as well. Researcher Kojo Sebastian Amanor, of the University of Ghana, told this touching story about an increasingly scarce tree species that burns well and is still found in some parts of his country: "In the Asesawa area, one household with an exceptionally small plot of land of less than two acres had an area on their land that they called their 'forest.' This consisted of a single *Celtis mildbraedii* tree, protected by three or four outflanking pioneer species. Branches from this tree were carefully harvested to provide firewood throughout the year."[21]

It is the rural people who tend to suffer when forests disappear. Villagers along the Dareda escarpment in rural Tanzania speak for scores of millions like them in many lands. Fully forested when it was originally settled by wa-Iraqw tribespeople early in the twentieth century, the slope gradually gave way to pastoral activities. On its lower portions land was cleared to run cattle and grow coffee and bananas. Higher up the forest was largely left intact, and it yielded fuelwood and timber and provided habitat for a diversity of wildlife including hyenas and leopards. To protect water sources, leaders gave forest areas near them special protection, and to remind people of their special importance, the skins of goats slaughtered and eaten at inauguration ceremonies were left to mark the sites. By the middle of the twentieth century more and more people had entered the region and had founded farms on the lower slopes, forcing the cattle up into the forest. Fires, always used with care to drive honeybees from hives or to clear small plots for cultivation, began burning out of control and killing large trees in the upper forest. Post-independence government rules compelled immigrants to clear land to avoid losing their rights to use it. The wild animals disappeared along with the trees.

Even without the heavy added pressure of commercial logging in the region, researcher Gill Shepherd learned in the mid-1990s, the cumulative effects of these changes were devastating. Supplies of fuelwood and timber grew scarce. Streams dried up faster in the dry season. When they flowed they were far more laden with silt and dirt than they had been in the past. A greater incidence of landslides was reported. As family economies suffered, the need to restore the forest as a means of stabilizing the landscape became obvious. Villagers were embracing with enthusiasm the arrival of outsiders who were eager to launch a new program of tree planting and more rigorous forest management including banning cattle in much of the region. How could a regenerated forest improve conditions? "Cheap fuelwood and more rain," said one villager.[22]

Far more than many realize, city dwellers the world over also depend on forest values and productivity. Many derive direct economic benefit from selling or trading forest products and resources. City dwellers in developing countries rely heavily on forests for assured supplies of fuelwood, charcoal, and building materials. Many sell or trade forest products and resources. Urban-based tourism ventures in Costa Rica, Belize, and many other lands profit from the beauty of forests and the richness of species to be found within them. By the 1990s, reports Martha Honey in her book *Ecotourism and Sustainable Development*, tourism was vying with oil as the world's biggest business, with overall travel expenses expected to reach $4.2 billion by the end of the century. Within the total market, Honey continues, there is no lack of travelers who prefer Las Vegas or love boats to the delights of quietly exploring pristine nature, yet she has little doubt that ecotourism has "become the most rapidly growing and most dynamic sector of the tourism market," and she quotes many authorities on the field's immense potential.[23] In industrial nations forests supply city consumers with a wide range of commercial products including timber, wood-based panels, and paper and packaging products. Urban dwellers everywhere depend on the capacity of forests to regulate soil and water conditions for agriculture and fisheries and to inhibit floods, fires, droughts, and desertification. Many others for whom forests offer no financial return value them for aesthetic, spiritual, and recreational reasons.

Forests offer great potential to improve current imbalances of wealth and power and reduce current levels of global poverty. No overall improvement in the planet's shocking poverty statistics appears likely in the near term. In some regions poverty is growing fast. Between 1990 and 2000 alone the number of destitute people in sub-Saharan Africa was expected to have increased by 40 percent. Bad as the situation is, it would be far worse without the access that some poor people have to forests and the resources within them. Women and children especially benefit from small-scale forest-based activities such as basket and mat weaving. Without corrective measures to eliminate extreme inequalities in income and power, growing numbers of the poor and landless will add to the escalating pressures on forest resources. But with more equitable access to forestland and resources, both they and forests stand to benefit. "Providing traditional communities with access to resources," writes the forester Donald A. Gilmour, "is simply restoring a system which previously had led to great biodiversity and, arguably, sustainable forms of relationships with resources."[24]

FORESTS AND DEVELOPMENT

The concept of sustainable development surfaced when the World Commission on Environment and Development (WCED) stated in its landmark 1987 report, *Our Common Future*, that "humanity has the ability to make development sustainable—to ensure that it meets the needs of the present without compromising the ability of future generations to meet their own needs." Sustainability is widely interpreted to mean that economic, social, and environmental objectives must reinforce each other to achieve what Jim MacNeill, secretary-general of the WCED, referred to as a requisite set of "strategic imperatives": reducing high rates of population growth, increasing equity, reducing poverty, improving eco-efficiency, reorienting technologies, encouraging democracy, and supporting human rights.[25] Often criticized for being too vague and too subject to misinterpretation, the idea of sustainable development has persisted for two decades and is indelibly incorporated into the conventional rhetoric of development policy. Arguments can be avoided if one simply defines it as the greater and wiser inclusion of environmental considerations in economic planning.

A cardinal measurement of sustainable development is the extent to which the world proves willing to transfer power from the strong to the weak, from the rich to the poor, from the literate to the illiterate. Equity and human rights are as essential to the process as economic advancement. The contribution of the world's forests to sustainable development could be vastly greater if significant numbers of local communities and traditional forest users—those who benefit from the standing intact forest, not from its removal or degradation—can win back at least partial control of these invaluable resources.

CHAPTER 2

Why Tropical
Forests Decline

In lowland Amazonia violence frequently breaks out when ranchers, loggers, and miners plunder the forests and poison the rivers in their quest for quick gains. During the 1980s, stated the anthropologist Stephan Schwartzman, some five hundred "peasants, union activists, Indians, and rubber tappers" in Amazonia were victims of what he called "targeted, political assassinations promoted by large landowners seeking to stop rural community organization and efforts toward land reform."[1] Until 1990, when rancher Darly Alves and his son were convicted for the celebrated 1988 murder of rubber tapper Chico Mendes in the state of Acre in Brazil's far west, no previous trial had ever resulted in a guilty verdict.

In the emotional wave of reform that followed the Mendes affair many positive developments took place in the Brazilian Amazon (see chapter 7). According to Acre state senator Marina Silva late in the 1990s, 75 percent of the local population favored "development without destruction of the forest." Highly destructive logging persists in many parts of the region, however, and it is increasingly carried out by migratory Asian companies with no concern for the long-term consequences of their actions. Fires of unprecedented ferocity have swept across many parts of Amazonia in recent years, many of them attributable to juxtapositions of logging and seasonal drought. Large landowners in Amazonia, as in Indonesia, have also deliberately set fires to prepare land for plantation agriculture—a practice highly contrary to the interests of local people. Soybean monocultures are spreading across the basin's southern rim.

In the biologically diverse Colombian department of Chocó, local communities suffer from guerilla and paramilitary attacks as well as from top-down development pressures. In 1997–98 twenty-five thousand people were removed from just one contested river basin. Assassinations and military air raids are frequent occurrences in the region. During the summer of 1998 a unit of the Venezuelan National Guard traveled from Venezuela to Brazil along a new highway and moved into the rainforest homeland shared by four indigenous groups. The soldiers used a tank to remove log barricades that the Indians had placed across the roadway in protest against what they called the illegal installation of a high voltage power line through their territory.

In southern Mexico, conflict between indigenous forest-using communities and central authorities has persisted since the Spanish conquest of the sixteenth century. The Tzotzil, Zapotec, and Mixtec peoples in the states of Oaxaca and Chiapas, who believed that some of their ancestors emerged from the roots of trees, have long suffered from government policies that favor foreign capital and overexploitation of forest resources by outsiders. The Mayan people of the Yucatán peninsula used their highly valued forests as a refuge from marauding *conquistadores*, and they later established farming systems that did not destroy massive amounts of the forest. For the past century they have been driven onto marginal lands by Army-backed commercial loggers, coffee growers, and other large and well-connected landholders. The land reform that followed the end of the Mexican Revolution in 1920 did the interests of these peoples little good, even though they were awarded collective landholdings called *ejidos*. The consequences of recent economic liberalization and the North American Free Trade Agreement have been negative, attracting oil, gas, and pulp and paper interests to shrinking forest areas and flooding the Mexican market with cheap U.S. corn against which domestic growers have not been able to compete. Conflict persists. In Chiapas, what has emerged from this dismal history is the Zapatista Army for National Liberation, a guerilla force that seems likely to endure in the region despite the bloody incursions of the Mexican army and new overtures from the more enlightened national government that came to power in 2000.

African villagers denied access to forests and nontimber forest resources feel they can do little more than look on helplessly while foreign concessionaires, equipped with valid government permits, open up vast stretches of primary forest as they search for small quantities of the most valuable wood. In the aftermath, following a worldwide pattern, migrant settlers driven by population pressures or environmental degradation in other areas travel the new logging roads into the forest, fell more trees to establish small farms, and set the stage for further local conflict with traditional forest occupants. In southern Somalia's rural Bay region, villagers use bows, arrows, and sometimes guns to defend their trees from charcoal burners seeking raw material for consumption in Mogadishu.[2] In Edo, Nigeria, the AT&P Company acquired logging rights to a 50,000-hectare tract in the early 1950s. Without consulting local people, the company clear-cut the entire area, leaving behind a desolate ghost village, a badly silted stream, and a poor and helpless populace. When a large-scale commercial farmer in Zimbabwe fenced off an area that villagers had long used for grazing and to harvest tree products, they retaliated not just by climbing over the fence, but by tearing it down and carrying off a section that the farmer estimated at fully 20 kilometers in length.[3]

Industrial foresters continue to strip eastern Cameroon, their heavily laden trucks standing out as stark symbols of governmental malpractice, yet a powerless local person can be arrested for felling a single tree. "Pressure from commercial logging interests," writes economist Korinna Horta, "represents the greatest threat to the integrity of the forest dwellers' way of life" in Cameroon. Contrary to the widely shared impression that most such damage is done only by fly-by-night operators from such countries as Taiwan and Malaysia, Horta reports that Dutch, French, German, and Italian companies who boast at home about their environmental records were responsible for much of the carnage. A German company called Feldmayer (HIF/TT), Horta continues, was purchasing "about 70,000 cubic meters of round wood every year, mainly from Lebanese entrepreneurs, whose logging practices are based on the sole premise of cutting as many trees as quickly as possible."[4]

In a remote area of Luzon island in the Philippines, I saw the deeply troubling reality of what can happen to a community in the aftermath of logging when no reforms are undertaken. One afternoon we drove to a town called Dingalan, located on the island's east coast. During the logging years jobs had been available at a large sawmill and at the port where the sawnwood was loaded directly onto Japan-bound ships. Now there was no visible economy. On the flatland below the bare hillsides were row upon row of abandoned trucks, tractors, and bulldozers, quietly sprouting weeds in the humid air. The gateway to the abandoned sawmill was locked, and two gun-toting teenagers inside motioned me away when I asked to enter and look around. There was virtually no commerce in this once-bustling village. Two women were hacking at large slabs of fresh tuna that, without ice, they could not keep for long in this climate. A group of children played with a wagon, pulling it in little circles, with five or six of them crowded aboard. Men were scarce, and there was hardly any motor traffic on the roadways. This is the fate of forest communities after the loggers have gone unless the government steps in to help or the local citizens find their own way out of the mess they have inherited. Scattered communities of this sort become easy targets for insurrectionists seeking support from local people.

Since colonial times Javanese peasants have found many ways to express their resentment over the government controls that bar them from access to teak forest resources. Local people in Indonesia have been complaining for many years about the practices of the many private logging companies working there under government concessions, but without effect. Smoke from the 1997 fires in Kalimantan (Borneo) clouded skies, closed airports and entire communities, and provoked complaints from as far away as Singapore and Kuala Lumpur. London's *Sunday Times* classified the disaster as "wholly man-made—because many of the hundreds of fires were started deliberately as a cheap way to clear land by companies with corrupt connections to government officials."[5] In India what began as a local dispute flared into the national Chipko, or "tree hugger," movement. Although nonviolent, it was bitterly contested, pitting local forestry officials against villagers who were determined to save forestlands. In Malaysia's tribal Sarawak territory, indigenous Penan and international ecowarriors joined forces to barricade logging roads.

From Papua New Guinea to Guyana authorities weigh the question of how aggressively to plunder the forest for the sake of lagging economies. In Papua New Guinea in the late 1980s apparent inefficiencies in forest administration and links between logging companies and public officials prompted the prime minister to launch a commission of inquiry. It concluded that some of the companies were "roaming the countryside with the assurance of robber barons, bribing politicians and leaders, creating social disharmony and ignoring laws in order to gain access to, rip out, and export the last remnants of the . . . timber."[6] Despite a 1991 overhaul of the national forestry law, similar abuses continue. In 1996, the issue took on global overtones when the World Bank refused to disburse portions of a $225 million "structural adjustment" bailout loan package unless the government agreed to stop awarding logging concessions to foreign private companies. Attaching such conditions, Papua New Guinea's finance minister stated, violated his country's sovereignty. National leaders in many lands use the same argument.

In cash-starved Suriname, at the northeast corner of the Amazon basin, the government is known for awarding logging and mining concessions without even informing local and indigenous people, let alone consulting with them. Consequences for them have included forced relocation to make way for the new extractive activities and cyanide poisoning of local rivers. In 1998 only the miraculously successful intervention of several international environmental organizations saved the country from handing over virtually its entire forest estate to hit-and-run logging companies from Indonesia and Malaysia. Conservation International, a Washington-based environmental organization, worked long and hard to persuade Suriname's officials to declare almost 10 percent of the country to be a nature preserve in 1998. The organization also convinced the Suriname government to establish a trust fund to ensure that the decision to set aside the land would pay off, easing the political pressure to exploit the forests of a poor country that is desperate for revenues. "A small ray of hope," said the *New York Times* in a lead editorial that went on to complain about the lack of governmental support to protect fast-disappearing tropical forests. "The task of saving the forests has thus been left to private conservation groups, whose resources are limited," the editorial concluded. "The very fact that one of these groups and one small country have joined to save four million acres might shame Western governments into broader action."[7]

Suriname bravely decided to sequester such a major portion of its remaining forest, but no such actions have spared the forests of neighboring Guyana or other nations in Amazonia, where the East Asian loggers, having exhausted the most lucrative commercial reserves in their own region, were establishing beachheads in the late 1990s wherever they could. Such companies are invading West Africa and the far eastern regions of Russia as well. All but remnants of the forests in Myanmar (Burma) and Cambodia are probably not long for this world. In Mongolia sharp conflicts have broken out between companies that are exporting raw logs to China at well below market prices and local communities that are pressing for local processing and better prices.

INEQUITIES

Beneath such conflicts lie patterns of inequity. Much tropical deforestation occurs because poor migrant farmers, pushed to the forest frontiers by population and political pressures, slash and burn trees to grow corn, beans, and other subsistence crops. But to blame these migrants for the bulk of the damage, as analysts frequently do, is to ignore the complex and interconnected set of broader forces that drive them. Loggers help trigger the process by building roads into the forest, then abandoning them after stripping out the most valuable timber. Governments subsidize and also build roads. They do so to ease access to forest resources, promote the colonization and development of wildlands, reduce population pressure and poverty in other areas, and enable military forces to subdue insurgent groups based in the hinterlands. These roads give the migrant farmers opportunities to occupy virgin lands deep in the forest. Once they deplete the soil the farmers move on, and the relentless sequence of poverty and deforestation continues. Without the roads they are more likely to be restricted to more traditional forms of lowland agriculture.

Poverty is more the result than the cause of forest losses. It is especially unfair to suggest that the culprits are the traditional forest users, who, unlike the recently arrived migrants, have a deep understanding of the ecosystem and employ well-developed methods to use it sustainably. The point is that neither group warrants a major share of the ultimate responsibility. In the tropics and in temperate regions as well, it is the "big" and not the "little" people who have condemned us all to a world of rapidly degrading forests. It is the powerful who have failed to perceive and manage the world's forests in ways that recognize and respect civil needs and goals. Tropical and subtropical forest use and policy usually favor short-term rewards for elites over longer-term environmental considerations that are of prime importance to everybody and that address the urgent needs of local people. Almost invariably those holding power have perceived the forest as a commodity to be consumed or an inconvenience blocking economic development, and they have little concern for the sharply divergent needs of local and indigenous forest dwellers and all the rest of us.

Pressures from the world's well-off consumers have much to do with current patterns of forest loss. Those who live in the equatorial countries, where large portions of these remaining forests still stand, use little processed wood. It is the consumption habits of people in developed countries that weigh heavily on forests. Currently the world annually uses about 1.6 billion cubic meters of industrial wood. It constitutes the raw material for sawnwood, wood-based panels such as plywood, and paper products such as schoolbooks, newsprint, packaging cartons, and paper bags. Intensive forms of plantation forestry, supplying yields many times those of the natural forest, cover a growing portion of the rapidly escalating demand from the developed world for forest products and resources. Eighty percent of all commercial wood products come from temperate, not tropical, forests. But to satisfy some portion of the demand, estimated according to one study to increase by 20 percent just by 2010, loggers gnaw away at the natural tropical forests as well. Brazil, Indonesia, and Malaysia already rank high among the world's top commercial wood-producing countries.[8]

In developing countries as much as 80 percent of the closed forest is in the hands of the government. Government landholders in weak, cash-strapped countries are often no match for commercial interests in search of resources. In the marketplace a single log of top-quality tropical hardwood can fetch a price that far outweighs the dollar value, at least as conventionally calculated, of any other form of forest use. In heavily wooded developing countries with low per capita incomes, forests can generate instant wealth. On the Philippine island of Palawan during the 1980s, just one logging company's revenues represented three-quarters of the province's total income—and twenty-four times the local government's annual budget.[9] As much as 40 percent of the total land area of desperately poor Suriname could be logged for a substantial financial reward.[10] The problems that stem from intensified logging, as well as from large mining and oil exploration operations, are hardly confined to South Asia. Transnational corporate power can override governments even in more affluent regions such as British Columbia, Alberta, the Pacific Northwest, and Siberia.

The terms under which governments grant forest concessions normally undervalue the timber, encouraging wood waste and forest destruction through the careless use of inappropriate logging systems. The damage caused can be substantial. Government revenue losses reached some $3 billion a year during Indonesia's Suharto era. Some logging companies, showing respect for the multiple values of the natural forest, use efficient technologies to cultivate trees on plantations that supply most or all of the trees they cut. They are mindful of the effects of their operations on local people and on regional ecosystems. Most who make their living by harvesting trees, however, show little appreciation for any aspect of the forest other than its ability to generate a quick financial return. Typically the loggers in Africa's forests who high-line—felling only the finest trees—extract only two to three trees per hectare while fracturing and tearing apart the entire landscape. In most forested regions the stability of the land may require that at least 85 percent of it remain in no more than lightly disturbed forest. Today, no more than 1 percent of all forest cutting obeys this rule.[11]

A survey of insensitive road building, which is often undertaken to benefit commercial interests, is one way to measure how governments tend to regard forests. Land tenure policy is another and a more fundamentally important yardstick. A principal reason why landless peasants invade the forest lies in the failure of government landholders to acknowledge traditional ownership rights. They have consistently ignored the tenurial rights of forest-dependent local communities and have allowed them no seat at the table during discussions about allocating forest resources and privileges. Stubbornly persistent national laws, based on the old assumption that forests are "dirty" and cleared land "clean," sometimes impede governmental efforts to empower forest-dependent people through improvements in land tenure security.

In Brazil land entitlements used to be valued based on the area of forest cleared. In Costa Rica, legal land titles could for many years be obtained more easily if more than 50 percent of the land claimed was deforested. Even when squatters somehow manage to overcome such difficulties and obtain legal land titles, big landholders with good connections to government officials too often forcibly buy them out for low prices.

Too many public officials, functioning in shadowy alliances with mining and logging companies and others whose operations harm the rainforest, have lined their own pockets to the detriment of the public interest. Such misuse of power undermines the efforts of those in government and the private sector who diligently seek to improve the situation. Most logging is carried out illegally, and connivance between logging companies and corrupted government officials is common. The corruption that is most damaging to forest resources is not so much the petty bribery affecting low-ranking officials as it is the large-scale misuse of public resources for private gain by top-level political elites. Corruption encourages "get rich quick" approaches, deprives governments and local communities of resources that could be used for development or improved forest management, and channels scarce public resources into private pockets. Common corrupt practices affecting forests include the concealed or secret sale of harvesting permits, illegal underpricing of wood from timber concessions, false documentation of species or amounts cut in public forests, illegal logging, and trafficking in sensitive government information related to forests.

In Papua New Guinea, underpricing by foreign companies was so prevalent that until 1986 not a single company operating there had declared a profit despite a booming timber trade. Virtually all timber exports from India, Laos, Cambodia, Thailand, and the Philippines are illegal. A third of those from Malaysia may also be illegal, and as much as 95 percent of exports from Indonesia are not completely legal. The World Bank conservatively estimated that in Indonesia, by 1992, about 500,000 hectares of tropical forests were being illegally logged every year. Corruption is hardly confined to developing countries. In 1994 the European Union charged several corporations for corrupt practices. A decade earlier, the European Union fined forty major pulp and paper producers for similar reasons.

Although areas that are allegedly protected for future generations exist almost everywhere in the developing world, these are often no more than "paper parks," as they are often called. Inadequate resources, obsolete skills, and weak political clout usually constrain the ability of most government agencies to manage and protect forests more effectively. For want of enforcement, many officially off-limits forest areas are in fact open to uncontrolled access by landless peasants and others for use as a free resource. Significantly, many countries follow the U.S. model by burying the forest service within a far larger agriculture department and by making food production its overriding concern and forest protection a low priority.

GLOBAL ECONOMICS AND POLITICS

The globalization of the world economy and the acceleration of world trade promote economic expansion and increasing consumption and impose heavy pressures on natural resources and forests. The efforts that forest-rich countries do make to shield their forests from excessive exploitation often lead to undesirable results. Bans on log exports are meant to protect remaining natural forests and motivate the domestic forest industry to increase levels of processing and value-added production. But closing the export market reduces the price of wood nationally and encourages the faster conversion of forestlands to more profitable uses. A protected domestic industry may become extremely inefficient, causing the country to lose more forest by exporting processed products than by exporting logs. Log export bans in some countries may accelerate deforestation in others.

Markets do not provide the correct signals for forest conservation. Many of the ecological services that forests and watersheds provide have either no market price or unrealistically low prices. A landowner in an upper watershed does not get paid for the protection against soil erosion—which produces sedimentation that can clog irrigation channels or hydroelectric power plants—that his forest gives farmers or urban dwellers located downstream. Nor does the forest landowner profit by capturing carbon and thus helping to arrest global climate change, maintaining the landscape's scenic beauty, or preserving biodiversity for the benefit of all. Conversely, the marketplace does not oblige those who destroy forests and convert them to other uses such as agriculture, mining, or oil exploration to compensate people whose lives have been adversely affected. Neither the owners of sulfur-spewing factories nor the millions of motorists who pollute the air have to pay for damage to forests. Some of these unpriced services that the forest provides, particularly carbon sequestration, can be substantial in importance. Landowners usually prefer to dedicate their lands to more profitable uses, however, and because markets do not reflect the hidden values of forest resources, consumers use larger quantities of forest products than they would if higher prices reflected their full value.

Agricultural policymakers are often insensitive to the influence that their decisions have on the well-being of forests. If the economic returns for farming or ranching increase, so do the incentives to convert forests for those uses. In Panama deforestation is directly linked to subsidized official credit for promoting cattle ranching in remnant areas of high environmental value. In Costa Rica the conversion of forestlands to pastures was also encouraged through subsidized credit for cattle ranching. Agricultural subsidies are often substantial. In Mexico, Brazil, and South Korea in the mid-1980s they reached 55 percent of the value of production. In many countries agricultural income is either taxed at very low rates or not taxed at all, while "unutilized" forestlands are taxed at higher rates. This policy further encourages the conversion of forests to agricultural production. Individuals and corporations often invest in agricultural production as a tax shelter. In some cases, labor policies can also have a detrimental effect on forests. One reason for the migration of Filipino swidden farmers into forest regions was the establishment of national farm policies that promoted capital-intensive techniques and created a surplus of farm labor.

Mining and oil exploration ventures, which governments often subsidize heavily, can be designed to minimize negative environmental and social impacts. These mitigating measures are frequently not adopted, and the effect on forests can be devastating. The large size and the toxic wastes associated with some mining extraction and oil exploration operations are daunting. High-cost foreign mining investments in Latin America imply the development of vast stretches of forestland.

For many decades after World War II international finance agencies such as the Asian Development Bank and the Inter-American Development Bank not only failed to support measures to protect the forests but also hastened their destruction by funding large dams, agribusiness, and commercial forestry projects. Policy at the World Bank and other multilateral aid donors and lenders was dominated by economists and engineers who maintained blind faith in the idea that "economic growth" would benefit poor people in developing countries, whether they be huddled masses in urban centers or subsistence farmers on the periphery. Investment in infrastructure—roads, dams, bridges, electric power—would lead to such growth. So would support for large, capital-intensive industrial ventures, even those such as mining and smelting that would tear up the countryside and disrupt local communities.

So-called structural adjustment programs, codesigned by the World Bank and the International Monetary Fund, are also often said to have been detrimental to the health of forests and the people around them. The intent of these programs has been to invigorate the economies of developing countries by curbing inflation and stimulating economic growth, principally through increasing exports. In some countries adjustment-triggered reductions in government expenses have ironically been a plus for forest villagers as forest departments, weakened by budget cutbacks, have been compelled to interfere less and leave more responsibility in local hands. In nations with weak natural resource policies and institutions, however, pressures to increase exports imposed by structural adjustment agreements have hastened forest decline. In Nigeria during the 1980s encouragement from the Washington institutions as well as domestic pressures to push exports led directly to the overlogging of hardwoods and the usual duress for forest-dependent local communities.[12] Deforestation, the World Bank itself calculated, was costing the Nigerian economy some $5 billion a year. After Indonesia's 1998 financial collapse the International Monetary Fund overruled the objections of the World Bank and insisted that the previous ban on whole log exports should be lifted to help shore up the balance of payments and better enable the country to grow its way out of the crisis. In other cases structural adjustment encourages countries to condone forest clearing not just to sell logs but also to make way for alternative ventures that quickly generate export income.[13]

Little has resulted from several global forest initiatives attempted during the 1980s and early 1990s. FAO and the independent World Resources Institute mounted a heroic effort in 1985 and produced the Tropical Forest Action Plan, which was aimed at helping countries prepare and implement national action plans for sustainable forest management. While some useful national planning was accomplished as a result, the overall project was widely criticized for being top-down, hostile toward nongovernmental participation, too oriented toward outmoded classical forestry solutions, and generally characterized by bungling, inaction, and paralysis.[14] The project collapsed early in the 1990s.

The International Tropical Timber Agreement, signed in 1983 by a coalition of producers and consumers, included a quixotic pledge from producers to achieve "sustainable forest management" by the year 2000. But only a tiny fraction of the world's forests is now being managed in what could be called a sustainable fashion. The International Tropical Timber Organization, formed as a result of that agreement, is best known for promoting tropical timber trade under the environmentally insensitive rules of the World Trade Organization.

As the 1992 Earth Summit approached, official delegations began discussing a possible forests convention to bind signatory nations to tighter forest controls. Negotiations broke down as a result of deeply differing perceptions between countries in the Northern Hemisphere and those in the Southern Hemisphere over two principal questions. One was sovereignty, with industrial nations tending to see tropical forestlands as a "global commons" and the nations owning them hotly asserting their right to use them as they pleased. The second was the quantity of "new and additional resources" that northern countries would be willing to provide to the countries of the south in return for their commitment to protect these forests and their ecological services rather than mine them for quick profits. What emerged from Rio was a watered-down statement of "Forest Principles" which, although non-binding, was said to constitute a "good start" for further discussions in the United Nations about a possible forests convention. The discussions droned on into the new century under the auspices of the United Nations's Commission on Sustainable Development. The Intergovernmental Forum on Forests, established by that commission, staggered on for four inconclusive and interminable sessions between 1997 and 2000. At its fourth session, it achieved a consensus whose meaning few could understand well enough to report back to the parent body. "The only thing worse than having to sit through these meetings as a delegate," reported World Conservation Union observer Kheryu Klubmikin, "was to be there in an absolutely powerless capacity."[15]

What the delegates mostly wanted to discuss were the pros and cons of creating a legally binding instrument to guide forest policy. One explanation for the mealy-mouthed wording on this subject in its report (see the introduction) is that no consensus now exists among nations on whether trying again for a forests convention is a good idea. Many of the nations that were opposed in 1992 later became supportive, and vice versa. The United States, which pushed hard for a convention then, has held more recently that differences between industrialized and poorer nations remain too great for fruitful negotiations. Many people think that no treaty is better than a weak treaty and argue that, in any event, the international system already offers sufficient protection to forests under such existing mechanisms as the global climate, biodiversity, and world heritage conventions. Others insist that only under an officially sanctioned global treaty can offenders be brought to heel.

One thing is clear: well-forested nations such as Brazil and Colombia are not likely to agree to a deal that fails to compensate them amply in return for not exploiting their forests. So if the north wants to get anywhere, it will have to make a serious financial commitment—one far more substantial than the small amounts currently available through the World Bank–managed Global Environment Facility and other limited sources of funding. One promising approach is what is called "joint implementation," which is being worked out under the terms of the global climate convention that was agreed to in Rio in 1992. The idea is that developed countries or companies needing to reduce greenhouse emissions could get credit for relatively inexpensive but cost-effective carbon-reducing investments in developing countries. What is attractive about this market-driven concept is that it requires no commitments from developing countries yet has the potential for substantial emissions reductions and protection for tropical forests. Since industrial nations are not obliged to participate, however, it is doubtful whether this creative idea can generate financial incentives that are large enough to satisfy cash-hungry tropical forest nations that still see forest mining as an easy short-term fix.

Overall it seems unlikely that government officials who are dependent on powerful special interests, and who often face severe constitutional impediments to action, will ever take it upon themselves to protect the forests. The most likely outcome of the continuing global policy discussions is that they will drag on for years, while forest degradation continues. If the world's forests are to survive, citizens will have to lead the fight for broad changes that range far beyond the boundaries of forest policy as traditionally defined. In this context a remarkable phenomenon of recent years has been the growth in strength and competence of civil groups and local communities seeking to regain control of forests and to use and protect them better. Private donors and even some national governments have become aware of the importance of these new caretakers of the forest landscape, and they have begun to devise policies and programs that conform to their needs.

BACK TOWARD LOCAL MANAGEMENT

Back in the 1980s, write forest management specialists Donald A. Gilmour and Robert J. Fisher, governments began to move away from top-down forms of forest management that had persisted since colonial days. What was then called "social forestry" boiled down to having local people participate in internationally funded government forest programs as paid (or unpaid) employees. As genuine concern for the needs and skills of local people gained ground, "community forestry" became the more fashionable term, and, gradually, "naive and simplistic (if well-intentioned) attempts to 'motivate,' educate, and organize local communities, began to be replaced with more sophisticated understanding of local dynamics and social processes." Technologies began to diversify at the same time. Where once this kind of forestry involved little more than plantations and seedling nurseries, today's community forestry can incorporate multiple activities including agroforestry, natural forest management, watershed management, and harvesting nontimber products as well as trees. The authors conclude that community forestry has already become "a major form of forestry in many parts of the world," and that it is "a very dynamic creature that will continue to evolve and adapt to changing internal and external influences."[16]

As figure 1 illustrates, there is no fixed pattern to the devolution of power to the community level. In some instances protecting the forest is an overriding consideration; in others commercial resource extraction is a principal goal. Power distribution ranges from full government control with community participation to full community control with government participation. Sometimes, to make it work, corrections in the original design need to be made. Sometimes the gender dynamics within village communities can be harmful. In tropical forest societies women usually collect fuelwood for cooking and household heating and many other forest products for diverse uses. Such women are likely to have a deep knowledge of the forest's medicinal and edible plants, fruits, nuts, mushrooms, and animals, but they seldom have a strong enough voice in how forest resources are managed. Since male-dominated decisions may give preference to the commercial utilization of forest resources and reflect poor understanding of how the family as a whole may be affected, the empowerment of women within communities, as well as the empowerment of the community itself, becomes an important imperative.

Community forestry works better if supporting technical-assistance advisers enter the scene unobtrusively, as I discovered on travels in the Philippines and elsewhere. In Nan, a quiet town in north Thailand, I visited the bustling office of an impressive, tightly organized nongovernmental organization called Hak Muang Nan (HMN), or "Love for Nan," that was founded by Pra Kru Pitak Nantakhun, a gifted monk who resolved to return to his village and embark on community development activities. With sixty affiliates in the Nan watershed, HMN has become an effective force for forest and watershed management as practiced in the region for 700 or more years. "Things hop here," said Gerry Duckett, a friendly Canadian who was working there. We visited a successful chemical-free farm that produces a variety of fruits, vegetables, and livestock. Formerly only heavily fertilized corn had been grown there. HMN had helped the farmer, Puyai Chusak, make the transition and had formed an "alternative agriculture group" whose thirty-eight members were following his model. In a village near Nan, a monk affiliated with HMN had formed a vigorous youth group. Among its activities was managing a community forest and confronting loggers who lacked respect for local knowledge and traditions. Frequent tree ordination ceremonies in the region are another indication of the influence of the Buddhist ecology movement.

Another group seeking ways to improve the lives of marginalized farm families and help restore this landscape was DANCED, Denmark's

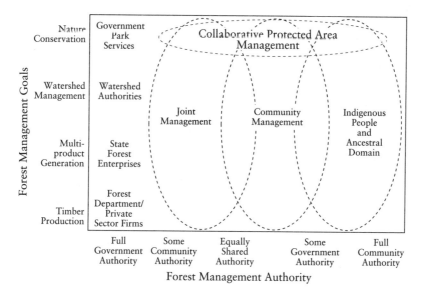

Figure 1. Forms of community forestry. Reprinted with permission from *Working Group on Community Involvement in Forest Management* (Gland, Switzerland: IUCN-World Conservation Union, 1996), 11.

foreign aid program. It is the principal sponsor of a seven-year effort called the Upper Nan Watershed Irrigation Project in which, according to the plan, tribal people in twenty-eight villages in the watershed will help plan and carry out the rehabilitation and protection of their forests. Australian project coordinator Peter Hoare, a veteran forester new to the region, said that he did not yet have much to show for his efforts except that a series of village workshops had sharpened the definition of the problems. What had become clear from these, a consultant's report emphasized, was that "the real challenge for the project is to hand over the responsibility and benefits for forest management to the communities themselves. It is widely accepted that this is the key to the success of forest management in rural areas, where communities traditionally have had common property rights."[17] Hoare's plan called for revolving village development funds, administered by village committees, to support projects leading to an "environmentally friendly livelihood" for the villagers. Much of the project's success or failure will depend on the performance of these local groups, the quality of the planning and management training they receive, and the extent to which those intervening from outside will be sensitive to local culture and traditions in animist societies where shamans and other religious leaders remain powerful.

Many of the ways in which Hoare planned to introduce concepts of participatory decision making and management came from models developed at nearby Chiang Mai University. Hoare told us that previous community stabilization and development efforts undertaken by the university had involved interactions between a rich mixture of people: indigenous community leaders, Royal Forest Department (RFD) officials, field representatives of nongovernmental organizations, monks, academics, and foreign aid workers. Unofficial doyenne of this unlikely melange was Dr. Uraivan Tam-Kim-Yong, the energetic director of the Resource Management and Development Center in the faculty of social sciences at Chiang Mai University. She is the originator of many of the ideas moving regional policies, like those in the Philippines, along a trajectory from ineffective top-down forest management toward more successful participatory approaches to ecosystem restoration.

A Cornell-trained expert on social aspects of economic development, Uraivan had been working to strengthen the use of these new forms of watershed management in northern Thailand and surrounding areas since 1986, when she launched her first experiments in partnership with ecologist Jeff Fox at the East-West Center in Honolulu. Now she and her staff were seeking opportunities to extend their efforts to Laos, Vietnam, and China. At the time of my visit she was working on several plans to create even broader linkages between nongovernmental groups so that mistakes could be more easily avoided and good, larger scale ideas could be presented to such funders as the Asian Development Bank and the World Bank. Encouragement could be drawn, said Uraivan, from the victories that her loosely structured coalition had scored in northern Thailand. Over the past decade, after the mismanaged pounding the region had suffered, forests have been regenerating and local economies are growing stronger in many communities at a cost far more reasonable, she said, than that of similar activities in the Philippines. Chiang Mai University had provided social and cultural input and facilitated the creation in 1994 of an increasingly powerful and egalitarian Northern Farmer Network, which had begun to show signs of becoming a real force in the region. By 1997 it included 107 villages in seventeen watersheds that were organized to confront the state's infringement of traditional land rights. Technical experts from other nations had introduced such useful concepts as "counter-mapping," which villagers could employ to confront authorities with accurate field-based data that they had collected themselves. Thailand's Royal Forest Department, like the Department of Environment and Natural Resources in the Philippines, had become far more sensitive to local concerns, and early in the 1990s it founded a community forestry division with a field staff.

As a consequence of the successes in northern Thailand, a national community forest bill had been drafted and was under consideration in 1997. Not universally popular, the law would delegate to local communities full decision-making authority over many aspects of forest use. In 1997 the national parliament scheduled a public hearing to debate the bill and especially the question of what rights indigenous people would have to the resources in national parks and protected areas. Karen tribal elder Pati Punu Dokchimoo, one of a delegation of some 300 hill tribal people who had journeyed to Bangkok to express their views, became persuaded that the minister of agriculture was irrevocably opposed to access for local people. In protest he twice attempted suicide, succeeding the second time when he jumped from a train. Although the government responded by appointing a new and less antagonistic agriculture minister, the fate of the draft law remained uncertain. At the least, through the efforts of such leaders as Uraivan, the northern farmers, and those in charge of the Hak Muang Nan movement, local communities in northern Thailand were achieving an ever stronger grip on their own future. Said one analyst, "Community forest will be the strongest sphere of social action for marginalized ethnic minorities towards social justice and ecological decentralization."[18]

PART II

Stirrings in the Field

CHAPTER 3

The Road to Bendum

From Cagayan del Oro, a port town at the north end of Mindanao island in the Philippines (map 3), the road to Bendum rises steeply. We wound around deep ravines before reaching the broad plateau where farmers cultivate corn, pineapple, and fruit trees.[1] In the distance were denuded mountains on whose flanks magnificent huge hardwood trees once grew. In the foreground, a nine-year-old boy stood by the roadside. He dangled an eel he had managed to catch from a fast-flowing nearby river, despite the growing scarcity of the species; he hoped that a passing motorist would buy it for a pittance. The road swarmed with traffic: antique buses, gaudily decorated minibuses called jeepneys, overloaded trucks carrying upland corn and good *arabica* coffee down to the seaside. Vehicles that had slid into a roadside gully at a grotesque angle or had been left wheels up after failing to complete a sharp turn were all-too-frequent sights. Every few kilometers we encountered a *barangay* (town), where the calm green of the open countryside and the pine and gmelina trees flanking the roadside gave way to the bustle of roadside commerce. Here the streets were filled with the snarl and dense blue smoke of motorbikes, which often pull canopied sidecars that serve as the local taxis.

After two hours of driving from the coast we passed through

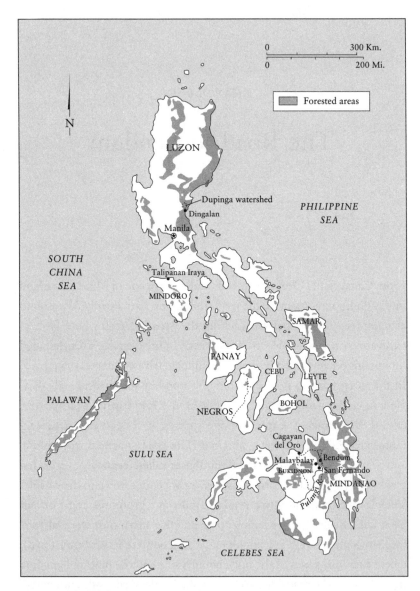

Map 3.   The Philippines.

Malaybalay, the capital of Bukidnon province. This town of some 17,000 people extends for several streets on either side of the main road. The wealthy and educated were congregated at places like Malibu Haus, a new hotel, to do business and talk politics. Then we turned onto a series of ever narrower dirt roads, passing ghost towns that had been largely abandoned after all the trees were harvested and rice paddies that were cultivated not by tractors but by carabao. TV aerials grew scarce and soon all but disappeared. As we climbed the road crossed rushing streams of water more frequently. Entering the upper Pulangi River watershed, we paused at a dusty place called Zamboangita to buy canned and dried fish.

Only four-wheel-drive vehicles with high clearance, such as ours, could proceed past the next village, St. Peter. Not even a sturdy jeepney could manage the rough stones of the abandoned logging road that we followed or traverse the stretches of white water that crossed the route. We proceeded, shooing away chickens and small naked children, until a fall of trees blocked further motor passage of any sort. An hour's walk through the patchwork of upland farms that had replaced the plundered forest brought us at last to Bendum, the last outpost along this line. Home to about seventy-five families when we made our visit in 1997, this *sitio* (hamlet) stretched perhaps a kilometer along a "main street" of compacted red dirt. Everywhere were reminders of degradation and poverty. Look carefully and one could also see tendrils of promise.

I arrived in Bendum at nightfall in the company of Peter ("Pedro") Walpole, an Irish Jesuit priest who has lived for many years in Asia. He left the formal Church long ago to work among the people, especially those whose lives have been devastated by excessive logging. Once a revolutionary, Walpole now directs an orderly staff of sixty people at the Institute of Environmental Science for Social Change, a development agency based at the Manila Observatory on the grounds of the Catholic University in Quezon City. While there, Walpole works the high end, tirelessly trying to persuade ranking public officials of the need to delegate possession of the land and authority over its use to the people who live nearest the islands' remaining forests and depend on them most. Since Bukidnon province is one of Walpole's principal project sites, his organization also maintains a lively office in Malaybalay. About thirty of the staff are based here and conduct activities in many parts of Mindanao. The wiry Walpole, whose slender frame disguises the throb of his energy, is most at home with the real flock he has chosen: the people of Bendum and many other Southeast Asian villages like this.

Walpole made his way to Bendum in cautious stages. He had been working in a parish in nearby Zamboangita. In 1992 he decided it was time for a move and "just began walking around" in search of a place where he could help bring about positive change. "I had no interest in imposing ideas on anybody during my visit," he said, "but I was prepared to try to support what a community had already shown interest in making happen, and I was looking for such a community."[2] He walked to San Fernando in southern Bukidnon province, where in 1989 villagers had blockaded logging roads to protest the disruption of their environment, then traveled all the way to Manila to fast before the office of the national Department of the Environment and Natural Resources (DENR) in an effort to get them to stop the logging in their old-growth forests. Walpole walked on to St. Peter. After six months of walking he strode alone into Bendum. He met a village *datu* (leader) with the Lumad tribal name of Man Ingga as well as a Filipino name, Nestor Menaling. Walpole saw that the Lumads with no help from outside had built themselves a little school. Walpole sensed he could accomplish something here.

INTO THE VILLAGE

By the time we reached Bendum it was pitch dark, with only the light of cooking fires and kerosene lanterns spilling out of the small houses. Confident of his navigation, Walpole led me up the main road, then across a ditch and downhill along a pathway to a primitive staircase leading up to a large house on stilts. We took off our shoes (hiking boots for me, rubber flip-flops for him), climbed the stairs to a rickety balcony, and entered an interior room. Here, to my surprise, were about twenty people ranged around a long dining room table who were preparing to eat. Most were children aged eight to fourteen. Walpole said a grace in English, then bowls of squash soup, platters of rice and vegetables, and a salad of ginger and sweet potato greens were passed around. The silence gave way to excited chatter as Walpole told the group where he had been and what was happening in Malaybalay and Manila. The children ate fast, cleared the table, helped wash dishes, then vanished into obscure corners of the house where they slept.

Walpole withdrew to a rocking chair on the balcony. The moon had risen, and now we could see across a beautiful wooded valley to the crest of a slope a mile away. Walpole leaned back, locked his hands behind his head, and began to describe where we were. Some of Bendum's residents, he said, are migrants from the lowlands who had followed the logging road nearly to its terminus in search of a place where they could build primitive wooden huts on publicly owned village land and try to grow crops on its outskirts. Three separate tribes of indigenous Lumads remain here as well. Lumads have lived in these mountains for centuries, long before the heavy logging began in the 1950s. They feel they own the mountains. Back when there was forest, much of what the Lumads ate and used came from within it: wild boar, birds, snakes, frogs, the occasional monkey, mushrooms, ferns, and honey for food, fiber to weave into traditional cloth, rattan—a long-stemmed climbing palm that has key economic importance in the region—to sell or barter. Sacred groves within the forest form the center of religious life for many Lumads. The bones of their ancestors are buried there.

Industrial logging disrupted traditional farming systems, in which long fallow periods enabled soils of poor quality to remain productive. The trees ordered the flow of water and inhibited erosion and landslides, which became a big problem on the steep hillsides and an even bigger one in the lowlands. In 1981, after extensive logging in the highlands, heavy rains sent vast amounts of mud down the Agusan River, at

Bukidnon's north end, and silted up its mouth. Severe flooding ensued. Hundreds were killed; thousands were left homeless.

The problem faced by Bendum's Lumads has roots that date to the sixteenth-century Spanish conquest of the Philippines. No sooner did the first governor general arrive than he and his entourage began handing out choice portions of land to Spanish citizens. Although subsequent land tenure legislation seemed to offer some protection to "Indians" with clear, if undocumented, evidence of ancestral occupancy, those natives without power were no match for land-hungry caciques, or local bosses, allied to colonial rulers. These usurpers systematically began to clear land, 90 percent of which had been forested when the first Spaniards arrived, to make way for sugar, coconut, rice, and corn plantations. By 1870 forests on the Philippine island of Cebu had been all but totally stripped, and erosion problems were noted. Local people were usually the losers. "In many cases," according to one summary, "peasants who had been using land for generations, but had not known about documentary titles, were suddenly confronted by influential people invoking colonial law and claiming their land. Many people surprised by this legal change were forced to flee their ancestral areas or became tenants."[3]

The situation worsened when the United States assumed control of the islands in 1898 as a result of the Spanish-American War. Soon afterward the new colonial administrators promulgated the so-called Regalian Doctrine, which alleged that Ferdinand Magellan had won total ownership of the islands when he stepped ashore in 1521. The Americans gave themselves the right to use more than 90 percent of the islands' landmass. Forest destruction accelerated as of 1904, when modern commercial logging on the islands was initiated. Clear-cutting soon became a common practice.

> U.S. lumber companies joined with Philippine businessmen to cut trees on Negros, in Bataan, and in other areas. Within a decade of independence, the Philippine government began a system of one-to-ten-year concessions wherein the lumber company was supposed

to replant some of its logged-over areas. Corruption, inadequate enforcement, and an interlocking of interests between loggers and government officials made a joke of this requirement. The 1920s through the 1960s marked the heyday of Philippine log exports; the Philippines was, during that period, tropical Asia's top exporter of tropical rainforest timber. As demand for wood in Japan grew rapidly in the 1960s, quick and easy money was made.[4]

During the 1950s and 1960s international theorists supported the emphasis on "scientific" industrial forestry that was practiced in the Philippines. Policies, which were administered from the top down, conformed to the accepted economic development standards of the time. In 1962 the influential forester Jack Westoby of the United Nations Food and Agriculture Organization (FAO) wrote that developing countries had neglected their forest assets, which could be converted into powerful engines for economic advancement.[5] Harvesting these resources more aggressively, wrote Filipino analyst Juan Pulhin, would result in a "new symbiotic relationship" between industrial nations and less-developed countries (LDCs): "The LDCs which abounded in forest resources could mobilize these for development, assured of markets with their more advanced trade partners. On the other hand the more developed countries would benefit from the relationship through the steady supply of forest products, particularly timber, to fuel and sustain their quest for further economic development."[6]

When human densities remained low, and few people other than scattered tribal communities ventured into the upland areas, none of this mattered much to the indigenous Lumads who had long occupied Bukidnon's upper slopes. For centuries they had lived there in relative isolation, venturing out occasionally to trade their crops for salt and clothing. Following World War II the population of the Philippines exploded, and after the choicest low-lying areas had been occupied to capacity, large numbers of migrants moved into the uplands. One-third of all Filipinos (more than 18 million people) now live in these highland areas. Farmers from Visayas, the group of islands in the middle of the archipelago north of Mindanao, migrated south to the area around Cagayan del Oro. As their settlements climbed ever higher, the Lumads fled before them, moving into even more remote areas.

The Lumads still had no land rights. As late as the mid-1980s the Regalian Doctrine remained the principal basis for land law, allocating all "undocumented" land to the public domain. Groups such as the Lumads were reduced to the status of squatters no matter how long they had occupied and farmed their lands. The logging crescendo occurred at the same time. U.S. companies like Georgia-Pacific, Weyerhaeuser, and Boise Cascade began operating in Mindanao's most important watersheds, including those of the upper Pulangi. By the mid-1970s these companies, and the national ones that eventually replaced them, had stripped Bukidnon of its timber. The companies then moved on to conquer new territories. The number of forest licenses issued to timber companies and the number of hectares felled each year reached record heights at the zenith of the Marcos regime, between 1972 and 1984, when the corrupt dictator's power was backed by martial law. By the end of the 1960s, half of the nation's original forest was gone. Only 20 percent of the country was forested in the early 1990s, and most of this was second-growth forest with far less commercial value or biological importance than the old-growth forest.[7] By the beginning of the seventies it was becoming apparent to Pulhin that "the hoped-for benefits for forest-based development were not being realized. More money was going into forestry; fortunes were being made; some forests were being ruthlessly exploited. But nearly all the developments were enclave developments; multiplier effects were absent; welfare was not being spread; the rural poor were getting poorer, and their numbers were increasing."[8]

In recent years the loggers and their Manila political cronies have not been the only threats arrayed against the villagers of Bendum. The Philippine army has long desired better road access to the Bukidnon highlands, where persistent bands of New Peoples' Army (NPA) insurrectionists are said to hide out. If built, the roads would attract new swarms of immigrants. Two hydropower dams have been proposed for the region; the scheme for the Pulangi, put forward early in the 1980s and later postponed, would have created the second-largest dam in Asia and flooded much of the region. Mining companies, some operating without government permits, comb the hillsides in search of new areas to exploit. More and more outsiders compete with the locals for the scarce rattan resources. The Asian Development Bank, accustomed to dealing in large amounts of money and still often insensitive to the needs of the poor in areas where it invests, has approved an "integrated" development project for the area. Large-scale initiatives of these sorts can easily trample the delicate watershed management regime that the Lumads have begun to create. The proposed development is "almost as big a threat as logging," Walpole said.

THE QUESTION OF RIGHTS

Perhaps worst of all, the Lumads have waged a long battle with rival claimants to regain formal title to the lands they have always considered to be theirs. Datu Aligpulus Timbangan, who bears the nickname of "Whirlwind," lives in Malaybalay, three hours' drive from Bendum when the roads are good, more when there is flooding or when landslides block some roads. He is connected to the lowland power elites—the politicians, the mining interests, the "educated." This man has hardly ever even visited Bendum, yet in the early 1990s he claimed to be the "designated chieftain" of a 30,000-hectare area within which the village falls. He collected thumbprints and other signatures in support of his candidacy to win the region as an "ancestral domain" for himself and his supporters, who were known as the Buhita Group. After Walpole's arrival in the village in 1993, the Lumads began a dogged counter-campaign for the restoration of their tribal rights. In 1994 they gathered to discuss the question of rights to gather rattan from remaining areas of forest that they think of as theirs. After the discussion Datu Nestor and ten other *datus* signed a letter to the government advancing their claim of an 8,000-hectare parcel within the area of the rival claim:

When the earth was created, God put us in this place called Bendum;
here where we were born. That is why we do not like Mindanao
migrants trying to make investments out of the land. The land we
have inherited from our ancestors. That is why we the Lumad unite
to protect the land of our ancestors. When their laws were not
violated, we did not go hungry, for our farms had enough produce.
Our crops were protected by the spirits. Our forebears told us to
take care of the forests and the water for it is here where we get our
food. Back then our livelihood was easy. The entry of different
companies to get trees and rattan marked the start of our hardships.
The forests were destroyed leaving nothing for us to live on. The
land we inherited from our ancestors has become a skeleton of
our beloved forest destroyed by logging. We are requesting from
the government that if there are any planned activities within
our land and the forests, such as the issuance of permits to extract
rattan, we would like to be consulted so that we are informed.
No one should take trees and rattan from the area without our
knowledge.[9]

In the balance of the document the Lumads requested the government's permission to develop a plan to manage the rattan that remains
on the region and asked for the license to harvest the resource. Two
years later, Bendum's Lumads took a broader initiative. In a letter to
Victor Ramos, secretary of the government's Department of the Environment and Natural Resources (DENR), Datu Nestor explained that
over the radio the people of the village had heard of a program whereby
some "ancestral domains" were being restored to traditional ownership
and management. At several meetings government officials urged the
Bendum group to merge their claim with the Buhita claim for a larger
area. The Bendum Lumads declined. Then Walpole helped arrange for
a government delegation to visit the village, and these officials were
impressed by what they saw. The villagers told their visitors that they
wanted to convey their "outmost desire to separate our claim," and they
advanced these principal reasons:

1. Because we are occupying the forest now. The Buhita group is already living in Malaybalay far from the forest and they could not take care of the forest.

2. And we recognized that this is the land passed on to us by our ancestors. The forest has been our church, market, and hospital, and so we will definitely claim it to take care of it until the end of the world. . . . We dream of taking care of our forest for the future of our children.

3. There were already several companies wanting to come in here but we have successfully driven them off because we take care of the forest in our domain.[10]

The Lumads' claim was at last resolved in their favor in 1998, but their problems were hardly ended. Walpole and his associates continue to work with the local community, and they quietly intercede on its behalf both in Malaybalay and in Manila. They do so because they passionately support the Lumads' cause, and also because they hope that their intervention will help establish a broader principle. "We are always trying to avoid uniqueness," Walpole said. "We want to be the center of a framework from which ideas can spread." The concepts of community-based land and forest management are not just "important" to the sustainable development process, he added. They are *fundamental* (a word a visiting World Bank official excised when redrafting an official document).

Life for Bendum's 200 Lumads remains precarious. Thirty-five percent or more of their children fail to make it past the age of five. A common cold can become tuberculosis or pneumonia and lead to death. Chicken pox can be fatal. The average life expectancy is thirty-five. People over fifty are rarely seen. They try to grow enough food to survive during periodic droughts and to make a little money by selling some of their harvest in the two tiny stores in St. Peter. They haul their produce to the village in carabao-drawn wooden sleds, which are handier on the often sodden pathways than wheeled carts are. Money is scarce and its use is still beyond the comprehension of many in the community. There is no electric power other than that produced by the odd auto battery or solar panel; there is no phone service, no resident doctor or nurse. One house has a television set. Many of the adults are illiterate and can write only their name. "Look what logging has done to us," said one of the *datus*, pointing at a denuded distant hillside.

These impediments are severe, but over the several days I stayed in Bendum I was able to see and touch the progress that Datu Nestor and his determined fellow villagers, with Walpole's quiet behind-the-scenes assistance, had made. After they had resolved to build a new water system, Walpole helped arrange a donation of plastic pipe. Now pipes link freshwater springs on the hillside to six pipe heads in the village, where women and children come to bathe and fill their buckets. Then the villagers built their second school.

Committees on land and forest management debate, set, and enforce intricate rules that govern farming and the use of the forest's resources: no one can legally cut rattan without the community's approval. While I was there, the men of the village were constructing two large buildings, following a long-standing tradition of *pahina*, or community work, in which they volunteered their time in return for corn. One building would be the village's third school; the other would be a meeting place for the "livelihood committee" and a place where community members can make handicrafts to sell elsewhere. The men used rented chainsaws and planes to fashion timber from logs that had been dragged in from the outskirts by carabao sled. Although they worked freehand, their boards were straight and true.

Walpole's field station serves as a boarding house for children from outlying farms and settlements who hike long distances to live in the village and attend classes at the adjacent school. The teachers, ten of them, are young parents from within the community. Walpole helped to get training for them. The learning is basic, but already these children are better educated than are their parents. The boys play soccer barefoot on a red-dirt field; the girls walk the village in twos and threes. School lets out during the harvest season, and the unaccompanied children walk home over the hills to help their isolated parents bring in the crops and to teach them to read and write. Older people in Bendum enthusiastically sign up for adult courses.

Late one afternoon, after it had grown cooler, I walked the old logging roads in the good company of Karen Lawrence, a young English woman who had been working with Walpole for several years. Some areas were planted with coffee and abaca, a banana-like plant that produces a marketable fiber for such products as straw mats. Some stretches of farmland, looking less well tended than they actually were, were dedicated to dry rice and corn and other basic food crops. The most affluent villagers haul in chemicals to supplement the meager supply of nutrients that the land provides. The Lumads observe long fallow periods, Karen said, and that too increases the fertility of the soil. Some old-growth forest, especially portions of it that hold spiritual value, had survived the cut, she added, and the community had shown great determination not to lose what remains. I looked across at areas where I could not walk alone since some of the local Lumads set snares to try to catch the scarce wild game. What is left of the forest still provides some resources: as we were returning to the village we passed a girl carrying a large basket of nuts that she had harvested.

The morning of my last day in Bendum was sunny. I sat for a while in Walpole's rocker on the porch, looking across the green valley, watching the birds. The familiar Philippine white-eyes foraged in the trees around the compound. So did a vividly yellow and black bird called the elegant titmouse and the flame minwet, an orange and black fruit-eater that resembles the northern oriole. It was the last day of the school term, and classes ended late in the morning. I joined Walpole and the children on an outing, walking down the precipitous hillside to the Pulangi River, where the boys in their undershorts and the girls in their dresses waded and paddled and swam in the crisp, clear, fast-flowing water. Some climbed and dove from a large rock. We found and attempted to photograph a large snake ranged along the branch of a tree

overhanging the water. Clouds were gathering as we climbed back up
the steep incline, making our way along the slippery pathways of red
mud. The children quickly scampered out of sight. "They move like a
troop of monkeys passing through the forest," Walpole said.

Later, after lunch and a rest, Walpole and I set forth down the village's main thoroughfare on the first leg of the hour's walk to a rendezvous with a vehicle that would take us to Malaybalay. As we left the
village the sky turned from gray to black. Lightning flashed, the wind
came in dust-swirling gusts, and then the rain arrived in large heavy
drops. We took refuge under the plastic sheet of a canopy outside a
grass house and watched as the drenched and chilled families of Bendum
splashed home. Little evidence of hope was apparent in this sodden
scene, but anyone operating under the illusion that Bendum is down-
and-out has it dead wrong. This community has cohesion despite its
poverty and remoteness and ethnic disparity. It has a sense of where it
wants to go.

BROADER ISSUES

Not many years ago efforts such as those of Bendum's Lumads would
almost surely have foundered, for authoritarian and centralized systems
prevailed in this archipelago until very recently. For government agencies it simplified things to work in larger units, to favor the interests of
the *barangay* over those of the *sitio*, and to respond to the elites and not
the masses. Corruption, which would escalate as one drew closer to the
palace, hardly favored village interests. Logging concessionaires wielded
power that was disproportionate to their limited ability to create jobs.
In the 1990s, as the Philippines began to favor more democratic and
more participatory social mechanisms, a greater degree of recognition
for the rights of remote local communities began at last to develop. The
Bendum *datus'* claim for their ancestral land rights now had a fighting
chance of success. And if the state actually places power in the hands of
the people who care desperately about improving the quality and sta-

bility of their savaged landscapes, the country just might avoid the eco-logical—and political and economic—disaster that beckoned only a few years ago, when the trees were tumbling down.

The transition dates from the 1970s, a time when very poor Filipinos in rural areas began to organize themselves in opposition to the central regime. Environmental issues moved steadily toward the forefront of national concern. Many analysts identified a cycle of environmental degradation in which the rural poor, in order to survive, follow a course of resource depletion that leads to harsher poverty, which in turn leads to even more severe assaults upon the environment. Closer examination, however, reveals many instances in which the rural poor have been very careful stewards of their environment in order to maintain their sources and supplies of food. Poverty, widely viewed as a principal cause of environmental decline, is just as often its consequence. If government-sponsored deforestation meant instant wealth for logging tycoons and wages for their employees, it represented the antithesis of "economic development" for most people, especially those struggling at the bottom.

San Fernando in Bukidnon, one of the communities that Walpole visited during the course of his walkabout, provides an example of the consequences of deforestation. Before the commercial loggers arrived, the people of the region could grow enough corn and rice to survive. Logging, however, produced the usual byproducts. Erosion removed the nutrient-rich topsoil. Creeks dried up and so did farming areas that previously could withstand long periods of drought. As the forests disappeared so did food supplies. At this point the region's formerly passive villagers began to stage anti-logging protests. They barricaded logging roads and fasted in front of a government office in Manila. One researcher who surveyed the area reported that "once environmental degradation began to transform poor people who lived in a stable ecosystem into marginal people living in vulnerable and fragile ecosystems, they acted."[11]

Incidents such as the San Fernando uprising, which were ever more widely replicated during the 1990s, gave evidence of how vehemently the rural poor were beginning to react to environmental degradation and excessive logging. At this point the Filipino leaders might have begun to grapple seriously with the issue that lay behind the unrest: the relationship between the nation's social and economic health and its forest management policies. Instead, when President Ferdinand Marcos responded to the mounting pressure, he did so more to control insurgencies than to work toward a more equitable society or to score environmental gains. Although the Marcos regime lacked the foresight to preempt the social revolution that began early in the 1980s, it did express moderately greater concern for the well-being of the indigenous upland communities than it had, and it made sporadic efforts to increase their land tenure security, treating them not as squatters but as deprived citizens with legitimate complaints. In 1982 "Integrated Social Forestry" became officially enshrined as part of national forest policy. It was touted as a step forward, although what it has usually meant is no more than the hiring of local people to establish community woodlots to give local people access to fuel and other resources. The government began awarding forest "stewardship certificates," which allocated user rights, to individual households or to communities in the uplands.

Vested political interests opposed the new programs to accord tenurial rights to upland families, and implementation remained painfully slow. The transition accelerated somewhat after Marcos was toppled in 1986 and the far more democratic Corazon Aquino came into power. During her incumbency the principle of community forest management was enshrined in a new national constitution, and a government directive mandated the decentralization of power. The DENR, an agency that had done little else than process an excessive number of logging concessions, showed growing enthusiasm for the idea that the welfare of the remaining forest, and all the environmental services that the standing forest provides, is closely linked to the welfare of the forest dwellers. In 1992 the government issued a document known as Administrative Order No. 2, which instructed DENR to initiate participatory planning processes that would lead to the award of ancestral domain certificates to qualifying upland communities. The Lumads were seeking this kind of recognition.

In 1995 an order came to consolidate all "people-oriented" forest activities into a single "community-based forest management program," to be regarded as the principal strategy for achieving the sustainable management of the nation's remaining forest resources. By 1998 three of DENR's four top officials were genuinely committed to the concept, Walpole reported. Plans called for its rapid growth—from 35,000 hectares[12] of forestland under the social forestry program of the 1980s, to 3 million community-managed hectares at 600 different sites in mid-1997, to a target of 9 million hectares by 2020.[13]

Local participation and village "empowerment" were becoming fashionable concepts at the international economic development agencies that support the Philippines as the nation swung away from investments in commercial forestry toward more "social" approaches. The World Bank, which since 1978 had been half-heartedly advocating something called "people-oriented forestry," took a step forward in 1991 when it cautiously admitted a willingness to endure "some sacrifice of short-term economic growth" for the sake of slowing deforestation in developing countries and in the future to "promote more active participation of local people . . . in the long-term management of natural forests."[14] In 1990 the United States Agency for International Development (USAID), for historical reasons a prominent entity in the Philippines, launched the $125 million Natural Resource Management Program (NRMP). The principal feature of the program was to "promote the sustainable management of the Philippines' tropical forests," in large measure by empowering local communities to protect the forest. In the four years of the program's first phase, which ended in 1994, USAID claims to have supported 250 separate forest protection programs managed by upland communities, reducing illegal logging in these areas by 97 percent and also reducing the rates of clearing and burning of forestland.[15]

For all the evidence of progress, contemporary community forest management remains in its infancy in the Philippines. Things move slowly even in government agencies with the best intentions. Politics and graft remain strong forces opposing the implementation of government policy. The more than 3 million hectares now under some form of community management is a small figure relative to the nearly 15 million hectares, including almost all of the remaining forest and many ancestral domains, that remain classified as "public land" under the control of the state. In the Philippines as elsewhere, says Walpole, cut-over *cogon* grasslands or second-growth forest of poor quality and limited economic importance are the lands that are most likely to have been handed over to local communities. Moreover, when local participation in land and resource management has been achieved there is no guarantee that wiser policies and practices will replace the squandering and carelessness of the past—even when large amounts of money are invested in efforts to achieve the transfer of power.

In 1990, for example, the Asian Development Bank and the Japanese Overseas Economic Cooperation Fund jointly committed $240 million to a project called the Low-Income Upland Communities Project (LIUCP), which was designed to improve the lives of tribal communities on the Philippine island of Mindoro. One-third of the island's people belong to an indigenous tribal group, collectively known as the Mangyan, who are admired for their peaceful ways and for their dedication to communal efforts to improve their villages. Reforestation and better management of eight critical watersheds would directly benefit 4,500 Mangyan families and render them better able to withstand pressures on their traditional lifestyles, which were coming from two directions. In the island's rugged mountains the insurrectionist New People's Army (NPA) had become the principal force, replacing both the Mangyan and Marcos's army. Along the shore and in the lowlands better-educated immigrants from other islands were taking work and land away from the Mangyan. Few signs of success were evident in 1995, however, when a group visited a Mangyan community. The occasion was the annual meeting of the Asia Forest Network, a loosely woven coalition of people and institutions interested in advancing the cause of community forestry in the region.[16]

The group had been heatedly discussing the matter for several days at the Mindoro Oriental, a pleasant reef-lined resort on the island's east coast. Three weather-beaten elders from the nearby Mangyan community of Talipanan Iraya had joined the workshop for a brief discussion of their situation and outlook. The next day a platoon of us boarded a small fleet of *bangas* (outrigger water taxis) for a visit to the village. After a short ride past several small resort and fishing settlements on the mainland and the small islands sprinkled offshore we disembarked on a beach and walked inland along a sandy path for perhaps an hour before we reached Iraya village. About fifty families lived in or near the village, which comprised a collection of randomly sited huts and a Puritan-style stockade used to discipline violators of tribal rules. Near this distinctive landmark we arranged ourselves in a semicircle around the elders. Women and children sat on the periphery in small, scattered groups.

We learned that although the village's stream was dry, we were at the foot of a watershed extending from the sea to the peak of an 8,500-foot mountain. Originally the Iraya were fishers and had lived on the coast. Starting in the 1930s migrants began pushing them back into the mountains, where the Iraya evolved sustainable systems of communal farming that were based not on land ownership but on each individual's ability to work the land. The villagers employed "agroforestry" methods in which trees not only yield resources but also protect the land and the smaller food crops cultivated in home gardens. Units of measure were neither used nor needed since there was plenty of land for everyone. During the 1970s new migrants invaded the highlands as well. Then, during the 1980s, the NPA insurgency drove the Iraya away from their lands on the upper slopes and left them pinned near the coast. The Iraya had forgotten how to fish, and they were able to continue farming only on some lands on the lower slopes.

To enable the Iraya to gain an ancestral domain certificate, which

would strengthen their position, Walpole's unit at the Manila Observatory, then called the Environmental Research Division (ERD), introduced mapping techniques. With a growing population in the region,
the Iraya needed to achieve more precise knowledge of what land had
been theirs. Better data would, the ERD hoped, lead to the award from
the DENR of an ancestral domain certificate that would strengthen
their hand. The Iraya were among the beneficiaries of the islandwide
LIUCP project, and some of their older men were consequently members of a district council with representation from all seven Mangyan
groups. Despite these efforts the mood seemed to be more one of apathy
and even despair, as opposed to the energy and determination I had
sensed in Bendum.

The traditional practices that had enabled the Iraya to survive had
been slowly eroding, and no services from outside seemed able to jerk
this community out of its stagnation. Pulhin had deliberately selected
this as one of his study areas because the community provided evidence
that "progressive community forestry policies do not necessarily guarantee good outcomes in practice." His text describes the broader failure
that may have contributed to Iraya's stagnation. The LIUCP scheme,
which was financed by the Asian Development Bank, had suffered multiple grievous wounds over eight years of expensive implementation,
Pulhin found. The bank and the DENR adhered to official preset targets
even after the locals articulated other priorities. The contracted nongovernmental organizations walked out and were blamed for the failure
to meet goals. Deadlines were missed. At the end of the project, Pulhin
concluded, the Mangyans may have been somewhat better off financially, but their lifestyle and value systems had suffered. And the government had failed to give them what they most wanted: rights to their
ancestral lands.[17]

It is important to note that there is also ample reason to believe that
the shortcomings of the Mindoro program represented an exception
rather than the rule for forestry management in the Philippines. The
movement toward more equitable forms of management and land tenure

is becoming increasingly evident in practice, in the field, and in policy as it is represented in published research. In 1998 this positive trend encountered setbacks, including a sudden halt in the awarding of ancestral domain certificates and the approval of management plans that bring funds to support community development initiatives. The president elected that year, Raul Estrada, has been better known for nightclubbing, girlfriends, and impeachment proceedings than for interest in any serious national development policies, including community forestry. The concept has gained a firm foothold, however, and its prospects improved after citizens forced Estrada out of office in January 2001. Surely, too, the Philippines is hardly the only country that is at last beginning to recognize that following this course has far greater environmental, social, and economic value than do the status quo and the limited benefits that previous forest policies offered only to a privileged few. Too much is at stake to leave the management of forests in the hands of foresters trained to cut down trees.

CHAPTER 4

Village Forests in India

I arrived in New Delhi late at night, surprised by the chill of winter in the smoggy air.[1] I peered through the crowd and spotted a small sign with my name on it, thankful that the director of the Tata Energy Research Institute (TERI), R. K. Pachauri, had arranged to have someone collect me from the airport. I had met Pachauri earlier that year at the annual World Bank conference on Environmentally Sustainable Development in Washington, D.C. "It will be your first trip to India?" he had asked. "Then I must help make your trip an unforgettable experience. You must come by the office and we will arrange visits to some of our forest projects. You will be greatly impressed."

The purpose of my trip was to learn how donors were integrating participatory policies into their forest projects. In particular, I wanted to assess how well the World Bank was integrating its policies on community participation at the field level. I planned to examine the bank's Madhya Pradesh Forestry Project, a new initiative that had been negotiated directly with Madhya Pradesh, India's largest state, rather than the national government. Madhya Pradesh is in India's heavily forested tribal belt, which spans the wide part of India from Rajasthan to West Bengal (map 4). All of the forest projects I planned to visit were aimed at helping India's poorest and most forest-dependent people, many of

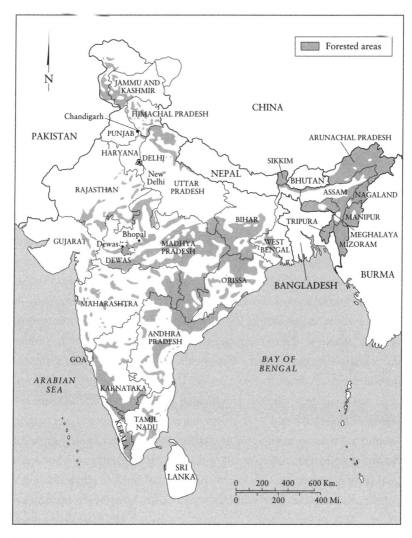

Map 4.   India.

whom are tribals. Tribals are groups of people that historically were geographically isolated and culturally and linguistically distinct from other Indians. Because they were non-Hindu—and hence without caste—they were seen as uncivilized. Like untouchables, they lived separately from casted Hindu communities. Today most tribals have adopted the Hindu religion and are distinguished more often by their extreme poverty than by any cultural or physical differences.

The broad objective of the Madhya Pradesh Forestry Project was to improve the quality of forest operations throughout the state in accordance with India's National Forest Policy Act of 1988, which recognized the need for local participation in forest management. The project promised to achieve a number of specific objectives: ensuring environmental stability and maintaining ecological balance, conserving India's biological heritage, substantially increasing the forest and tree cover in forest and farmlands, increasing the productivity of the forests, and—a key new addition for World Bank projects—ensuring the participation of local people in the management of forests and trees.[2] By including participation in the project's design, the World Bank made a fundamental departure from its usual projects, which had typically supported large-scale, timber-oriented production forestry. World Bank experiments in the 1970s and 1980s with social forestry projects were often limited to hiring local villagers to establish plantations of quick-growing fuelwood under the management of the forestry department. The bank's goal for the new project was to change the vision of Madhya Pradesh's forestry department. This ambitious goal was to be achieved by increasing the department's technical capacity in forest management and planning and by implementing training to improve relations between the staff and local forest-dependent communities.

The positive experiences of a few foresters in India triggered this focus on improved relations. These foresters made huge breakthroughs in forest protection once they began working with local people rather than viewing them as forest poachers. By embracing the concept of working together, which came to be called "joint forest management," the forest departments realized that they could achieve cost-effective means for reforestation while also improving local livelihoods. Pioneered in India, joint forest management relies on creating partnerships between rural people and forest agencies, with clear rights and responsibilities for each.

ORIGINS OF JOINT FOREST MANAGEMENT

About two thousand years ago the Indian subcontinent had an estimated 50 million people, and as much as 85 percent of the land was covered in forest. Today less than 10 percent of the land possesses good forest cover.[3] The population, already approaching 1 billion, is expected to reach 1.5 billion by the year 2050.[4] Almost 80 percent of this population lives in rural forest communities and depends on equitable access to forest resources.

Since the introduction of joint forest management, India's rural communities have steadily increased their control over and protection of forests. Nonetheless, only about 3 percent of India's 40.5 million hectares of reserve and protected forest is under community management.[5] Mark Poffenberger, long an advocate of local community forest management rights and an analyst of forest policy in India, finds the country's forest resources to be under mounting pressure. He argues that the failure of state forest management systems to include local communities has led to the erosion of biomass, declining timber and fuelwood productivity, habitat destruction, and biodiversity loss. The deterioration has been slow but continuous. Poffenberger supports turning more forest management responsibility over to communities.[6]

As early as 1860 Dietrich Brandis, founder of the Indian Forestry Service, warned India's governor general, B. H. Baden-Powell, that a policy that excluded local users would fail to protect forests.[7] Nonetheless, exclusionary policies and practices continued until well after India achieved independence from Britain. Throughout the 1970s, a period when donor agencies were supporting the Indian Forestry Service reforestation efforts that were supposed to involve local communities, local conflicts over forest resources increased. These social forestry models failed to recognize local rights of access to and control over public forestland and created many of these conflicts, particularly where traditional community control over forests had been strong. Meanwhile, in eastern India thousands of villages were taking unilateral control of public forests in defiance of existing policies and with the support of local politicians. Populist leaders at the local and state levels were beginning to represent the interests of tribal communities and other forest dwellers who were demanding a greater voice in how local forest resources were managed.[8]

Village forest protection efforts blossomed early in three regions where forestry officials were willing to share power: eastern India (West Bengal, Orissa, and Bihar), western India (southern Rajasthan and Gujarat), and the Himalayas (the Siwalik Range and the middle hills of Haryana and Uttar Pradesh).[9] In these areas the concept of joint forest management emerged from conflicts in which district forest officers, confronted by irate villagers, concluded that turning over forest responsibilities to local communities was the best way to maintain both peace and forest cover. A number of terms were used interchangeably to describe the concept: "participatory forest management," "community forest management," and "joint forest management." The last, conveying the idea of an equal partnership, came to prevail.

In 1988 the national government began to encourage local participation in reforestation. In 1990 it issued a new resolution on joint forest management, declaring that "tribals and other villagers living in and near the forests are to be treated as first charge on forest produce." In other words, these forest-dependent groups should have access to and control over forest products. The resolution called on state governments to establish use rights for local communities in exchange for their participation in the regeneration of public forests. It also encouraged the forest department to work with "committed voluntary agencies" that were "well suited for motivating and organizing village communities for protection, afforestation, and development of degraded forest land."[10]

The resolution sent an important message from the national government to state forest departments, and by 2000 almost all Indian states had implemented some form of policy. Donors have been quick to endorse the new strategy, in some instances with such haste and exuberance that many committed advocates of joint forest management fear that the concept is losing its force through co-optation and misinterpretation even as it achieves top ranking in forest policy debates. The World Bank has become one of the biggest proponents of joint forest management, making huge loans to state forestry departments with specific conditions that require local participation. I wanted to see how these conditions were being received at the field level, to what extent they were possible or even desirable in implementation, and whether the Madhya Pradesh project was in fact different from those that had gone before it.

NEW DELHI

I began by meeting with a number of people in Delhi to ask how they thought the World Bank's investment in joint forest management, or "JFM," was working and what trends they saw emerging. Kamla Chowdhry, a member of the World Commission on Forests and Sustainable Development and founder of the Society for the Promotion of Wastelands Development (SPWD), received me at her simple apartment in downtown Delhi. Sitting on the floor amidst piles of field reports and project documents, she told me,

> My real concern is that this new generation of JFM-oriented projects from large donors is built on the earlier social forestry plantation models, rather than the innovative institution-building approaches upon which JFM was founded. It's a problem of scale. The World Bank is determined to scale-up the successes of JFM. I worry that

the heavy funding of the JFM concept and the drive to expand numbers of village forest protection committees by the forest departments will detract from the genuine successes that emerged spontaneously as a response to real conflicts over forest resources.

She explained how different donors handle funding and noted the recent trend of Japanese aid that had begun to flow into India's forestry sector in large amounts with neither requirements for its use nor specific support for the joint forestry management concept. She sighed, "All things being equal, bad JFM is better than no JFM." She urged me to speak with Syed Rizvi, then the executive director of SPWD. Even though the following day was a holiday, she told me, he was always working and would be happy to take the time to talk with me.[11]

Meeting with me early the next morning, the spry Rizvi expanded on Chowdhry's explanations. "First of all," he said, "I must emphasize a distinction that local nongovernmental organizations are increasingly making between the spontaneous forest protection committees that emerged from customary traditions and those formed by the forest department, which in my opinion tend to lack a sense of ownership and purpose."[12] Committees that have formed on their own initiative have compiled an impressive record. In many instances nongovernmental groups like Rizvi's helped local people organize their communities. Rizvi described the success that these communities have had.

Some 2 million hectares of India's state forestland are said to be regenerating under the forest department–endorsed protection of community groups. With virtually no investment from the state or outside agencies, local communities in India have already done at least as much to restore degraded forest environments as have development agencies and forest departments, which have invested about 1 billion dollars in social forestry projects over the past two decades.

Rizvi told me how the Madhya Pradesh Forestry Project got started.

In the 1980s an enterprising forest officer in Jabhua district paused to consider how much forest department money was being invested in fencing to keep cattle out of the forest. The cattle were destroying the fencing as well as the forest, and the forest officer wondered whether there might be a better way to deal with the problem. He began to talk to the villagers in a new way and to listen to their solutions. The villagers volunteered to keep their livestock from devouring the forest by tethering their animals and collecting fodder for them. The forest began to recover. The officer then sat with the villagers to work out alternative uses for the money saved in fencing costs. They decided on a number of social projects. The news of this success began to travel through the ranks, and the attitudes of forest officials started to change. The World Bank got wind of it and decided to underwrite joint forestry management projects clear across Madhya Pradesh, India's largest state.

Approximately 20 percent of the state—135.8 square kilometers—is covered with forest. Rizvi told me that, strangely enough, the officer who started all this had been transferred to another state. "No one mentions him," Rizvi said. "They mention the region of Jabhua, but they fail to give him credit. You will see when you go to Madhya Pradesh how they deny his critical role."[13]

MADHYA PRADESH

I set off by train from New Delhi. During the long journey to Bhopal, the capital of Madhya Pradesh (map 5), I was surprised by the endless expanse of flat, dry terrain. When I arrived in Bhopal I made my way to the Indian Institute of Forest Management to find Dr. Prodyut Battacharya. I had met Battacharya through the Asia Forest Network, a group of forest practitioners, donors, and policymakers from across Asia who meet biannually to discuss trends in forest policy development, particularly policy that supports enhancing the role of communities in

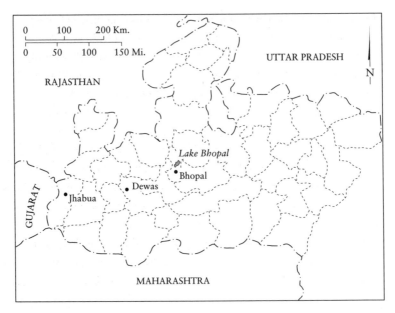

Map 5. Western part of Madhya Pradesh State, India.

managing forests. Battacharya had studied at the Regional Community
Forestry Training Center in Bangkok, and we had many friends in common. Battacharya immediately set to work. He helped me arrange meetings at the forestry department, warning me to brace myself for the
sharp-tongued principal chief conservator of forests, and arranged
lodging for me at the institute's dormitory. He then invited me to dine
with his wife and another colleague from the institute.

Before dinner we climbed up to the roof to take in the sunset over
Lake Bhopal. The peaceful view and the cool breeze on the roof were
refreshing. Battacharya's colleague was eager to give me some background on the training components of the Madhya Pradesh Forestry
Project. "Most of those fellows at the forest department know nothing
about training," he told me.

> They talk about the need to have the forest officers sit with the
> villagers, but they are all mired in their own ambitions to move on

to a more glamorous district. The only training that interests them is the high-tech Geographic Information Systems course for which they must go to Germany. They are not interested in understanding caste and gender differences among villagers and how they influence forest use. They are hopeless. They have too much money now to do what is needed to get foresters to change their mindset.[14]

Both professors lamented the continued obsession of forest officials with what they called "hardware"—technology—when what the foresters need to focus on is "software"—human relationships. They argued that the foresters need to develop real human relationships with the villagers, understand their point of view, and learn the skills required for participatory management. Instead they want to spend their money on the latest technologies and infrastructure projects. "An even more difficult problem," Battacharya added, "is that the Indian Ministry of Environment and Forests and most state forest departments continuously rotate their high level officers." Battacharya explained that every year or two the top officers are transferred to a different state. Consequently leadership tends to be erratic. Policy implementation can stagnate, or it can become tied purely to personal gain. He continued:

Even more ludicrous is that as soon as a district officer has gained the trust of villagers in his district and has begun to make changes in the department that improve the forest base and address people's livelihoods, the chap will be moved. Just like the district forest officer from Jabhua that got this project started in the first place. It makes no sense. At any rate, changing the mindset of foresters is really a complex undertaking. Ask them about their training programs and it will all sound very good. But in the end, what is really needed is time and commitment to changing the culture of the forest department right down to the lowliest beat officer based in the village. This is no easy undertaking. There are no quick fixes.[15]

The next morning I took a motorized pedicab to the Madhya Pradesh forestry department. After making the acquaintance of the trainers and the Madhya Pradesh Forestry Project task force, some of whom were friends of my contacts in Delhi, I was escorted in to see the principal chief conservator of forests, D. P. Singh. True to his reputation, he gave me a frosty reception. After cross-examining me on my intentions, on my qualifications, and on the basis of my interest in community forestry, he concluded, "You have no business in coming to spy on the World Bank project, and you are obviously up to no good!" He insisted that there was no way a foreigner could ever understand India's long and complicated history. "Did you know that India was colonized by the British?" he asked condescendingly. Most impressive were his assertions that the World Bank's views are completely irrelevant to what happens at the village level, and that he had no intention of paying attention to any of its policies. "We managed to get a loan from the World Bank because they wanted to fund a project. We were interested in expanding our activities. We are using the funds as we wish. The World Bank cannot dictate what we do with the money." He continued:

> Now all these donor agencies come in talking about community
> participation without even knowing what that means or what sort of
> obstacles might exist at the community level. They are trying to
> sell "participation" when they themselves are not at all participatory.
> If you want to understand how participation is working at the
> local level, then come back with some sociologists and plan to be
> here for a few years. I cannot see how you can get anything out of
> such a short field visit.

Pompous and arrogant as he was, I had to concede his last point. I explained that I had heard about the district of Jabhua and would like to visit. Singh looked at me, his eyes widening.

> You are not going to Jabhua! Do you know how many hundreds of
> foreigners have gone parading through Jabhua? People of all
> colors, even in full national costume, have gone to gawk at these
> poor people in Jabhua for their forest. I say enough! No, I will send
> you to one of the areas where we have just begun. Unfortunately

the district officer will not be able to accompany you. You will go to Dewas.[16]

I spent the remainder of the afternoon with the members of the project task force. They seemed to grasp the enormous difficulty in implementation, as the task officer explained: "The problems we have are on the 'social' side and not the technical side. Real participation means the forest officers and the villagers each have to agree on rights and responsibilities."[17] The training coordinator concurred:

> The real difficulty is in trying to explain why to the subordinate officers. The higher ups understand that we need change but the less-educated beat officers at the bottom do not want to give up the power they hold over other villagers. Furthermore, there are cultural barriers for a beat officer, or any officer, to sit with low-caste villagers or non-caste tribals. These things are what we must work on. The higher ranking officers have dispensed with wearing a uniform to help them seem less imposing, but the beat officers seldom want to do that. Psychologically, wearing the uniform gives the beat officers their power. Sure there are problems in getting upper level officers to listen to the villagers but, surprisingly, that has been the least difficult part. These district forest officers also know that once they have shown good effort, they will be transferred out. We can't offer that same kind of incentive to a beat officer.[18]

At the end of the day I managed to meet with the district forest officer from Dewas, Mudit Kumar Singh, who was on his way to a training seminar elsewhere in India. M. K. Singh apologized sincerely that he could not accompany me to his district, and assured me that his lower ranking range officers would be able to show me around. I learned that joint forestry management had been introduced at Dewas only three years earlier. The district has about 50,000 hectares of forest and about sixty-three state-initiated forest protection committees. The district forest officer told me that to reduce pressures on the forest his range officers had been promoting the use of fuel-efficient stoves that could burn cow dung. Singh explained that following Jabhua's model, range officers had been encouraging villagers to tether their livestock as an alternative to the costly wire fences that the forest service had been building around the forests. He explained that district forest officers across the state are now supposed to encourage villagers to tether their animals and to use the money that had previously been allocated toward building costly fences around forests to support the construction of schools and irrigation channels and the development of projects to provide drinking water.[19]

DOMESTICATING TRIBAL VILLAGERS' TASTE IN TREES

The next morning a quiet forest guard fetched me in the vintage car that I had rented for the day. As I gazed out the window onto a countryside once known for fierce tigers and abundant wildlife, I was struck by how the dusty landscape stretched for miles without even a shade tree to break up the monotony. As we drove along, the terrain turned into graceful hills spotted with green. After about three hours we arrived at a forest department rest house in the district of Dewas. Among the people who greeted me were the range officer, dressed in casual trousers and a button-down shirt, and his subordinate beat officer, who was in uniform. We sat down on the veranda. Over tea I launched into my questions about the technical and economic aspects of what they were doing in forestry. They answered dutifully, but I sensed a certain impatience, or perhaps eagerness, in the range officer. Finally he stood, insisting that I see the forest.

The lanky range officer was keen to show me as many corners of the teak plantation as he could manage, and he set off at a rapid pace toward the distant sloping hills, which were dotted with young trees. I followed behind with the beat officer. The range officer told me that the forest department had used pilot project funds to establish this forest three years earlier. They had planted the teak seedlings on degraded land with the help of local villagers. The spindly young trees, each with a few large dry leaves, were taller than I was, but they hardly looked like they would qualify as a forest. The range officer explained the techniques that were being applied to control erosion and protect the young trees. He assured me that this "forest" needed constant vigilance to protect it.

I looked across the plantation and saw a man in the distance. As he approached I asked who he was. The range officer replied, "That is one of the villagers who is guarding the forest." As the range officer pointed to another teak sapling I witnessed a strange interaction between the villager and the beat officer. I saw the beat officer rush over to the villager and strike him with a stick. I turned toward them and asked if I could take their picture. The two men posed side by side, expressionless, one in uniform and the other in a simple sarong. When I turned away the beat officer began speaking aggressively to the villager. I gathered that this apparently uneasy relationship between the beat officer and the villager was the sort of difficulty that the trainer in Bhopal had described as a factor complicating the advance of participatory policy in the field.

Bringing my attention back to the teak plantation, the range officer explained the technical side of the forestry operations, beginning with the details of how teak "coppices." As teak trees grow, multiple shoots grow from a single stump. Villagers remove smaller and deformed shoots, allowing the sturdier shoots to grow straight and tall. The original rootstock is not damaged, and it continues to grow. Planting coppicing trees is popular because these trees can provide a continuous supply of fuelwood. I saw a great many examples of coppicing, and I diligently photographed all variations in response to the range officer's enthusiasm. He also pointed out young bamboo, a few varieties of quick-growing acacia, and the occasional mahua tree. Mahua is particularly valuable to local villagers for its multiple medicinal and food products, but according to the foresters it is a nuisance because the villagers fight over the products. The foresters declared that there was no way to equitably allocate these products. When I asked if the villagers had been asked how they might allocate the products, I got blank stares in response.

During February, when I visited, Dewas was exceedingly dry, and the leaves on the trees were sparse. Overall, the plantation appeared to fulfill only the minimum requirements of fuelwood, fodder, and basic building materials for the local people. The teak grows slowly. The range officer said that eventually, in thirty years, the forest department would harvest it. "Villagers will get 30 percent of the revenue and possibly a daily wage for the cutting," he said. Until that time the villagers are not to cut any teak, apart from thinning out the coppices. The villagers' main incentive for protecting the forest, say the foresters, is to have access to fuelwood and fodder from around the plantation. I could not see any difference between this project and the heavily criticized social forestry project model that also failed to give forest-dependent people any stake in forest protection.

It seemed to me that reforestation that will benefit local people requires more than simply involving them in establishing teak plantations that earn income for the forest department. Unless the local villagers can gain basic use rights, the forest protection committees will have little incentive to do more than follow orders. The villagers were fulfilling their end of the bargain by tethering their cows and collecting fodder for them, limiting their gathering of fuelwood, and helping with the preparation of seedlings. Yet the forest department had not given them many rights despite the fact that they had taken on these responsibilities.

Later in the afternoon we met with some of the villagers. I was surprised that they had gathered in a compound outside the village walls. I asked the range officer why, and he explained that the tribals live separately from the casted villagers. We sat with the tribal villagers, sipping chai and discussing their forest project. When I asked the villagers if they had any questions for me, one very old wisp of a man wrapped in a white loincloth asked, "Can you help us get rights to our land? We want land rights. We want to know it is ours to manage. Until we have land rights, this makes no sense." The range officer explained to the man that having rights to collect fuelwood and fodder is almost like owning land. The man shook his white head sadly.

Before I left Bhopal I met again with Battacharya, and I asked him about the targeting of tribals. He explained that in the cases he had seen, projects were directed at tribals and involved them in the daily work of planting, managing, and protecting the "forest." More often than not, however, it was the casted villagers—the local elites living inside the village compound—who indirectly reaped the benefits from these projects in one way or another.[20] I realized that any good project had to confront the realities of village power relations to succeed. I also recognized that my understanding of social organization in India, and specifically in Madhya Pradesh, was grossly deficient. Although I did not think the project in any way resembled the joint forest management projects that I had read about, I knew that the project had officially just begun, and I tried to keep that in mind as I evaluated it.

TERI PROJECTS IN HARYANA

Battacharya ferried me back to the Bhopal station on his Vespa, and I returned to Delhi on the express train. Upon arrival in Delhi I headed across town to TERI, where O. N. Kaul, the astute director of the biodiversity program, was awaiting me with express train tickets to Chandigarh (map 6). He told me that Dr. Bakshish Singh would collect me from the station and take me to see Haryana's Ford Foundation–funded community forestry projects. Kaul asked for a quick rundown on what I had seen in Madhya Pradesh. He nodded his head knowingly as I described what I had seen and guaranteed me "a completely different picture in Haryana."[21] He loaded me down with literature on the projects to prepare me for my visits and rushed me out the door to catch the afternoon train. I hailed another pedicab and found my train at the station. When I arrived in Chandigarh it was dark. Singh, a turbaned

Map 6. Haryana State, India.

Sikh, met me as promised and welcomed me warmly to northern India.
He took me to a hotel and, leaving me to a late-night supper, told me
I should be prepared to start early the next morning.

In the two ensuing days of village visits I gained a picture of community forest projects that differed significantly from what I had seen
in Madhya Pradesh. Singh is a former forestry official who commands
great respect within the forestry department. He is also a gifted and
experienced community organizer and had been visiting villages in the
region for over six years as part of his work for TERI. In each village,

he said, tribal people had succeeded in forming a forest protection committee, which in this region they call a "hill resource management society" to distinguish their committees from the initiatives sponsored by
the forest department. In some instances the villagers had formed a
society after a year of weekly gatherings. In other villages it had taken
as many as five or six years to achieve this step. In all cases participation
of the village communities in forestry management led to the formation
of grassroots institutions that have assumed a definite role with clearly
defined rights and responsibilities. Singh explained that these societies
were founded on the basis of traditional village institutions, not built
around the suggestions or requirements of the community organizer.

The first village we visited made the deepest impression on me. It is
located in the hilly belt of the Siwalik mountains that form the foothills
of the Himalayas. On the way to the village Singh explained that the
villagers were Bhandjas, a tribal group who carry on a tradition of making bamboo baskets and depend on the local forest for bamboo. Singh
said that the Bhandja society is not as hierarchical as village societies in
Madhya Pradesh. Nonetheless, including women was not easy. He explained that although women play a strong role in resource management
in this area, he initially could not get the men and women to sit together.
Singh told me that he had brought in women organizers to help incorporate the women into the process of village meetings. The organizers
had to convince the villagers that since forest problems concern both
men and women, men and women should consider the problems together. After a year of involvement, the Bhandjas formed a hill resource
management society to protect the forest from fires and illegal felling
and to secure their source of bamboo.

When we arrived, the president of the hill society, a small woman
with a commanding presence, introduced herself. The villagers gathered
eagerly around Singh, barraging him with questions and their latest
problems. I could not follow the discussion, but as I sat with the villagers, observing the meeting, I noticed that everyone had something to
say. I also noticed that the women, even when speaking forcefully,

covered their heads and faces with the corners of their scarves and did not look directly at the men as they spoke. I asked Singh about that later, and he explained that this region has had centuries of heavy Muslim influence. Although the Bhandja society is Hindu, they had acquired some Muslim mannerisms. Despite these customs, both the previous president of the hill society and the village head were women. This was a big contrast to Madhya Pradesh, where women were scarcely a part of the project. But then again, this hill society had been active for six years and had gotten a lot of attention from the dedicated Singh.

Another part of Singh's work is to set up a village bank. The Bhandjas have collected member dues for five years. They use those funds to administer small loans to the members at a minimal borrowing rate of 2 percent per month, considerably lower than the rate that had been charged by middlemen. Singh said, "Unfortunately, most of the villagers are in debt because they take out loans for important celebrations or wedding ceremonies rather than develop money-making activities. But I am reluctant to interfere. I feel the people will eventually learn to invest in business ventures. The important thing is to allow the hill society to develop its own sense of priorities."[22]

Later in the day Singh took me to another forest-dependent tribal community in the Siwalik belt, where he had used this same patient approach. This was a community of Banjaras that traditionally make rope from bhabbar grass (*Eulaliopsis binata*). Singh explained that they had only recently formed a hill society to secure their own supply of bhabbar rather than buying it from middlemen. For almost five years the villagers were reluctant to form a hill society and hesitant to contribute to a village bank. At last, in the fifth year, a few people in the village began leasing bhabbar fields directly from the forestry department and earning more money. Once the other villagers found out, they were suddenly interested in joining. Singh explained that this process required patience. "It was worth the wait. The committee that has formed has been very effective in the end, much more effective than it would have been had it been mandated by the forest department."[23]

It occurred to me that the success of joint forest management in many places in India has often depended less on money than on time and dedication. Building trusting relationships between villagers and forest department officials requires a commitment to communities that most forest department officials do not have. Involving local nongovernmental intermediaries like TERI as key players may help. As Chowdhry stresses, perhaps it comes down to a question of scale. It is not enough to pump more funding into projects to increase community forest protection. What is needed is a combination of a commitment to the process and the resources to keep committed organizers involved. I asked Singh what he thought. "I am personally heartbroken that in a short time this project will end," he replied. "The hill societies will have to continue without my guidance. I wish the project were longer term so that I could be sure these groups will survive, but such is the nature of project funding."

Singh bid me farewell at the station the following day, and I made my way back to Delhi, thinking about the major differences between these projects. Because of the contrasting nature of their funding and their scale, they really were not comparable. Although it would be tempting to dismiss the World Bank projects as a failure based on what I had seen in the communities that I had visited, these projects were still in an early phase. Furthermore, they faced different challenges with respect to the people and their forest resource base. All the same, the very premise of the two projects, who the projects benefit, and how the communities were organized left me feeling that Chowdhry's concern that joint forest management could lose its meaning in large projects was very real. Although much depends on the community organizer's approach, the original concept of joint forest management—that communities and foresters work together—was apparently more difficult to establish in the field than the World Bank project organizers realized.

FOREST PROTECTION COMMITTEES
IN EASTERN INDIA

Almost a year later, in December 1996, I returned to India to attend a meeting of the Asia Forest Network, held just outside New Delhi. Many of the country's most experienced and committed advocates of joint forest management attended. Also present were Indonesian colleagues with whom I was working on a forest policy study in eastern Borneo. The Indonesians were stunned by the buzz of conversation about the latest trend in India: the emergence of federations of community forest protection committees. I had planned to travel to eastern India, where joint forest management was born, after the meeting ended. As it turned out, this was also where the federations were most active.

At the meeting I met with Neera Singh, who runs an organization called the Vasundhara Institute, which is based in the capital of Orissa, one of India's eastern states (map 7). She told me that the most exciting development in the past decade had been the emergence of these federations of local villagers, which were making local control a political demand. "It's really quite a radical departure from joint forest management," she said.

> In the case of the federation we are working with, the local people have declared their forests off-limits to the forest department officials. They won't let the forest department enter their forests. They feel that the idea of joint forest management is a way for the state to claim 50 percent of the forests that these communities have been protecting for the past fifty years, and they won't have it. They even prefer to take the high-value trees like teak out of the forest before they grow bigger and become more valuable. This way, as they see it, the forest department has no excuse to make claims on the forest, and there is less risk of forest poaching.[24]

I was surprised that villagers would remove high-value species from their community-protected forests before they could become valuable,

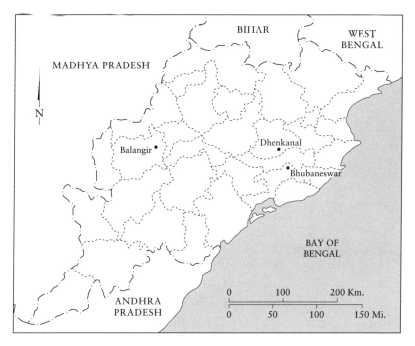

Map 7.   Orissa State, India.

and I asked about the legality of their act. Singh explained that the forest service only had an interest in valuable species that they could sell. These acts of resistance by local communities against the forest service were not strictly illegal, and they were very difficult for the forest service to counteract or control. I later discovered that this was a recurring practice in Orissa. The reason is simple: the enterprise arm of the Orissa forest department has organized the nationalization of all high-value forest products—they have full control of the trade of these products. Villagers are not allowed to sell them. Many villagers across Orissa would like to be able to collect and sell nontimber forest products themselves, and they resent the state monopoly on these activities. Some protest this nationalization by removing products with potential value to the forest department. In the meantime they continue to protect their forests for the sake of the services they provide, such as watershed protection, as well as for subsistence needs.

The state of Orissa has by far the most progressive joint forest management laws in India, mostly as a political response to spontaneous formations of community forest protection committees. Social and political factors have strengthened local efforts to protect forests in Orissa. Forests there have traditionally been subdivided among various users so that tribal peoples and casted villagers protect separate areas of the forest. Although caste skews the distribution of resources among those protecting and using forest goods and services, organization along caste lines seems to have minimized conflict both among castes and between villages.

During the Asia Forest Network meeting Singh had introduced me to another colleague, Sankharsan Hota, who runs a community organization in central Orissa called the People's Institute for Participatory Action Research (PIPAR). Hota told me that federations were emerging quite rapidly in his area. "My field coordinator called me up last month. He said that he had been invited to a meeting of forest protection committees in his district that they had convened with all the villages in their forest block. They wanted to organize into a federation. They wanted more control over their forests! We have never talked to them about federations!" Hota continued:

> The villagers lamented that some villages in the block had not created forest protection committees and were tempted to invade all the nice forest that is under community protection. They argued that if they had everyone in the area joining together to protect the forest, they could reduce local conflict. They also thought they would have more bargaining power with the forest department if they were a solid front. It all makes perfect sense, but their move took us by surprise. They had representatives from every village in the entire range. We would never have thought to organize something like that.[25]

The day after the New Delhi conference ended, I flew with Singh and Hota across India to Bhubaneswar, the capital of Orissa. Orissa is one of the most important forest states in India, but commercial exploitation and a rural population that has grown tremendously in the past thirty years have accelerated forest degradation. This exploitation has come in waves in different places in the state. "From 1962 to 1968," Hota explained, "there was a period of intense degradation from commercial logging. Community efforts were made to restore and protect the forests from 1968 to 1972. That was followed by another period of degradation from 1972 to 1978 by companies that had obtained licenses by the forest department." In the 1980s the Orissa forest department established a social forestry program. Referring to the forest department as "FD," Hota continued:

> The villagers had a lot of conflict with the FD over the planting of eucalyptus trees around Mahapada. They complained that the FD wanted to clear the forest areas that they had been protecting.
> So the villagers sent them packing. They had no use for fast-growing varieties of tree. The FD later decided there could be no plantations in areas that were demarcated as forest, so the program was stopped.[26]

Hota explained that Orissa has four types of forest: reserve forest (48 percent of the state's forested land); demarcated protected forest (29 percent); undemarcated protected forest (23 percent), also known as *khesra*; and degraded forest. Until recently strict laws forbade communities from entering reserve and demarcated protected forests but encouraged them to adopt and protect *khesra* forest. By 1980 many village-based groups had emerged to protect their adjacent forest resources and, in some places, to take over the protection of some reserve forest. In 1988 the state passed a resolution recognizing the role of these communities and giving them responsibilities to guard against theft and fire in return for being allowed to collect fuelwood and other minor forest products. In 1992 the state passed a second resolution that allowed for the registration of forest protection committees. Within a few years the forest department registered some 6,085 forest protection committees in Orissa.[27] Meanwhile, hundreds more groups that were not registered with the forest department were functioning as forest protection committees. In 1995, owing to the poor condition of the state's reserve forests, the Orissa forest department stopped issuing permits for commercial felling. This moratorium allowed communities to expand their protection to include some of the state's reserve forest as well.

FEDERATIONS OF VILLAGE FOREST PROTECTION

The next day Hota and I went to PIPAR's office in Dhenkanal, in the heart of Orissa. As we began the half-day's journey from Bhubaneswar we drove past scrubby fields with bald hillocks. Gradually the landscape transformed into graceful hills dotted with trees. Dhenkanal has the highest number of forest protection committees in the state. Thousands of villagers spontaneously formed these committees in response to the waves of logging and social forestry programs that excluded the villagers from their traditional forest domains. The people organized themselves according to traditional village guidelines so that they could combat fuelwood scarcity and protect their watersheds for irrigation purposes. Hota was eager for me to meet the Bejibolua villagers, who had initiated the latest federation. He sent me off with one of his field coordinators, Samarendra Satapathy.

Satapathy was as serious as Hota was jovial. He immediately began to talk about Bejibolua and how the villagers had mobilized some 150 villages around the Chandipada forest. The events he described provided a living example of the most remarkable feature of community forest protection efforts in India: their ability to spread from one village to another with little outside intervention.[28] The movement began in Bejibolua when the villagers decided to organize at the forest-block level to form a federation of village protection committees. A forest block comprises twenty-four *panchayats* (village administration units), with each *panchayat* representing 10,000 people. Satapathy had been stunned when they invited him to the block-level meeting to plan their next steps. "I had no idea they had moved so quickly!" he said. Satapathy told me that at the meeting, after lengthy debate, the representatives from the 150 villages had decided that despite their misgivings about the Orissa forest department, they wanted to register their forest protection committees under the joint forest management legislation passed in Orissa. As a registered forest protection committee, referred to as an "FPC," they would have the backing of the state to defend their forest use rights, but it would mean that the department would also have certain rights over the area. The villagers were still talking about this recent decision when we visited Bejibolua.

We drove to Mahapada village, where the Bejibolua Chausa caste lives. We pulled off the road near a small hut with an old bicycle resting against it. It was midday, and despite the early morning chill of hours before, I could now feel the sun licking at my neck. We settled in the shade of a tree and waited for the villagers. Satapathy told me that ordinarily they would be busy harvesting their fields in December, but because this year's drought had wiped out 75 percent of their harvest, the villagers had time to talk with us. Soon nine men emerged from the foliage across the road, where I could just make out the edges of the typical round-edged mud-brick houses. Those who joined us first were the older men with white hair and leathery faces. Their wiry bodies were draped in bright colors. A few younger men arrived wearing madras sarongs. We were making introductions, with Satapathy translating, when a spry older man, his head wrapped in a hot pink cloth, ran up, saying excitedly, "I was in the fields and had come home for tea when I heard someone was here!" His name was Govindo. He nodded his head eagerly as I explained that I had come to learn about their forest and how they had decided to protect it.

I asked them what the forest had been like when they were young men. Spreading his arm out energetically toward the forest in the distance, Govindo recounted tales from the past. "In the fifties the forest was quite dense. There were tigers, peacocks, and deer. From 1955 to 1960 the forest was massively degraded by logging, and then people took the rest. It took only four years to degrade the hillsides around here." He explained that during the sixties there was a severe shortage of fuelwood: "It took three days to collect a cartload of fuelwood, walking twenty-four kilometers, roundtrip."[29] The rest of the men chimed in, describing how the forest department officers used to harass them and fine them for taking logs from other places. The men recounted how the villagers finally decided to protect their forest and formed their first village protection committee in 1972.

I walked with the villagers through thickets of shrubbery on the edge of the forest and then into a forest of sal (*Shorea robusta*), which, like teak, serves as an important source of fuelwood because it coppices, or naturally regenerates, from the same rootstock if cut carefully. My companions proudly pointed out the girths of the trees and the abundance of leaves and fruits and barks and roots that they use on a regular basis. These nontimber forest products are especially important to the tribal populations. Fourteen percent of the district of Dhenkanal is tribal, with Juang, Munda, Saora, and Santhal inhabitants. When I asked why the block had been organized, a fellow who wore a pale red cloth loosely over his shoulders responded.

> Our biggest problem is that we need the forest and we need the FD
> to cooperate with us. They won't register us as an official forest
> protection committee, but we need our forest demarcated. Only the
> FD has the legal authority to do that. We will do it ourselves, but
> we need to be legally protected from marauders. The FD wants the
> village government to be the same as the FPC leader. That won't
> work for us. We want them to recognize that our FPCs are working.
> We want legal recognition of our village forests. And then we
> want to be able to market minor forest products that the state forest
> development cooperation monopolizes. This is why we joined

together to represent 150 villages—enough for the state to pay attention.[30]

REAL STORIES OF FOREST PROTECTION

Back in Bhubaneswar I met with Neera Singh. She told me that she had originally come to Orissa to assess the impact of social forestry programs for the Swedish International Development Agency in the region of Balangir in western Orissa. She found that villagers who were not involved in the projects were achieving far more effective forest protection through their own informal initiatives than were those working with the forest department.

> Some of these villages have remarkable stories of protection. In one area a woman in her mid-forties was single-handedly protecting twenty-five acres of public forest. In the same region, a man of fifty-five had been guarding a patch of 1,800 acres for some ten years, fighting off pilferers from twenty different villages in sometimes violent confrontations. He finally prompted the formation of a forest protection committee in his village that could share the protection responsibility. This patch is said to look much denser than a ten-year patch should look.[31]

Singh told story after story about energetic individuals who had organized forest protection committees. It seemed that behind every forest protection effort was one of these individuals. Singh suggested that I meet a man in one of the nearby forest ranges who had single-handedly organized a federation. He convinced his village to protect its forest years ago, in 1955. In 1994 the villagers protecting the forestlands along the range formed a federation to demand formal legal recognition over their community forests. According to Prateep Nayak, Singh's colleague at the Vasundhara Institute, this federation was the first in the state to record a formal demand for tenurial rights over their forests.

"This is no small thing," said Nayak. "We have only a minimal fa-
cilitating role in all this. The demand for full ownership was entirely
their initiative." I asked what their main motivation was. He answered,
"They want legal recognition from the Orissa forest department so that
they can prosecute illegal loggers. They also want to strengthen their
capacity to market the nonwood forest products in the area." Nayak
explained that the Vasundhara Institute has representation on the state-
level joint forest management steering committee for Orissa, and it is
active on a number of levels in attempting to strengthen the rights of
communities over the forestlands they manage and over forest products.
"We have found that villagers are very skeptical of joint forest management, which they see as a means for the state to take back the forest
that these villagers have protected at their own peril. They want tenurial
security."[32]

The next morning I set out with Giri Rao, the community organizer.
As we drove along, he told me that before independence the area was
part of the Nayagarh princely state. Some of the reserve forest was
brought under forest department management in the 1930s, but the area
was basically undisturbed by commercial logging interests until the
1950s. By the late 1960s the area was denuded. He told me he would
take me to two villages along the Ranpur range. The first had been
protecting its forest for twenty years, the second for fifty-five years.

One villager named Arjunrout initiated the efforts in the second village. In the 1950s he encouraged his fellow villagers to protect the forest. After his village had established use rules and had begun to actively
protect the forest, Arjunrout moved on to neighboring villages. The
neighboring villages were initially suspicious of his motives, but eventually came to agree with him on the need for forest protection. His
pioneering efforts laid the groundwork for the Vasundhara Institute.
Field organizers from the institute have had a hard time explaining that
they are interested in strengthening the voice of the villagers in policy
making and increasing forest ownership or forest rights and market access for the villagers. Initially, the villagers did not understand why the

institute was interested in their village. Rao explained that the villagers are learning that they can rely on the Vasundhara Institute to explain forest laws and to support their legal efforts.

Samar Singapur is a good distance from the main road, located at the foot of the hill where the village forest begins. Fifty or sixty villagers gathered on the porch of the temple to talk with us while their children sat on the cool earth in front of the temple. We were served warm chai in small glasses. I asked a few simple questions about the history of the place, with Rao translating. Our hosts soon grew bored, and one begged me, "Why don't we go to see the forest and walk through it? Then you will be able to ask us better questions." We set off immediately. Adjacent to the community-protected land is an old rubber plantation. It jutted out into a small valley just below the dense, cool forest that the community has been protecting.

The forest contained trees that stretched over our heads and had girths too large to wrap my arms around. These trees are mostly sal, which is similar to teak. One of the villagers listed some of the committee's rules, including "No axe is allowed into the forest!" He explained that trees cannot be taken without approval of the committee and that they use bamboo instead of wood for most practical or ceremonial needs. As we began to descend from the forest, cutting across a wide expanse of scrub filled with chattering birds, I asked whether the women take part in their protection efforts. One man replied, "The women guard during the day as they collect the dead wood and leaves on the ground or the fruits and other products they need. The men guard at night." They explained that they took turns guarding the forest. "What happens if a villager violates these rules?" I asked. "No one in the village has violated the rules," said one of the villagers. "Have you ever caught anyone?" I asked. "Oh yes. We did catch red-handed a man from the neighboring village. He had the goods. First we confiscated them. Then we invited him to confront the village as a whole and apologize. A fine was determined together with the villagers." Rao said that the combination of social pressure and financial penalty works fairly well for small-scale violations. I asked Rao if the women were part of the village council. He replied:

> No, nor are they involved directly in the forest protection committee.
> Although Vasundhara would like to see that change, we feel it
> could be counterproductive to work on this. We are trying to facilitate
> the villagers' efforts to get clear tenure over their land, and not to
> interfere. Part of our job is to build trust and if we start telling
> them to change how they do things, we are going to lose that trust.[33]

As we returned to the village, I saw a group of women carrying enormous bundles on their heads. They were heading up the path toward a group of mud-brown houses, their orange and green cotton saris standing out against the golden fields of rice in the distance. I asked the men why these women lived here. A villager answered, "They are tribals, who always live a distance from the village." I remembered Madhya Pradesh as Rao explained that the tribals were outside of the caste system and hence lived in this small compound, which was called a *sahi*. As we neared the collection of houses, we saw that a group of men were sitting in the tribal compound. They were darker-skinned than the villagers I was with. Several of them wore simple cloths of bright red and blue around their waists, and the others were dressed in white cotton undershirts and plain white sarongs, hitched up. The women arrived at the compound, and as they took their bundles off their heads I noticed that their appearance was strikingly different from other women I had seen. Both sides of their noses were pierced, and they had dozens of bright bangles around their wrists. One woman also had tattooed hands and a geometric design on her chin. They smiled widely at me and continued to unravel their bundles. Rao reminded me that we needed to move on to the next village.

THE WATER GODDESS

As we traveled to the next village, the sun began to set, filling the sky with deep crimson and orange hues. We drove past vast fields of dry rice. By the time we arrived in Bajarkot it was nearing dusk. We pulled up to a tea stand and had an impromptu meeting with some of the oldest villagers who had started forest protection efforts in 1955. I asked them what had motivated them. "There were many things," one said. "The scarcity of fuelwood and other forest products, lack of rain, but mostly the lack of water for irrigation. We could no longer harvest enough to feed our families." The water had a special meaning, and before they would continue they insisted on taking me to the edge of the forest that they had been protecting for the past fifty years. They nimbly clambered over the rocks and led me to a stream with a small waterfall, which trickled down through a crevice of rocks from the forest above. In the dusk I could see offerings of flowers and incense on the rocks. "This is the place where the water goddess lives," one villager declared. "If her temple dries up, there will be severe drought. Because of the forests in the hills above, she has kept the rains at bay in the monsoon and has saved some water from them to give to us even in the catastrophic drought of this year." Nearby villages had lost 75 percent of their harvest in the drought, but the farmers in Bajarkot lost only 25 percent. They attributed this to the water goddess. In talking with the villagers it was clear that they understood perfectly the relationship between protecting the watershed and having water for their fields. This relationship was inseparable from the wrath of the goddess, and that guaranteed the forest's integrity.

As I looked up at the forest above me I could see, even in the twilight, that the forest canopy was thick. I could make out large trees and heavy vines. This place was not far from a main road, and the villagers told me that protecting it can be a dangerous business. Sometimes armed gangs arrive with truckloads of "headloaders," women from outside the district who are hired to carry cut timber out of the forest on their heads. The gangs drive off with the stolen timber, destroying decades' worth of forest protection. On one occasion, they told me, the village forest guards actually captured one of these armed trucks, and the whole village held the gang captive until someone came from the forest department to prosecute them. I had heard that often these gangs have links to the forest department that ensure their escape. This technique of timber poaching is common across India. It is so common, one forest officer told me, that "even the most honest FD officials often let some of this activity go on. Personally, I am compelled to accept a certain number of bribes from the wood mafias lest I find my own life threatened."[34]

The villagers explained that it was more difficult to catch the persistent poachers from neighboring villages who come into the forest to collect on a regular basis. This is another reason why the villagers are trying to organize on a block level. If every village in the block took responsibility for protecting a patch of forest, poaching from other villages would stop. Arjunrout, I learned, had been traveling between the villages to convince his neighbors to think about bringing together as a block the villages that are already protecting their forests. He had also been encouraging adjacent villages still without protection committees to start them. Arjunrout's vision includes organizing the block to market nontimber forest products. As we were leaving, Arjunrout ran up to our vehicle. The man, who had to be in his eighties, was full of life. He had wrapped a wool blanket around himself, creating an outlandish hood around his head. He nearly hopped with excitement. He was very charismatic. I wished we could stay and talk, but Rao was eager to get on the road and back to Bhubaneswar. At least I was able to meet the man who made it all happen.

Later, over dinner at her home in Bhubaneswar, Singh explained that she sees federations as an emerging force to precipitate many of the changes that need to take place to strengthen local control over forests and forest resources. The institute would like to see representatives of the federations sit directly on Orissa's joint forest management steering committee. In that way the federations could gain more political clout, the concerns of the local communities could be heard, and policy changes could be created that might revolutionize the way the forest department operates. At the same time, Singh fears that the joint forest management steering committee could become a place for token membership, which would undermine its useful political role. Her fears reminded me of the discussion of different donor agencies that I had with Chowdhry. Chowdhry was worried that as the World Bank co-opted the idea of joint forest management, it might lose its original meaning. Chowdhry thinks that joint forest management should support the spontaneous community forest protection committees and not simply scale up and increase the number of committees. Singh's husband, Kundan Singh, added, "The one strength of the World Bank is the potential for their projects to transform the policy environment for forestry, precisely because of the large scale."[35] Although the Singhs emphasized that changing policy requires political mobilization and cannot be achieved simply through the largeness of scale, the size of the project does have the potential to provide political leverage at the top for initiatives that come from the community level. Singh encouraged me to keep studying what was happening at the village level to learn how policy change really takes place.

SCHOOLTEACHER'S FEDERATION OF TREES AND LIVING BEINGS

As promised, Singh helped me arrange meetings with a few other organizations that work with forest protection federations in Orissa. The state has struggled to keep up with the innovative villagers. Although most of these villagers can explain that they protect their forest to secure their livelihood, it is not easy to separate these "rational" explanations from more traditional accounts—such as the presence of the water goddess—of what motivates villagers to protect their forests.

I had heard about Oxfam India's work with one grassroots forest protection movement from a friend of mine from graduate school, Ted Lawrence, who had worked briefly with Oxfam India Trust in Orissa. I was pleased that Singh could arrange a meeting with the forest support

officer there, Sarthak Pal. Pal told me that Oxfam India Trust had been
providing very modest funds, as small as $50 or $100, to support the
protection efforts of the movement. Joginath Sahu, headmaster of a
middle school, had started this movement in the late 1970s, working
through the schools. In 1976 his village had begun to protect a small
hillside patch of forest. Its regeneration attracted pilferers from nearby
villages, and when it became clear that action was needed, the environmental campaign was born. Villagers spread the word about the need
to protect the hillside. In 1982 twenty-two villages came together to
form the Bruksho O'Jeebaro Bandhu Parishad (BOJBP—Friends
of Trees and Living Beings), a voluntary organization with an open
membership, to formalize the efforts of forest protection and environmental conservation. This organization is much more than an environmental group. Its members consist mostly of small and landless
farmers in several villages, and it has become a vibrant social movement
in the region.

BOJBP began to reach out to protect forests that were not immediately adjacent to their villages. Members used popular means like street
theater to educate the residents of other villages about the need to protect forests. At the time of my visit the organization was working in 450
villages through its thirteen sister organizations, and approximately
20,000 hectares of forest were being managed as common resources.
Based on Gandhian philosophy, the organization has been able to protect forests in the area without imposing fines or requiring intervention
from the forest department. The organization employs embarrassment
and public ridicule to punish offenders. To deal with intervillage problems the village council directs elders to fall at the feet of the offender,
a major embarrassment in the Hindu-Oriya (Orissa) culture. BOJBP
mediates intravillage conflicts through local arbitration and Gandhian
approaches. They also use the Gandhian tools of fasting and prayer to
avert threats to the forest and local environment. All twenty-two villages
have informal village councils that manage a number of other village
resources.[36]

FEDERATIONS FOR MARKETING
FOREST PRODUCTS

Singh specifically wanted me to meet with members of a nongovernmental organization, the Regional Center for Development Cooperation, that was working in the district of Balangir with a federation that had in a very short time become the most powerful in the state. Part of what makes Balangir's situation unusual is the determination of key individuals who came together in a coalition early on. The federation was pushing for an end to the monopoly held by the Orissa Forest Development Corporation—the enterprise arm of the state's forest department—on the sale of nontimber forest products. The Regional Center for Development Cooperation had an office in Bhubaneswar. Singh explained that because the federation in Balangir was already quite strong, it had received a great deal of political attention.

Balangir was targeted heavily for timber commercialization in the 1950s, which brought about a fuelwood crisis in the 1960s and severe drought every two to three years after that. Manoj Pattanaik, a center staff member, told me that after plantation efforts initiated by the forest department in the 1970s failed, large-scale conversion to agriculture followed. Social forestry efforts during the 1980s generated enthusiasm and community plantations, but ultimately the quick-growing eucalyptus plantations established by the forest department did nothing to take the pressure off the forests because the local people were not really benefiting from them.

The Regional Center for Development Cooperation has a very specific set of concerns, as Pattanaik explained.

Having formed as a coalition of nongovernmental organizations that were working with communities who wanted clarification of the status of their land and legal rights to market nontimber forest products, we feel the forestry department has to become a fundamentally different sort of institution. The forest department has to change from being a landlord to being a service organization and they must support rather than undermine the efforts of villagers interested in protecting the forests. The communities want to market the products that they are protecting, some of which have very high value.[37]

In fact, the value of these products is so high that the state has nationalized—barred the private sale of—a number of lucrative products: bamboo, a basic multipurpose product used by villagers for construction, firewood, and fodder; *mahua*, which has important medicinal and nutritional value; *sal* seeds for reforestation; and *tendu* leaves, also called *kendu* leaves, used for rolling *bidis*, a kind of cigarette. *Tendu* leaves from the region of Balangir are the best in the country. The Orissa Forest Development Corporation handles the marketing of all these products. The villagers are not allowed to sell any of these products themselves, nor are they allowed to collect them in an amount larger than what they can use in a day or two.

The revenues for *tendu* leaves from Orissa bring in ten times the value received from timber in the state. The Regional Center for Development Cooperation has estimated that about 80 percent of Orissa's nontimber forest products are transported illegally by private traders from outside the state. The center is trying to show the forest department that the local communities would have an incentive to help control the illegal harvest of these nationalized products if they could participate in their marketing, as Pattanaik explained:

> These communities do not want or need to own the resources they
> protect, but they do need recognition from the forest department
> of rights over management and marketing of those products. Without
> those rights the problems of illegal trader and corruption, as well
> as of forest degradation by outsiders, will never end, and the local
> communities will remain dirt-poor subsistence farmers![38]

The foregoing examples indicate that in terms of protection at the grassroots level, Orissa is far ahead of other states in India. Yet, the state still needs to develop policies supporting community-based forest enterprises. Joint forest management, which is a useful starting point for the development of partnerships, cannot be applied without extensive organization and training within the forest communities and reorientation and training within the forest department. Neera and Kundan Singh and Shashi Kant stress this point in a report written in 1991.

> Forest communities possess a wealth of knowledge regarding their environment and how to sustainably manage forestlands to meet their needs. However, the community-based forest management systems are in the evolutionary stage. Current levels of research, field experimentation, policy study, and financial investments are woefully inadequate in responding to forest management problems. A massive increase in efforts to decentralize forest management and establish viable controls at the village level will be required if forest use is to be stabilized before the ecological functions and productivity of these natural resources are lost.[39]

CONCLUSIONS

Forest management systems in India, as in many other nations around the world, are in transition. Rural communities across India are demanding formal control over local forest resources that they have restored and protected. Many professional foresters are recognizing that rural Indians are committed to protecting their resources, and they too see the value in formalizing the rights and responsibilities of local communities. The colonial legacy of strict forest regulation is slowly giving way to more inclusive forest policies.

The many different experiences in Orissa show how rural communities faced with resource scarcities are imposing strict controls on their access to the forest resources they depend on. These controls are designed and imposed through group consensus. Without outside intervention, rural communities in Orissa and elsewhere are developing federations of forest protection committees to strengthen their political voice. These community-based efforts to gain control over forests and forest products appear to be far more effective at protecting forests than the efforts of forest department–sponsored committees. Although outside intervention can help communities form effective groups, the formation of protection committees is not automatic. It requires time and dedication.

In Haryana visits with the hill societies showed the importance of recognizing that different communities evolve at different paces. The bhabbar collectors in Haryana were initially reluctant to pool their resources through a committee, even if it was in their best interest. Eventually they formed strong independent committees only because of TERI's patient approach. TERI did not push them, nor did the community organizer interfere with their decision to spend their initial earnings on activities he thought unwise. If he had, they might have stopped listening to him. In the end, by letting the process unfold at its own pace, the villagers were able to assume full ownership of the idea. TERI was also able to make real changes in gender dynamics by persuading women and men to acknowledge that they share the responsibility for resource management. When compared to the committee in Madhya Pradesh, which was mandated by the forest department, the hill societies appear to be far more dynamic.

The Madhya Pradesh forestry project is still quite early in its development, yet it clearly has serious problems at the level of village implementation. Based on what I saw, it appears that the Madhya Pradesh project is emphasizing the technical side of reforestation rather than attempting to deal with socioeconomic factors that lead to forest degradation. This project risks repeating some of the same mistakes experienced in the era of social forestry projects. By failing to make any real changes in the economic, social, and political bases of power, or in the structure of power relations between villagers and foresters and among castes and elites within villages, the project is little more than a way for the forest department to make money.

In my brief assessment I did not attempt to measure the results of the project. My goal, rather, was to see how participation is being implemented at the field level. The foresters in Madhya Pradesh are attempting to implement the idea of managing forests jointly without really changing the terms of access to the forests. The foresters are mobilizing the villagers for reforestation, but they do not understand that they will not be successful until they address the economic circumstances of the villagers and their need for clear rights. The real issue is not whether people are involved—people will always be involved—but which people are involved, and how, and why.[40] These questions seem to be beyond the foresters' professional mandate.

What are the factors shaping forest protection movements in India? The particular social and economic histories of each area play a critical role. The ecological resilience of forests is crucial. The enabling legislation has a great deal to do with how communities perceive forests and their relationships with forest resources. Much also depends on individual foresters and local forestry departments and how they choose to use the resources available to them. Taken together, my field experiences in India demonstrate that the shift toward greater community control of public forestland has begun in earnest. Nonetheless, because the state has controlled the use of the public forestlands in India for 150 years, bringing communities back into the management picture fully will take many years.

The control of natural resources is a political issue for rural India. Growing democratization has helped the central state to begin devolving forest authority to communities. Given the expanding population of rural India, the sustainable management of water, soil, and forest resources is necessary for the survival of rural communities. Rural communities and many foresters alike are recognizing that sustainable management of those resources is most likely to occur when the users themselves make and enforce the rules.

Since 1990 the number of professionals in forest departments, nongovernmental organizations, academic and training institutions, and donor agencies who understand the importance of village participation has grown steadily. Although the World Bank is in a position to finance the widespread implementation of joint forest management projects, the introduction of policies that promote participation requires time and dedication more than money. The forest service must build the trusting relationships with local communities that are needed for successful co-management, and this will require a new approach from top to bottom. Although the scale of World Bank projects may encourage India's forest service to support community control over forest resources, policy development requires the participation of constituencies. This participation carries high political stakes. Donor agencies are slowly moving toward increasingly flexible funding arrangements that can facilitate a deeper commitment to social and political change and a willingness to provide continuity for a transition that may require decades.

CHAPTER 5

Conservation in Indonesia

Once known for its exotic spices, fertile volcanic soils, and teak forests, the island nation of Indonesia is probably better known today for coffee from Java, surfing in Bali, and Nike sweatshops rather than the tropical forests that I had come to study.[1] Indonesia has one of the largest expanses of tropical forests in the world, second only to Brazil's. Because these forests possess some of the world's most unusual flora and fauna, Indonesia plays a very important role in global conservation (map 8).[2]

I first went to Indonesia in 1988 to work for WALHI, the Indonesian Environmental Forum. During the four years that I was there, I grew to appreciate the complexity of the international conservation agenda and its implications for Indonesia's rural people. After that time, I returned regularly to Indonesia to research forest-based communities. In recent years I observed nongovernmental organizations like WALHI evolve from their earlier struggle to gain political voice under a repressive regime to their current, increasingly sophisticated policy supporting community rights over state forest. The collapse of Suharto's regime transformed the political climate in Indonesia and rapidly created new space for rural and indigenous communities to place claims on the state and on state resources.

Map 8. Indonesia and Southeast Asia.

In February 1996, after completing field visits in India, I flew to
Indonesia to visit another World Bank project that was designed to
support the role of local communities in forest conservation. The project aimed to strengthen the integrity of Indonesia's largest national park,
Kerinci Seblat National Park, partly by working with the World Wildlife Fund (WWF) Indonesia. By chance, my old boss from WALHI was
WWF's new director. Despite my bias against large-scale projects, I was
interested in this one because the World Bank planned to use its leverage at the provincial level to stop mining and logging activities that
threatened the park on its border, while WWF worked at the local level
with communities around the park.

From conversations that I had with people in Washington, D.C., I learned that the WWF's component was to be supported through the Global Environment Facility (GEF), the grant-making arm of the World Bank (and the United Nations), which had been established at the Rio conference in 1992 to support the global conservation of biological diversity. The Kerinci Seblat project would combine conservation and development and would be one of the first World Bank initiatives incorporating this kind of grant into a loan agreement. The total project cost was estimated at $47.3 million—not large by World Bank standards. The bulk of the financing came from a World Bank loan of $21.3 million, with the GEF providing a $15.5 million grant and the government of Indonesia contributing $10.5 million.[3]

When I arrived in Jakarta I met with the WWF staff person who had set up the WWF's Kerinci Seblat field office. His name was Erwin. Describing his approach to community organizing, he told me, "I recognized early on that many of the communities already had indigenous concepts of conservation. For example, some of the communities had protected 'sacred' groves around their villages. So I worked to strengthen community control over the forests they were managing in the buffer zone area of the park."[4] Erwin had trained a cadre of energetic young community organizers to map community lands, work out conservation agreements with local communities, and establish community-based ecotourism around the park, which included training trekking guides to give cultural and ecological tours of the area. Erwin was being transferred to a new WWF field office, but he told me that the field coordinator in Kerinci would be able to help me with my study.

PEOPLE VERSUS CONSERVATION

I knew from my field visits in India that several factors would influence my assessment of the World Bank project in Indonesia. First, compared with my experience in India, I had a much greater understanding of Indonesian culture and politics, not to mention a much greater familiarity with the language. I knew that in terms of supporting community forestry, Indonesia's forest policy was years behind India's. I also knew that Indonesia's forest resources were far richer ecologically and in far better condition than India's were. On the one hand, the richness of these resources meant that rural communities in Indonesia were not struggling over access to fuelwood and subsistence use. On the other hand, it also meant that commercial timber exploitation remained an extremely lucrative venture. Indonesia's abundance of forest resources has also attracted international conservation organizations, adding another dimension to the struggle over resources. These international groups consider Indonesia's forests to be of global significance, and they have been actively involved in the creation of parks and protected areas with the mission of saving large tracts of unique forest ecosystems from degradation. In many cases people were living inside the boundaries of these protected areas long before they were declared parks. Some conservationists see the activities of people and logging industries as equally strong threats to the integrity of parks.

Despite decades of debate over the compatibility of people and parks, many ardent conservationists still argue that people who live within the parks present an unacceptable threat to their conservation, and they argue that resettlement will protect globally important biodiversity.[5] Nonetheless, growing evidence demonstrates that the sites with the richest biological diversity are not necessarily those isolated from interference by humankind. A recent survey of World Heritage sites concludes that

> [m]uch of the world's forest biodiversity is the product of millennia of manipulation of the forests by people. Sites of major significance for biodiversity may be located in the remotest forests of the Amazon or New Guinea but others are in areas with high densities of human populations. Some of the worlds' most valuable forests are outstanding examples of a harmonious and sustainable relationship between forests and people.[6]

These debates about people and conservation continue to play out in Indonesia. In addition to the Indonesian forest service, many international conservation organizations have yet to fully accept that local people might have the capacity to protect and manage forests. Struggles over these resources among international conservation organizations and timber interests have often overshadowed consideration of the management capacity of local communities. To redress this lack of consideration, in recent years international agreements have stressed the important role that indigenous peoples have in managing forest resources. For example, the International Labor Organization's 1989 Convention No. 169, which concerns indigenous and tribal peoples, recognizes their rights of ownership and possession over their customary lands. In addition, the convention on biodiversity that originated from the Rio conference acknowledges the importance of indigenous knowledge for the conservation and sustainable management of biodiversity. Despite these realizations, moving from recognition and acknowledgement to action remains a challenge.[7]

CONFLICTS OVER FORESTLAND

Although the exact number of forest-dependent people in Indonesia is impossible to determine, between 80 and 95 million people—close to 50 percent of Indonesia's population of 216 million—are directly dependent on forest resources.[8] Of those, perhaps 40 to 65 million are indigenous peoples living on land classified as public forest and managing their resources through customary law.[9] Customary law is a dynamic system based on an oral tradition in which the community makes laws and changes them by group consensus to respond to evolving practices or circumstances.[10] The Dutch colonial administration supported the idea of customary law to some extent, allowing local communities to establish some local rules, but the post-independence Indonesian government considered customary law a threat to its authority, particularly where it could conflict with state interests in forest and mineral wealth. Consequently, once Indonesia gained independence and the state found itself increasingly involved in disputes over land, customary law was no longer tolerated except in limited form, and state law took precedence.[11]

Since the colonial era conflicts over forestland between the state and local people have been a problem, particularly on the highly populated island of Java, which is no bigger than California but holds some two-thirds of Indonesia's population.[12] In contrast, disputes over forest resources on the larger forested islands have emerged only in the past few decades, when logging companies began decimating millions of hectares of prime forests. The loggers harvested commercially lucrative tropical hardwoods like the dipterocarp, a dominant tree species in most of Southeast Asia's lowland evergreen forests.[13]

Many Indonesian nongovernmental organizations point out that local indigenous communities possess intricate customary forest management systems, regularly collect an array of forest products, and cultivate many useful trees while adding to (or at least not detracting much from) the structural complexity of the forest. Studies show that local communities do play a decisive and positive role in conservation. Foreign researchers—notably those associated with the WWF, the Ford Foundation, and the French forest research institute, known as ORSTOM—have validated the complexity of the knowledge and skills of forest dwellers across Indonesia in order to introduce new models for forest conservation that include local peoples as partners. The World Bank project included WWF in its project at the Kerinci Seblat National Park partly because WWF had successfully involved local communities in conservation efforts. I wanted to see how well this World Bank–WWF partnership was working at the field level.

KERINCI SEBLAT NATIONAL PARK

Kerinci Seblat National Park was established in the mid-1980s by WWF and the Indonesian government. Stretching across four provinces in southern Sumatra, this area is home to the endangered Sumatran tiger, along with countless other species (map 9). In 1992 the World Bank began planning to support biodiversity conservation together with economic development around the park. The goal was to link park management with regional planning and rural development initiatives in target villages on the park boundary through the so-called Kerinci Seblat Integrated Conservation and Development Project (ICDP).[14] Plans called for establishing a buffer zone around Kerinci Seblat, and the World Bank hoped to draw on the experience of the WWF Indonesia field office to carry out the organizing that this would require. The field office had been working with local communities for six years, mapping customary lands and developing jobs and opportunities for local people in ecotourism.

I met with Asmeen Kahn, a World Bank officer in Jakarta, who told me that the bank sought to combine WWF's community organizing skills with the influence that the World Bank has to halt damaging logging, mining, and road development activities around the park and gain community support. Kahn felt that the project's design of working at both the state and community levels could be very effective. She explained that by addressing the income needs of the rural communities who live adjacent to the park and are dependent on the forest for their livelihood, the project designers hoped to reduce any further deterioration of the area around the park. She said they also had plans to assist provincial governments in restructuring mineral and logging activities in the four provinces bordering the park. Kahn was committed to making this project, with its unusual partnership, work, and she saw the local partners as more than capable.

Kahn had a pretty good reputation among the environmental activists I knew in Jakarta because she was sensitive to their criticisms of the project. She also had some concerns of her own. Kahn pointed out that one major difficulty was the need to broaden the efforts of the local partners: "There are some good people out there, but they have been working in ten villages for a long time, and the project needs them to

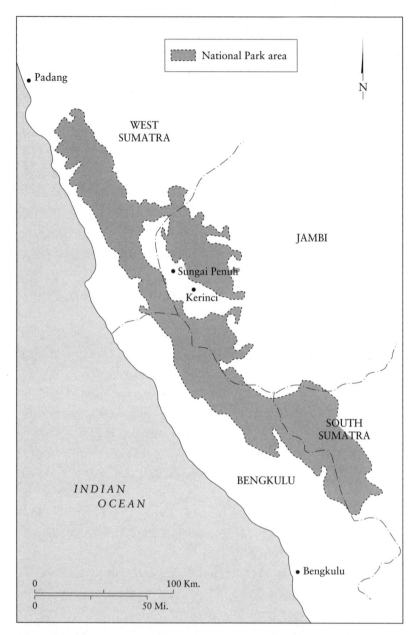

National Park area

N

Padang

WEST
SUMATRA

JAMBI

Sungai Penuh

Kerinci

SOUTH
SUMATRA

BENGKULU

INDIAN
OCEAN

Bengkulu

0   100 Km.

0   50 Mi.

Map 9.   Kerinci Seblat National Park, Indonesia.

organize 134 villages in just six years." Although six years is a little longer than the span of most World Bank projects, Kahn recognized that it was still a very short amount of time for organizing at the community level. Furthermore, she was not sure that brokered agreements with provincial governments to relocate logging and mining operations would last.

> We managed to introduce a moratorium on activities in concessions immediately bordering the park. We have also halted the construction of a major road through the park. However, these provincial governments, for the most part, are difficult, and personally, I don't know that the moratorium will actually put any stop to the illegal incursions . . . into the park.

She confided that it was no secret that many bureaucrats had a financial stake in the companies that were involved in these activities.[15]

THE WWF FIELD OFFICE

WWF's Kerinci Seblat office is in Sungai Penuh, a town tucked deep in the mountains of southern Sumatra and far from the provincial capitals. I flew into West Sumatra and climbed on a tiny bus that careened over a narrow, curving mountain road for twelve hours. During the journey I met a university student named Herry. I told him I was planning to look at the WWF project and discovered that he lived near Sungai Penuh and was a big fan of WWF. He explained that because of WWF's efforts he had become a trekking guide and his family had started a homestay that provided modest accommodations to tourists visiting the park. He was worried about my arriving in Sungai Penuh in the middle of the night. He encouraged me to stay overnight with his family, assuring me that their house was on the main road and that I could easily catch a bus to Sungai Penuh in the morning. Herry's family had lived in their ancestral village inside the boundaries of the park until recently, when they had moved close to the road. The family was wonderful, treating me like a long-lost relative.

In the morning, enveloped by the cool morning fog, I waved goodbye to my new family and climbed on a bus for the last half-hour ride to Sungai Penuh. I sat in front so that I could stretch out my legs. Indonesian pop music blared through the speakers as we drove past rice fields surrounded by densely forested mountains. The mountains were tinted in places with red foliage that stood out amid the rich green. I later found out that these red patches were illegally planted cinnamon trees, the bane of the park manager.

I went directly to the WWF project office after arriving in Sungai Penuh. My visit coincided with the preparation of a two-week course titled "Community Participation in Conservation and Development," which was delivered by Bina Swadaya, a Jakarta-based nongovernmental organization specializing in community development training. This was lucky. Many of the community organizers would be in town, and I would be able to meet some of the government officials from the other provinces involved in the project, who might otherwise have been difficult to track down.

The field coordinator for the WWF project, Nurhalis Fadhli—"Al" for short—greeted me, and we sat down in the meeting room. The walls of the office were covered with colorful posters advertising the park and newsprint replete with work plans scribbled out in detail. Al told me that things were going well. He was very excited about the project, particularly its emphasis on regional planning and community participation. He was also pleased with what it meant for WWF and its local partner, WARSI, a conservation group based in the city of Jambi in southern Sumatra. Al felt the project would surely build their capacity for conservation work. He did have concerns. "A cookie-cutter approach will not work," Al told me.

Very much depends on the incentives for villagers to participate. If they do not see any benefit in participating, they will not participate.

It takes a good organizer to find what will work in each place.
Usually we work in one village in a very thorough way. This project
will require us to change our methods to encompass 134 villages.
To be honest, I am not sure we can find that many qualified
community organizers. To say that we're worried that the quality
of WWF's involvement at the village level will decrease is
an understatement. But, it is a great challenge, and we are willing
to try.[16]

Al arranged my accommodations at the WWF women's dormitory,
then helped me set up some meetings. We determined what field visits
would be feasible before the workshop began. He thought I should see
Sungai Keruh, one of the most successful project sites, where native
Kerinci people were actively protecting the forest, and Muara Hemat,
one of the least successful sites, where the forest was inundated with
new settlers. These villages represented the extremes of the challenge
that WWF and WARSI had undertaken.

That afternoon I met with Pak Wawan, director of the Kerinci Seblat
National Park. He was pessimistic about the involvement of local communities. "There are big problems with this park," he said.

The area of the park is about 1.5 million hectares, and I only have
sixty-nine men to manage it. It is impossible to know what is leaving
the forest illegally until it is gone. My biggest concern is the
degradation of the park from planting large cinnamon plots. Since
the late 1980s everyone started planting cinnamon around the
park and then within the park. There were huge enclaves of settlers
within the park who were legalized in the most recent redrawing
of the boundaries in 1992. Even excluding those areas there are
approximately 12,000 hectares of cinnamon inside the park!

It is embarrassing to look over the vista of the park. All you can
see are those distinctive red leaves of the cinnamon trees. The
satellite images do not show the difference between the monocrops
of cinnamon, but it's insidious. The cinnamon is creeping in,
diminishing biological diversity and wildlife habitat. The farmers

burn the park forest to clear land for cinnamon. It is a serious ecological problem.

According to Wawan, 85 percent of the cinnamon bark from Kerinci is exported. He explained that he understood why people were planting it.

> It is better than money in the bank. With an absolutely risk-free investment of 200 rupiah [$0.10] per seedling, a farmer can pick some up at the market, throw them in his basket, hike up to his plot of land, and put each in a hole. Without fertilizers or chemicals, without mind to how many centimeters deep the seedling is planted, without concern for the steepness of the hill, the tree will grow. Within five years, the bark on that tree is worth about 30,000 rupiah [$14.00]. In ten years its worth will double, and triple in fifteen.

I asked him why everyone was not rich if they were planting so much cinnamon. Wawan, exasperated, looked at me and continued.

> The ones making the money and causing the greatest damage are not the small farmers, who are, after all, making a wise investment. I have a problem with a few large landholders who are very difficult to identify. They pay migrant workers to clear hundreds of acres to plant cinnamon. Some local people can work on these plantations, but for the most part the harvesting is done by migrant workers who are not living in the area. When my staff encounters them, regardless of where they come from, the people do not know, or do not want to say, who owns the fields. For all they know the land could belong to a local government official or, worse, some army general. And what is the park staff supposed to do about that? They cannot blame the workers for the clearing. The workers are just trying to make a living. But the park staff does not have the resources to track down the owner and the damage is done—the forest has already been cut. Technically, these activities should not even be going on in the area adjacent to the park, which is supposed to be a buffer zone. But it happens anyway, and it is a hopeless battle to

stop it. For example, in the village of Muara Hemat, where are we supposed to begin?[17]

I embarked on a day trip to Muara Hemat with Firdaus, the director of WARSI. Muara Hemat is on the main road to the province of Jambi, and it hugs the border of the park. As we drove Firdaus explained why this village is one of the most difficult to organize. Stretching along thirty kilometers of the main road and including settlers from all over Sumatra, Muara Hemat is about as spread out and heterogeneous as villages get along the park border. It is difficult to know how many people actually live here and who owns land. Most people in the area do not have titles to their land. Many live in small huts in their fields to avoid contact with authorities. Others may have a house along the road but spend much of their time on land they are working illegally inside the park. These people are not interested in talking about their livelihoods. Finally, much of the land around Muara Hemat belongs to people who live in distant cities and hire others to work the land. The workers they hire may be only temporary residents. According to Firdaus, approximately 300 families come through Muara Hemat during the year for work. Only some 50 are registered as residents, and few are originally from Muara Hemat. They come from all over and are divided by culture and ethnicity.[18]

These are not gentle forest people. They are rough frontier settlers. On the day we visited, a man had been stabbed and had nearly died because of a rumor that his large cinnamon plot had been sold. The assailant had planned to rob the man, thinking that he had the money from the deal in his pocket. I learned this from a West Sumatran settler in a coffee stall in Muara Hemat, where Firdaus and I finally caught up with Damsir, the local WWF community organizer. The settler told me that this kind of thing happened all the time "up in that part of town, where people are brutal."

Damsir had started working in the Minangkabau (or West Sumatran) part of town because he is of Minangkabau background and thought he might have a better chance of making headway there. One of the problems, he said, is that only a few of the villagers, if any, understand what he is trying to do. "People don't tell me what they honestly think. I am trying to build trust, but so many people have been in and out of Muara Hemat, talking with people about WWF, that they don't expect anything to come of this. I don't blame them. Why should they waste their time?" As we sat at the coffee stall Damsir pointed to a letter that had been posted.

> Last week all the target villages of this World Bank–WWF project received a letter from the district government stating that they were to be included in a World Bank project. These local-level officials do not know what the difference is between a branch bank and the World Bank. So, now I am suddenly busy trying to explain that the villagers are not about to get big bank loans. Explaining the ICDP concept is very difficult over and above the general confusion in a place as scattered as Muara Hemat.[19]

It seemed to me unlikely that any coherent model for village land use could be hammered out in Muara Hemat, much less one that would be consistent with the broader scheme. The large landholders have little vested interest in Muara Hemat. The people who live in the village do not have any customary claim to the land. Neither do they seem to want land titles because, they say, they would then have to pay taxes. Where, then, is the incentive? These villagers will continue to clear forest to plant cinnamon until they have a surer way to gain an income. Damsir told me that these people are not interested in being organized and that the last thing they want is for someone from the outside to find out how they make a living. Nonetheless, Damsir has begun to make small gains in the Minangkabau section of town. People there admitted that they would like to have some security over their use of the land. They are convinced, however, that if they agree to conservation their activities and their access to the forest will be curtailed. Damsir said that he thought progress would take some time in Muara Hemat.[20]

KERINCI VILLAGE

We went back to Sungai Penuh that evening. The next morning Al told me that I would have just enough time for the trip to Sungai Keruh before the workshop began. In contrast to the people at Muara Hemat, those who live at this site are indigenous Kerinci people who have customary claims over an area that is now part of the national park. I left with Desrizal Alira, or "Das," the community organizer, by bus. Sungai Keruh is part of a larger village, Pesisir Bukit, which is located in a lush green valley.

We reached Pesisir Bukit in ninety minutes. Then, beneath heavy clouds, we set off on a muddy footpath to hike the remaining ten kilometers to Sungai Keruh. Das told me that about fifty-five families live in the village. They work their rice fields in the valley and manage their upland fields on the hillsides. I asked Das if the villagers cultivated cinnamon. He said, "My guess is that every one of them has at least one hectare of cinnamon trees growing in the hills above the village, either adjacent to or within the park."[21]

Das and I reached the house of Pak Wun, the headman of Sungai Keruh. Das had been living with Wun for three months. We climbed up the ladder of the small wooden house on stilts, removed our muddy shoes as we got to the doorway, and went inside. After brief introductions Wun's wife served us hot sweet coffee in tiny glasses. The mountain air was brisk, making the hot coffee taste particularly good. The village elders, sarongs and prayer rugs draped over their shoulders, gathered to meet me before they went to pray and to gather other villagers at the mosque. While we waited for their return we talked with Wun, who related some of the history of Sungai Keruh.

The meeting with the elders and the villagers was conducted in the local Kerinci language, and Das translated for me. No more than five women, nine men, and a few children filled the small room. In general the women did not take part in the discussion. Wun had urgent business with Das. He had received a letter informing him that the village might lose its administrative status because it was too close to the park. He was concerned that this change would deprive the village of the chance to get government services like electricity or roads. Das and the villagers talked about the letter and discussed the conflict over the boundary of the village. They also talked more generally about conservation and their traditions. As the meeting ended, one woman who had spoken up during the meeting announced that she would put me up for the night.

As she took my arm she told me that first we had to go to a village wedding party and that I, as an honored guest, would sing. A band had assembled at the other end of the village. Sungai Keruh does not have electricity, so the band had a generator for the amplifier and the speakers. It was a strange juxtaposition to go from talking seriously about land rights with the village elders to being surrounded by the village youth rocking and swaying to Indonesian *dangdut*, a popular type of Indonesian music with an Arabic beat. The bride and groom were seated solemnly to the side of the band, where everyone could keep an eye on them. Everyone took turns singing karaoke except the bride and groom, who honestly looked a little bored. When my turn came, I offered John Denver's "Country Roads." The crowd cheered. The woman must have known I was exhausted after my big debut, and soon after she took me home.

The next morning Das and I set off with Wun, walking up to the boundary of the park, which was an hour's hike from the village. According to the villagers the real boundary is marked by a knee-high cement post that was installed in 1988 by the local and provincial governments in agreement with the local people. It took some time to find the marker since it was surrounded by dense forest. After fifteen minutes of searching, Wun discovered it hidden under a fallen, decomposing tree. He took out his machete and hacked at the dead tree until the marker was visible. There was no other sign that we were at the boundary of the park.

Wun emphasized that this was the marker that the village had agreed upon with the government. They were unhappy about the second boundary, closer to the village, that had been added five years later. It was confusing, explained Wun. It seems that as part of one of the national armed forces' campaigns to promote development, the army took instructions from the provincial government to extend the boundary of the park. The government wanted to put down what they called a living boundary, so that no one could claim that they did not know where the boundary was. The army hired workers to help them plant palm trees as a new marker. Local people were not consulted, and Wun said that some villagers got a thick swath of palms planted right through the middle of their fallow fields.

Wun told me that the villagers say they are still unsure which boundary is the real one. He said that the villagers want land certificates to prove that the land they are working is theirs and that it is outside the park boundary. He also said that the villagers were using the park forest only to harvest fruit and rattan vines for household uses and other plants for medicines and other necessities. Wun explained that the villagers were afraid to take trees except to repair their houses every few years. He pointed to a patch of trees in the area between the disputed boundaries. This, he said, is original forest, proof that the villagers are respecting the new boundary.[22]

Although the villagers seemed sincere in their concern over the boundary and their desire for land certificates, a primate researcher who had been working in the park near the village for eight months suggested otherwise. She said she had hired a team of former illegal poachers as research assistants, hoping to get the scoop on local activities. She told me that while villagers say they do not touch the forest and point to the trees standing near the village as evidence, they are going farther into the park to clear land for cinnamon. She said flatly, "I don't think any incentive will outweigh the planting of cinnamon."[23]

In short, several levels of deceit are at play in the region. Neither community organizers nor government officials hear the full story, and I heard only what the villagers wanted me to hear—or what they thought I wanted to hear. It was difficult to know what was going on.

The villagers say they feel left behind by the government because they have not been given electricity or paved roads. The government faces a dilemma. If the government gives the villagers what they want, park officials say, the village will become more permanent and will eventually grow. Because the village is located at the boundary of the park, officials believe growth will automatically mean further degradation of the park. They acknowledge that the degradation may be caused not by the villagers but by outsiders who move in because of the road. The government hopes the villagers will relocate. Over the past decade many of them have moved to nearby towns to have access to schools, health clinics, electricity, and roads. Nevertheless, the villagers who remain in Sungai Keruh seemed determined to stand their ground.

Das and I headed back to Sungai Penuh the following day. When we reached the WWF field office Al told me that the head of the regional planning and development board in Jambi had cancelled his plans to attend the workshop. Al thought that this man could give me some important insights into the project and that I should go to Jambi to meet him. Getting there, though, would require another all-night bus trip.

Before catching the night bus to Jambi, I spent the day at the workshop, and between sessions I had a chance to talk with some of the park officials from neighboring provinces. Over coffee one of them told me, "The only way to police a park is to constantly patrol it. Most of these park guards are too lazy for that, and they want to sit in their office and count the money they have earned in bribes. Not me; I am always out there, and in my part of the park no one dares to try planting cinnamon."[24] This man was a talker, but he seemed very earnest in his commitment to forest protection and his antipathy for people inside the park boundaries. I asked him about the participatory policy of the World Bank and drew a blank. Many of the officials at the workshop did not seem to know what the World Bank is, let alone understand its new participatory approach.

I left for Sungai Penuh by bus that evening. I arrived the next morning and checked into a hotel to get some rest. When I showed up at the WWF office a few hours later, there was confusion. The man I was to interview had been called away unexpectedly to a meeting in Jakarta. I was disappointed. I asked to speak to his staff and was escorted down the hall to meet with them. I wanted to hear what they thought about the project. When I asked about the policies of the World Bank they looked at each other nervously. Finally one of them said that they were not qualified to answer questions about policy, certainly not without a letter from my organization explaining my purpose. I tried to coax them, but they could not be budged. It occurred to me then that they might not know much about the project. Sure enough, they were not even familiar with the World Bank. I explained what I knew about the project, and they thanked me profusely. One added candidly that their boss did not share anything with them.

WWF JAKARTA OFFICE

When I returned to Jakarta I called on my old boss from WALHI, Agus Purnomo, who was now the Indonesian country representative for WWF Indonesia. I told him about my visit to communities around the park and asked him what he thought about the project overall. He summarized the situation:

> The park is a magnet for frontier settlers and corrupt bureaucrats. There are many conflicting interests in the four provinces that share the park. At the macro level there are mining and logging interests; there are infrastructural developments, population growth, plantation expansion, industry, and paper manufacturing plants, all of which affect the park. At the micro level, if people are benefiting from maximizing the short-term profits, they will continue to do so. I do not believe there is enough incentive for people to give up the short-term benefits in favor of the long-term conservation of the park. If these conflicting interests are to be negotiated, the

results will be disappointing to both the conservationists and the "developmentalists." But what does this mean for the future of the park?[25]

Purnomo explained that community involvement is clearly necessary, but asked how WWF could approach these communities when its real goal is to convince them to stay out of the park:

> The idea that the local people should be educated about the benefits of conservation is patronizing. It is not that they don't know about conservation, but rather that their needs are more immediate. How can WWF guarantee that by agreeing to community mapping and certain restraint in their consumption that they will benefit in the long run? These are not stable communities, and neither are the forces at play. How will we determine the maximum sustained yield for every activity? How do we at WWF carry the burden of pushing sustainable development? We are supposed to be a conservation organization. We are finding we cannot do conservation without addressing development and politics, but this falls outside our mandate. The members that support WWF are not asking for integrated conservation and development programs. They want to see WWF saving the Sumatran tiger. How far can the definition of wildlife habitat be stretched to accommodate the need to address these larger questions?
>
> The most troubling question is, are we facing a losing battle? The land and natural resources in those provinces are rich. Those who can are skimming off the profits. There are many opportunities to develop industries on a large scale. The people are anything but passive; they are actively engaged in trying to increase their sources of livelihood.

Purnomo explained that the settlers recognize the richness of the land inside the park boundary. The incentive for them to restrict their farming activities in this sort of setting is very small. He added that these settlers might even happily relocate if they were offered enough to do so, but that was not likely to happen. Anyway, he concluded, "It is all a gamble. There are so many factors to control for . . . political, social, economic. It is quite possible that within twenty to thirty years there will be nothing left of the park."[26]

COMMUNITY FORESTRY IN INDONESIA

The situation in the Kerinci Seblat region contrasted so sharply with what I had seen in India that I hardly knew where to begin to compare the two. In both countries attempts were being made to address the problem of the loss of forest and local livelihood and to change the way that the state manages natural resources. In India I saw stunning examples of spontaneous grassroots movements. The people's demands for control over their resources and their defiance of forest authority appeared to come from a sophisticated democratic tradition.

Indonesia's forest resources are richer than India's, which may be one reason that conflicts over forest resources have not reached the same pitch here that they have in India. Cynically, I thought perhaps Indian foresters are prepared to hand over management to local communities only because the commercial value of the forest has been depleted, leaving little incentive for the foresters to maintain it. In such cases the forests often flourish again, once communities take over their protection and management. Would events have to follow the same course of degradation before Indonesian foresters would turn control over to communities? Or could Indonesia, with its wealth of local community-based forest management systems, forge a different path?

In the 1980s the Indonesian forest department sought to integrate community management into the mix of production forestry through several major social forestry initiatives that were concentrated on Java, where a mere 3 percent of the country's forests are located.[27] Nancy Peluso, who studied villagers' resistance to social forestry in Java, found that although these programs have been very successful at putting trees in the ground, they have been less successful at keeping them there, largely because most villagers' economic circumstances have remained precarious.[28] Although social forestry programs have removed some of the antagonism between foresters and villagers, and perhaps initiated a change in attitude within the forest department, the issues of forest access and control remain problematic.[29] Furthermore, most Indonesian foresters continued to assume that local villagers do not have the capacity to manage forests and hence should be given no rights over them.

In the early 1990s a consortium of nongovernmental groups came together to support the documentation of community forest management across Indonesia. This consortium estimates that there are at least eighteen distinct types of community forest systems managed by ethnic minorities throughout the archipelago.[30] The nontimber products from these mixed "forest garden" systems, or agroforests, provide both cash and subsistence needs for the communities managing them. At the same time they maintain the ecological structure and function of the natural forests. These indigenous management systems may be traditional, but they are also dynamic. Village managers are continually experimenting with new techniques and management strategies and adapting their customary rules to meet new challenges.

KRUI'S DAMAR RESERVES

In 1997 I visited Krui, where local communities have been managing forests of damar trees (*Shorea javanica*) for generations. Damar trees are a type of dipterocarp that yield valuable resins for export. Krui is on the southern tip of Sumatra, close to Java. Nestled between a protected forest and the Indian Ocean, Krui has become famous for its community-managed reserves of damar. In one of the most recent developments in community forest policy, the forestry ministry gave Krui special status in recognition of the sustainability of its management system. This was a turning point for community forest policy in Indonesia because it supported the idea that communities can be quite capable forest managers.

In 1987 Indonesian exports of the highest quality damar resin, called *mata kucing* (cat's eye), were valued at an estimated $4.5 million, a substantial portion of the estimated $26 million garnered from the nation's total export of nontimber forest products. Most of this high quality *mata kucing* damar, which is used for varnishes for fine woodwork and as a binder in paint and linoleum products, comes from Krui.[31] The price of *mata kucing* in international markets remained stable during the 1997–1998 economic crisis in Asia.[32]

In July 1997 I went to Krui by bus with a community organizer named Dirman. Dirman worked for WATALA, one of a team of institutions that facilitated the negotiations with the ministry of forestry for Krui's special status. We visited three different communities managing damar reserves in the district of Krui, only one of which had received special status. At the first village we spent the day hiking through forest gardens with the customary leader's son, Mustafa. He showed us damar gardens in various stages of growth and explained how they develop. "Usually we start a damar garden at the end of the cycle of shifting cultivation," he said, "or where there is a large opening in the forest canopy." Mustafa went on to explain that the gardens increase in complexity over the years, influenced by natural ecological processes and by planting and selective cutting by the farmers: "Normally we begin by clearing an old garden or secondary forest to make a new garden. Primary forest is off limits under customary law, and anyway it is too much work to open primary forest. We prefer to open something that we have used before."[33]

After clearing the forest, the first crop that farmers plant is upland rice, followed by corn, cassava, and other food crops. After a third or fourth year, coffee or pepper may be added. Between three and seven years into the cycle, damar seedlings are interspersed with the other tree crops. The coffee and pepper seedlings provide shade for damar seedlings, and as the damar trees grow they provide a suitable microclimate for shade coffee and pepper production. In fifteen years the damar overtakes the coffee and pepper trees. Farmers add other fruit trees to the garden, and many natural timber species grow spontaneously.[34] In addition, many varieties of rattan and high-value woods are planted to meet basic household needs for fuelwood and building materials. This system of cultivation is common to almost every community forestry system in Indonesia.

The damar reserves that I saw looked like natural forests, and they were some of the nicest tropical forests I had seen. With their mixture of spontaneous and cultivated trees and plants, mature damar reserves resemble natural forests in structural complexity and species richness. Forest ecologists comparing adjacent forest areas estimate that Krui's damar reserves retain close to 80 percent of the original biological diversity of natural forests.[35] Researchers studying Krui's agroforestry systems have also found that as nearby natural forests have been degraded by logging, damar gardens have become an important habitat for endangered mammals such as Sumatran rhinoceroses, Sumatran tigers, goats, tapirs, gibbons, and *siamang* (monkeys).[36] These damar gardens are an excellent example of the important role that forests outside protected areas can play in protecting biodiversity.

Families in Krui manage the forests through customary law. Mustafa explained to me that an individual can claim a particular tree in a natural forest if there are no pre-existing claims on that tree. Generally, however, the tenure of plots of trees within the reserve is held by a family clan and is passed down through family lines. Mature damar trees begin producing resin after twenty years, and the owners of the tree can tap the resin for about thirty years. Damar production falls off when the tree is between fifty and sixty years of age.

Families in Krui have been managing the damar reserves and harvesting the resin in this way for several hundred years. Although most of Indonesia's natural forests are legally under the administration of government forestry agencies, millions of hectares of forestland are actively managed by forest-dependent households and communities. In the mid-1980s agroforests like those found in Krui covered about 3.5 to 4 million hectares in Sumatra.[37]

In the early 1990s local farmers in Krui began experiencing pressures on their damar gardens. A logging company planned to clear 3 million valuable dipterocarp trees planted by Krui villagers. In 1996 one oil palm company clear-cut dozens of hectares of community-planted damar on the southern border of Krui in order to prepare land for plantations. One recent report notes that plantations present the most serious threat yet to community-managed systems: "Oil palm and timber plantations may have more negative consequences for local communities than previous logging operations. To some extent communities had managed to co-exist with logging operations, but the plantations consume vast areas of land and may displace their traditional activities entirely."[38]

In the mid-1990s rumors that damar gardens in neighboring villages were being clear-cut at night and during Friday prayers fueled the local people's anxieties.[39] Many research institutes that worked in the Krui area feared that these systems could be destroyed by the plantation companies. A coalition formed by the Indonesian Tropical Institute (LATIN), the International Center for Research on Agroforestry (ICRAF), the Ford Foundation, Indonesian nongovernmental organizations, and several universities worked together to help villagers map and document Krui's reserves and customary land claims. The villagers, with the coalition's help, took this information to the forestry ministry with a proposal that Krui be granted permanent rights over the land. With technical assistance from ICRAF, the minister crafted a new special use zone in January 1998, granting Krui communities control over 29,000 hectares of damar reserves.[40] Although the special use zone does not give Krui permanent rights over their reserves and does not include all Krui's damar reserves, the legislation is viewed as an important step toward government recognition of the ecological and economic benefits of community-managed forests and the need for devolving forest management authority to local people.[41]

FOREST FIRES AND POLITICAL CRISIS

In 1997, after visiting Krui, I planned to research community forestry systems in Kalimantan, the Indonesian part of Borneo. Many of the places that I had hoped to visit were inaccessible because of huge fires that initially burned between 500,000 and 2 million hectares. These fires were intensified by a drought associated with the El Niño effect. As destructive as they were, the fires in Borneo in 1997 and 1998 were not the worst fires on record for that part of Indonesia.[42] Fires in 1982 and 1983, which were exacerbated by the worst drought since 1878, razed about 3.6 million hectares.[43] Drought allows the normally moist peat and swamp forests to dry up, catch fire, and burn underground, which makes the fire very difficult to extinguish. Peat also produces a thick haze, which in 1997 blanketed Southeast Asia and affected several international meetings, including the annual September meetings of the World Bank and the International Monetary Fund, which took place in Hong Kong. The haze was health threatening, and it interfered with shipping and air traffic across a 4,000-square-kilometer area.[44] Studies reported that carbon gas emissions from the fires were estimated to equal a year's worth of carbon emissions from all of Western Europe.[45]

At the height of the fires a young graduate student from an Australian university, who happened to be the son of the minister of environment, asked his father why the forestry ministry was not tracking the fires by satellite. The minister promptly called his colleague at the forestry ministry. Within days they had set up an emergency office to track the source of the fires. With access to official records, a team of young experts, largely from outside the ministry and gathered by the minister of environment's son, was able to trace the source of the fires to 176 plantation companies. Most of them had apparently been using fire to clear forestland.[46]

Analysis of land satellite images from the United States National Oceanic and Atmospheric Association (NOAA) later supported that evidence. According to NOAA, the fires that burned in Sumatra and Kalimantan in 1997 and 1998 decimated a total of 9 million hectares of land.[47] Furthermore, an analysis of the number and the location of the fires—detected as "hot spots" by the NOAA satellite imagery—indicated that the distribution of fires in Sumatra spread during a very narrow amount of time. One-third of these hot spots were recorded during the single week of 12–18 October 1997.[48] Nearly all of the hot spots were in areas designated as logging or plantation concessions, not in the natural forest.

The fires brought attention to years of corruption in the forestry ministry that included the illegal issuing of permits to cut timber, particularly those given to the operations of logging czar Bob Hasan, a golfing partner of Suharto. Hasan used his influence to mastermind the creation of a heavily subsidized timber processing industry and establish a cartel through which all timber had to be sold. Hasan, who misappropriated some $244 million in state funds, was the first of Suharto's cronies to stand trial for corruption.[49]

A 1988 ban on the sale of whole logs combined with heavy industry subsidies resulted in a proliferation of local sawmills and led to unprecedented and unsustainable rates of logging in the 1990s. The World Bank and the International Monetary Fund demanded the reversal of these policies and the dismantling of Hasan's cartel in the wake of the economic crisis. Large-scale commercial logging in Kalimantan was already reaching a turning point at the end of the 1990s because most of the valuable timber had been depleted. The ministry of forestry attempted to punish concession holders for years of overcutting and mismanagement of timber by revoking their licenses. Yet many of these same companies obtained new licenses for plantations on the same locations. These companies, who were looking for short-term gains, recognized that logging could not begin on timber plantations for twenty years or more, whereas investments in oil palm would begin yielding within three to five years.

DAYAK STRUGGLE

In 1997, despite the fires, I was able to go to East Kalimantan, one of Indonesia's most important timber regions and a place where indigenous Dayak people had been struggling for rights over their customary forestland. In East Kalimantan communities who had contended for years with the logging companies now were pulled into bitter struggles against oil palm plantations. I went to a community where I had earlier studied the traditional planting calendars and mixed forest garden practices that were used by the indigenous Dayak people. I stopped to see a friend of mine who had been working with these communities for more than ten years. He told me that things were not going well for the Dayak. I wanted to meet Nonda, the seventy-six-year-old customary leader of the Dayak Pasir Adang community. He happened to be in town administering a traditional medicine cure to a sick neighbor, and he invited me to return with him to his village that afternoon.

Nonda and I traveled by minibus to the harbor, where we boarded a speedboat to take us across the bay. We then caught another bus to the district of Pasir. We passed endless fields of oil palm plantations for a few hours and finally reached a large dusty logging road. We climbed out of the bus and walked along the road to Nonda's daughter's house, where he stayed when he was not attending to important Dayak affairs. Although Nonda did not have many teeth left, he had a lot of energy. In the days that followed he took me to visit two other villages that faced threats to their customary forests. The most striking case was Nonda's own village.

In the 1970s the forestry ministry had granted a timber concession to Balikpapan Forest Industries. The concession included the customary land of Nonda's village. The logging operations had slowly pushed the Dayak out of their customary lands, but once logging operations finished in a particular area, the Dayak were usually able to continue their mixed forest garden farming. Then plantation companies began to move into the area. They offered the Dayak the opportunity to become part of the company by clearing their own land and then planting it with oil palm bought on credit from the company. The people could then sell the oil palm back to the company at the company's set price. The company promised that they would be rich in no time and that in three years they would all be driving their own motorcycles.

The indigenous families of Nonda's village wanted no part of this scheme and refused to clear their land. Nonda's daughter told me, "Well, we thought it was a stupid idea. If we clear our land, what are we supposed to do for food? Where are we going to get our medicinal plants?"[50] Had Nonda's village accepted the company plan, they would have lost not only their medicines but also hundreds of other forest products and fruits. All of that would have been replaced by the inedible oil palm trees. Furthermore, the villagers would most likely have been in debt from the credit scheme offered by the company. Nonetheless, local officials were furious with the villagers and began to send military brigades to threaten Nonda. He told me that the district military officer shook his finger at him, saying, "You will go to prison for this. You are an antidevelopment communist subversive!"[51]

I returned to Nonda's village a year later, in August 1998. Despite a few visits to the local prisons over the past year, Nonda had not been dissuaded. When I met with him I asked him about the fires that had raged for most of the previous year. Nonda told me that the fires did not really affect them. They burned only small portions of their forest gardens adjacent to the new oil palm fields. This was true across Kalimantan and Sumatra. As Nonda's daughter Nilai cooked some bitter roots and "Indomie" noodles, she related that the people had been affected more seriously by the long drought: "It has been a tough year. Normally, I would be planting rice right now. I have not been able to plant rice in our fields for the whole year. We have used up our reserves. So, now we have to buy rice to eat and rice to plant. The monetary crisis is making it tough. Rice costs three times what it used to."[52] The villagers were left without rice to plant, and they could not afford to buy it. The Dayak Pasir are known for their planting calendars, which coincide with the stars and have been unfailingly accurate. The drought and the coinciding monetary crisis occurred at a time when their traditional planting routines had been disrupted by the struggles against the plantation and logging companies, putting an unusual strain on the Dayak community. Nonda explained:

> We are used to this El Niño drought thing. We are used to eating cassava or other things when this happens, but the children are hungry. So, we are trying to get wild birds and other goods from the forest to sell in the market so that we can afford rice. Even so, they say that La Niña effect will make it rain much longer when it does start. I know it is true because I can read into the future, and I see that all this trouble will pass. But some people are impatient and they want to sell their land to the oil palm company and move away.[53]

Across Indonesia, lands under de facto community control did not burn in the devastating fires, but the drought and land struggles disrupted planting schedules. This problem was exacerbated by the sharp devaluation of the nation's currency. Yet these people believed that, in the greater scheme of things, if they could gain rights over their customary forestlands they could regenerate and protect them.

CONCLUSIONS

As Indonesia struggles to restructure its economy and set a new course for democratic transition, the change in regime offers possibilities for new policies, particularly in the case of community forestry. Local and national conflicts and international concern over the loss of forest in the aftermath of the fires have caused a major rethinking of forest policy, including the formulation of a new forestry law, which was introduced in 1999. Although attitudes within the Indonesian forest department are not as progressive or unified as those reached by some Indian foresters, some individuals within the Indonesian government are pushing for greater community control over forest resources.

A new reform oriented government committed to a democratic Indonesia cannot guarantee the resolution of conflicts regarding forest resources, but it may give local communities an opportunity to manage their customary forests. The political environment has enormous implications for local people who are working to assert local priorities in conservation and development projects. It may mean that local people can gain recognition of customary claims over forests, and in some cases communities may even be able to gain formal legal title.

Coalitions of nongovernmental organizations that have been mapping customary claims and documenting customary resource management systems across Indonesia are using this documentation to demonstrate that many communities still have strong and flexible social institutions and should be granted the right to continue governing the use and protection of forest resources. Some conservationists fear that these efforts will undermine years of protection. They argue that well-meaning nongovernmental organizations that promote community rights vastly underestimate the sensitivity of these fragile ecosystems and the speed with which they can be diminished. The organizations involved in helping communities document their claims and management systems argue that it is the ardent conservationists that underestimate the vitality and resilience of the tropical forest.

Each side would do well to investigate the other side's claims. Each argues from a different political stance. The conservationists argue from a global perspective, claiming that these forests must be preserved for humanity because they are some of the last of their kind on the planet. The community rights advocates argue from a local perspective, saying that they cannot accept conservation efforts that take precedence over the way of life of forest-dependent people. Both sides want to protect the forest, but for different purposes and through different means. The only way to resolve these conflicts is for each side to recognize the other side as a necessary ally.

The case of Kerinci Seblat National Park demonstrates the complexity of conflicts between people and conservation and the multiple levels at which those conflicts play out. The World Bank has the leverage to restructure the provincial investments in ways that could strengthen the park and remove a significant threat to conservation, which would be a great achievement. Conflicts at the local level, however, can be resolved only by ascertaining the real concerns of local communities and determining what kind of responsibility communities are willing to take on in return for secure rights to land.

Conservation is not simply about protection. It is about the reallocation of resources and the restructuring of social institutions. If conservationists understand that they cannot save precious forests by excluding people and that, like it or not, they must work with people to achieve their goals, then much more progress will be made. It is not enough to pour money into an effort to protect the Sumatran tiger. Conservation implies a struggle over resources, and struggles over resources are simultaneously struggles over the meaning of those resources and over the identities of the people who depend on them.

Until conservationists understand that struggles over resources require constant negotiation, progress will be nil. Efforts to enforce arbitrary boundaries of parks and protected areas dreamed up in national capitals with international backing will fail to protect these special places. Paper parks with little relation to reality on the ground will create the opposite effect of the one that is intended. Progress might be made when conservationists fully understand two vital points: protection cannot be achieved by setting out ideal management plans that ignore the reality of settler populations, and it cannot be ensured by zoning away the rights of local forest-dependent people who want to preserve their access to the nontimber forest products that they use. As long as conservation is seen as a one-way set of inflexible rules laid down by some outside authority, conservation efforts will fail. Once conservationists understand the stakes based on field realities and learn that they can rely on local communities to help manage and protect forests, then there is hope for the resolution of conflicts over these resources.

The case of Krui is important because it has helped government planners and scientists understand the value of traditional agroforestry practices in Indonesia in terms of economic productivity as well as ecological sustainability. It has also shown that it is possible to develop new ways of legitimizing claims over land managed through customary law. At a time when Indonesia desperately needs stable and productive systems of forest management, indigenous forest garden technologies and customary resource management institutions not only provide an attractive alternative to large-scale timber extraction but also respond to the ecological and economic needs of local residents.[54]

There is no better time to support the endeavors of local people throughout Indonesia. There is much to be done to encourage the national government to support the democratic participation of local communities. This is the most important contribution that can be made to the effort to conserve Indonesia's forests.

CHAPTER 6

Africa's Cornucopia
and Scorpion

Ancient Romans depicted Africa as a woman holding both a cornucopia and a scorpion.[1] Early in the continent's precolonial history, traders were already hauling gold from there to Mediterranean destinations. Later bountiful quantities of ivory, copper, and diamonds, and plantation crops such as rubber, cocoa, cotton, palm oil, peanuts, and cashews were exported from the continent. Even as late as the early 1970s, when I first visited East Africa, there was a stunning grace and beauty to the golden meadows flecked with striking flat-topped trees and populated by giraffes and baboons and antelopes of every description as well as the majestically tall and strikingly dressed Maasai tribespeople and their herds of cattle.[2] Africa is rich in biodiversity, and, despite the pressures of population growth, it still has plenty of unused cropland to be cultivated and rangeland to be used. Only 1 percent of its vast and renewable water resources is being used for agriculture.[3]

Alongside such evidence of African splendor, riches, and promise there festers the "scorpion" side of the equation. The climate is steamy along much of the West African coastline and in equatorial Central Africa, where 90 percent of the continent's tropical rainforest is to be found. In most of East Africa and in much of Central Africa, grasslands and fractured forests alternate in what is often referred to as a "mosaic" landscape, where domestic livestock and wild animals graze and browse in woodlands (map 10). Food for them is often scarce. Dryness is the principal characteristic of the climate in these regions, and droughts are frequent. Sixty percent of the entire continent is desert. Great fluctuations in rainfall cause many Africans to migrate from place to place in search of water. Epidemics of disease—yellow fever, dengue, malaria, sleeping sickness—have frequently ravaged portions of the continent. Livestock is threatened by foot and mouth disease and the diseases carried by tsetse flies, which prey on cattle and humans alike. "Few regions have a poorer endowment of productive soils," wrote one author recently. Glaciers that left fertile mineral paths across Europe and North America never reached Africa. In much of the region exceptionally heavy seasonal rains over thousands of years leached nutrients from the soil and left hard pans of iron oxide beneath the surface layer.[4]

It is often stated that the cultures and societies of precolonial Africans were precarious, buffeted severely by weather fluctuations, disease, and the savagery of intertribal warfare. In fact, the vast continent had enormous variety and some very complex and advanced societies. Along its west coast, the Yoruba and the Ibo in what is now Nigeria, as well as many other groups, had highly specialized crafts and trades. Recent studies find evidence that without the expert rice cultivators that were brought to the New World as slaves, the plantation belt in the southern United States could never have developed. Slave trading began among early societies such as the Sumerians, the Romans, and Greeks, and it occurred throughout Asia and in the Arab world long before Europe and the United States picked up the habit. Where slavers did not venture, local warfare was often a disruptive force. As long as the population remained relatively low and fresh land was readily available, however, many African societies were able to use the techniques of shifting cultivation (or bush-fallowing, as the practice is better known in Africa) for subsistence. Since these societies were nestled in fertile river valleys and alluvial plains, agriculture abounded. In forest societies food crops were

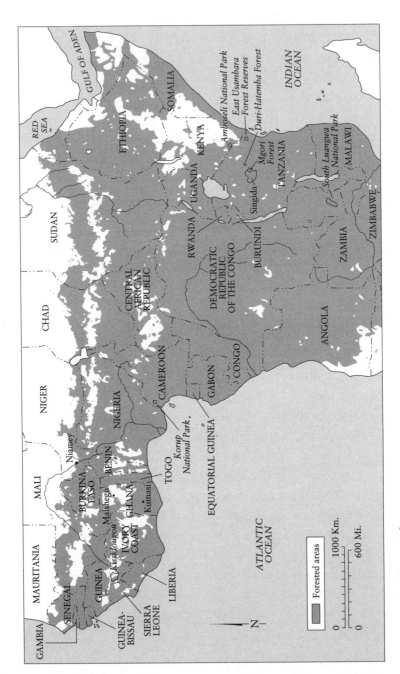

Map 10. Sub-Saharan Africa.

integrated into the natural ecosystem of the forest. These mixed crop-ping systems made the best possible use of the nutrients that were avail-able. The fallow or intact forest provided meat and many other foods, as well as fuel and medicine.

It is all too easy to romanticize and exaggerate the degree of "har-mony" that traditional Africans maintain with their natural surround-ings. There is nothing fixed about the spiritual and cultural ties between the indigenous peoples and nature. Aside from tribal warfare and weather disruptions, the Africans' own communal institutions have of-ten been in flux as different tribal leaders come to power. Under modern economic duress, villagers may do what it takes to survive. "Given the chance," said two keen observers of village life in Africa, "indigenous people will exploit their environment to their advantage, using whatever technology is available."[5] Yet when almost all sub-Saharan Africans lived nomadically or in scattered villages, the prevailing communal forms of governance did much to safeguard the supply of what people needed.

Local chiefs or elders would set rules to ensure that the community would not exceed the capabilities of often fragile ecosystems. Dynamic and flexible common property regimes regulated villagers' access to re-sources and grazing areas. As in Asia and elsewhere, certain areas were designated as "sacred groves" that served as burial grounds or places where medicinal and holy plants were protected from the harvesting activities permitted elsewhere. These places often became pockets of biological diversity. Customary laws regulated through communal knowledge of cultural taboos and inheritance systems, and enforced through tribal institutions, governed a great diversity of resource own-ership and use.

Rules and sanctions against excessive individual use were often part of overlapping layers of customary law, and sometimes the cost of break-ing them was high indeed. In precolonial kingdoms within what are now Mali and Niger, those who were caught illegally cutting a prized tree species had their hands lopped off.[6] To this day in the community of Malshegu in Ghana's Northern Region, farming and grazing are entirely prohibited within or near a grove within which, it is believed, resides a fetish god who drives away evil spirits. Only an important priest and his assistants are allowed within the grove to pray or collect medicinal plants. In older times transgressors violating the space were lynched. In the mid-1990s offenders had to pay stiff fines of several cows or goats and suffer severe adverse social consequences for breaking the rules.[7]

The slave trade was the first force from outside that severely distorted and weakened Africa's traditional systems. Soon after the Portuguese navigator Pedro Alvares Cabral stumbled upon Brazil in 1500, Portuguese adventurers began combing West Africa's backlands in search of human cargo to send to their sugar plantations in South America and the Caribbean region. Even priests became practitioners of this ghastly practice. Men, women, and children were captured in the hinterlands (or purchased from local chiefs), chained together, and herded to coastal ports for transfer to the slave markets. Entire regions were depopulated and their cultures lost. European settlers, fanning out from the coast to the interiors of many lands, began to do further damage. The ravages that imperialists from England, France, Germany, and Belgium committed are fully catalogued in Thomas Pakenham's chilling book *The Scramble for Africa*, a lurid tale replete with severed hands, severed heads, and fractured societies. In the more recent *King Leopold's Ghost*, Adam Hochschild zeroes in on how the cerebral, power-crazed Belgian monarch was able to convince many in Europe that he was bringing enlightenment to savage societies, while in fact, with the American adventurer Henry Morton Stanley as his principal agent in the field, he was commissioning grotesque atrocities in his quest for wealth and political control.[8]

Everywhere they went the roving armies dispatched by the imperialists shot, slashed, and hacked their way through resisting kingdoms and chieftains, raising the flags of Europe over the towns and cities they sacked and claiming all they found as their own. In Europe scorn greeted those few who doubted the validity of these claims. The consequences for often remote and far less disruptive societies were severe. Northeast Gabon was once well populated and extensively farmed by local people using traditional methods, authors Jonathan Adams and Thomas MacShane report in their book, *The Myth of Wild Africa*. After colonialists forced the local villagers to work for them, famine, disease, and severe distortions of village life ensued. The region's population was halved; many of those who managed to remain alive abandoned their traditional lands and migrated elsewhere.

Not only did the Europeans enslave the African villagers; they perceived them and their well-established traditions of shifting agriculture as despoilers of the "paradise" they now claimed as their own. "Scientific" foresters and planters brought in under the colonial administrations showed a profound misunderstanding of tropical ecosystems and the careful resource management techniques that local communities had developed. They failed to attribute any value to the nontimber products that villagers harvested from the forest and disdained traditional food crops, substituting exotic plants such as coffee, tea, cacao, tobacco, peanuts, and other monocultures destined for the European marketplace. The new plantations demanded quantities of cleared land far in excess of that required simply to grow food for local use. Ignoring women, who in most of Africa did most of the farm work, even well-intentioned colonial administrators often preferred to try to train the inexperienced men. The abandonment of traditional crop rotation systems and fallow periods of adequate length exhausted soils in many regions. Famine substituted for relatively secure subsistence life styles. Human populations shrank from the onset of colonialism until well into the twentieth century, when modern medical methods kicked in to curb the ravages of previously unchecked diseases. And when human numbers once again grew, although opinions vary about the often-cited role of population growth in environmental decline, additional pressures were surely placed on some already weakened landscapes.

INDEPENDENCE, BUT NO RELIEF

When sub-Saharan nations won liberty from their colonial masters during the 1950s and 1960s, one might have hoped for better times. Instead, in many lands things only got worse as the population explosion intensified and as dictatorial kleptocracies run by small numbers of "big men" replaced colonial administrations in country after country. Such leaders as the infamous Mobutu Sese Seko in the former Zaire, Hastings Kamuzu Banda in Malawi, and Félix Houphouët-Boigny in Ivory Coast plundered national treasuries and foreign-aid accounts to build costly palaces and line their own pockets. Houphouët-Boigny, wrote Jennifer Whitaker, "led his compatriots for over three decades with a patriarchal majesty even his French mentors could not rival."[9]

Centralized political control remained predominant. In many parts of Africa forest departments were closely linked to military units. Postcolonial forest services carried forward the repressive practices of the colonial "forest police," ignoring local communities' needs and traditions.[10] Specters of "tribal warfare" were frequently conjured up by Africa's new "leaders," who staged wars and cloaked their own thuggery within widely broadcast allegations of ethnic conflict. Behind a gruesome foreground of refugees, starvation, heinous killings, and brutal power brokerage there frequently lay sophisticated public relations exercises in disinformation in which "informants" on cellular telephones manipulated the international media with fictitious accounts of atrocious killings and visions of hell. To carry out these staged wars, rebel groups and governments alike relied on international warfare consultants from Britain and South Africa. Mercenaries from the unemployed ranks of the former Soviet Union were also in abundant supply during most of the 1990s. These schemes, played out in front of the world's television cameras, were often said to be fueled with money from mineral and timber interests. Real wars, adds one observer, have frequently occurred as a result of "a mobilization of youth on behalf of a small group of people angry at their exclusion from an opaque political system serving mineral extraction interests."[11]

During those decades, and even more recently, the policies and programs of the international development agencies helped place stress on African landscapes and on rural people. Here, as elsewhere, they called for capital-intensive forms of industrialization and monocrop, export-oriented agriculture and for major infrastructure investments in roads and dams. When these programs failed to achieve sufficiently rapid "development," structural adjustment policies calling for "export rehabilitation" efforts were installed in Ghana, Nigeria, and elsewhere; these encouraged overlogging and environmental decline. Although development agencies have become far more alert to environmental considerations and the needs of local people than ever before, recent transgressions have been noted. In the report issued after its regional hearing in Cameroon in 1997, the World Commission on Forests and Sustainable Development (WCFSD) cited the example of the World Bank–financed oil pipeline between Chad and Cameroon, which crosses the most fertile lands in arid Chad and displaces local people. And very recently, after the FAO had worked out very elaborate arrangements to save the forest and also address the needs of charcoal makers in a section of Uganda, negotiations abruptly stopped when an international development agency, the Commonwealth Development Corporation, intervened with a less sensitive rival proposal that offered the charcoal burners and some government officials a better deal.

How deeply this dismal history has affected sub-Saharan Africa's forests is a matter of considerable debate among scientists and conservationists. In many circles it is conventional to think that many countries of the region, especially in the West African tropics, were blanketed with primary or "virgin" forest three hundred years ago. Many researchers feel that as the region's human population has grown over this period, the conversion of forests to open savanna has accelerated at a more or less equivalent rate. Others calculate that there has been a far greater fluctuation in both forest cover and in population. As late as 1650 as many as 100 million people, or 10 percent of the world's population, may have inhabited the continent. In many regions at that time people were cutting down forests to make way for agriculture. Then populations crashed, down to as much as 50 percent of historic highs, thanks to a combination of local warfare, the slave trade, and the spread of disease. As pressure on them lightened, forests regenerated to the point where many observers believed them to be pristine and their land never used.[12]

NEW IMPRESSIONS

The baseline for many recent estimates of West African forest losses, according to anthropologists James Fairhead and Melissa Leach, is often placed at the years 1900 to 1920, a time when forest cover in many parts of the region had in fact achieved historic highs.[13] These researchers found, for West Africa at least, that if one looks back far enough, the extent of overall forest loss has been massively exaggerated. Even if forest losses in the precolonial period were not as precipitous as some have suggested, there is no doubt that those of the past fifty years have been vast. As in Asia and in Latin America, sweetheart deals for large-scale industrial loggers have resulted in heavy losses. The tropical forests of the Congo Basin, which are being cut at the rate of 4 million hectares a year, will survive only another two decades if losses continue at the present pace. Much of the rainforest has already vanished from such West African countries as Mali, Ivory Coast, Gabon, and Nigeria. While industrial logging is less of a problem in the dryland and montane forests of eastern and southern Africa, forest clearing in those regions has also been intensive, with fuelwood gathering, charcoal production, and the quest for farmland ranking as principal causes. Overall, according to World Conservation Monitoring Centre (WCMC) calculations, 90 percent of the intact forests that Africa had 8,000 years ago have vanished.[14]

Many observers still find the movement of human populations into forest areas to be the major culprit of forest degradation. During the 1980s, according to data collected by the World Commission on Forests and Sustainable Development, 70 percent of all forest change in sub-

Saharan Africa was attributable to "rural population pressure through subsistence farming, grazing, and wood extraction" (58 percent of all energy use in Africa comes from fuelwood). In 1996, the World Conservation Monitoring Centre calculated that 76.8 percent of all Africa's remaining "frontier forests" ("large, relatively intact forest ecosystems") were already "threatened." And regardless of the accuracy of population statistics from the past, the future forecasts for still largely rural sub-Saharan Africa are ominous: the United Nations figures are 179 million in 1950, 629 million in 1998, 1,832 million in 2050.[15] Some fear that this explosive population growth will put at risk a substantial portion of all the remaining forest in the region.

What the work of Fairhead and Leach suggests, however, is that at least in large measure the blame for forest loss lies elsewhere. The authors argue that "much of the forest that has been lost during the twentieth century, and indeed much of that which remains, covered land which had earlier been populated and farmed, calling into question the commonplace view of population growth and deforestation as a linked one-way process."[16] Degradation has often resulted, they find, less from the actions or numbers of people living in or near West African forests than from the imposition of state control and other interventions from outside on rural and forest regions. Many of these were once owned and managed by local people who were actually creating pockets of forests that the colonialists and their successors assumed were mere remnants of a formerly vast expanse of forest. Arguably, then, it was the misguided intervention of colonial and postcolonial foresters and administrators, as much as or more than the actions and growing numbers of rural people, that lay behind much of the loss of African forest in the past century.

In a remarkable book-length case study, *Misreading the African Landscape*, Fairhead and Leach tellingly review a full century of such interventions into the farming and forestry traditions practiced by people in Kissidougou prefecture in the West African nation of Guinea. Forest patches alternate with savanna grasslands in this region. Arriving late in the nineteenth century, French colonialists assumed that these bits of forest were "the last relics of an original dense humid forest which once fully covered the landscape," as Fairhead and Leach put it. They and many of their successors agreed that local villagers' actions were responsible for ongoing further degradation that "justified state action to take resource control from local inhabitants, and repressive policies to reorientate what has been seen as destructive land management."[17] In recent years it has been ever more commonplace for academic researchers, officials throughout the national education system, environmental nongovernmental organizations, and international aid donors to reach similar conclusions.

After careful research Fairhead and Leach came to a different understanding of the situation. They found that the Kissi people depend on these "forest islands" for many things. They shield the village from wind and heat, provide food, medicine, and fuel, shelter tree crops such as coffee, and are useful as protection and fortification during wars. Far from stripping these islands, the villagers had been painstakingly nurturing them, in part by planting trees, but more so "by creating fire and soil conditions which favour forest regeneration in savanna." Further evidence emerged that the area had been populous and quite intensively farmed since well before European occupation, perhaps for hundreds of years, but certainly long enough to determine the sustainability of traditional land and forest management methods involving elaborate rules and intricate webs of human relations. Twenty-five informants told the researchers of no fewer than 147 medical treatments, for ailments ranging from toothaches to convulsions, that are available from the wild plants that the Kissi cultivate and nurture.

Systematically over the past century, the ability of the Kissi to manage their landscape has been compromised by the usually wrongheaded actions of colonialists and state administrators. Successive waves of colonial and postindependence forest officials engaged in forms of "environmental repression" that misperceived the positive role of fire as a land management tool compelled the Kissi to fell trees and plant crops in the wrong places, wrested land ownership from local hands, allowed industrial loggers to overharvest the forest islands, and imposed heavy tax burdens on the villagers. One consequence was hunger.

Misguided thought in other sectors also has attracted the attention of scholars Fairhead and Leach. Late in the 1980s, when foreign aid donors became more influential, and during the post–Earth Summit 1990s, when greener forms of foreign assistance came to Guinea, World Bank officials continued to blame degradation on local farmers' actions and on growing rural populations. Fairhead and Leach are hardly the only researchers to argue that "use itself can lead to 'improvement'" among the Kissi and perhaps under similar ecological conditions elsewhere, but, as they point out, "few of the findings or discussions of modern ecological science" are available in the information bulletins issued by multinational and nongovernmental organizations, the development journals, or the media, "the sources on which most development personnel rely for environmental science information." Tagging the farmer as environmental destroyer, the authors conclude, "helps to justify the self-distinction of urban intellectuals as modern" and "reflects donors' needs to satisfy home political constituencies heavily influenced by media images and northern environmental pressure groups." They stress the obvious: "the importance of consultation of local populations."[18]

For forest-dwelling communities in many parts of Africa, a further major source of conflict has for many years been the actions and policies of those seeking to protect wildlife and biodiversity. Africa's first national parks and protected areas were created, early in the current century, not for their value to local people but simply to serve as shooting galleries for European hunters who took enormous pride in slaughtering vast numbers of game animals. In more recent years, while the hunters have become less bloodthirsty, the parks have attracted growing numbers of camera-toting wildlife viewers, and the safari business has become important in many national economies. Alliances were formed between tour operators, national parks, wildlife departments, and international conservationists to improve the management and security of these regions. Governments seized control as well as ownership of these lands and of the animals on them and worked hard to deprive local people, to the fullest extent possible, of access to resources that they had long considered theirs for the taking. It was widely assumed that few local people could interact with the land as the Kissi of Guinea had, and that given access they would simply destroy their environment.

For the sake of wildlife and biodiversity, felt by many to be more important than the well-being of local communities, international conservation organizations supported militaristic forest police forces by supplying them with vehicles, weapons, and equipment. Denied access to the forests and their resources, without allies of any description, and unable to gain material benefit from the safari or hunting operations, many local people not surprisingly turned to game poaching, illegal logging, and the ivory trade as their only remaining means of making a living. Some among these predators were well armed and well financed. Many were ordinary villagers, bearing primitive weapons and simply trying to get along within a system that gave them few alternative opportunities. Polarization and conflict intensified as human populations grew and, as recently as the 1980s, as the numbers of such species as elephants and rhinos, whose "horns" are prized aphrodisiacs in many parts of Asia and the Middle East, plummeted. Modern environmentalists, wishfully thinking that pristine wilderness was there to be preserved, failed to grasp the sustainable but forceful ways in which native people manipulated the forest landscape, and they joined ecotourism operators in hoping (although usually in secret) that these "tribal innocents" would simply step aside in favor of the gravely threatened plant and animal species.

CHANGE AT LAST

In the mid-1980s governments and conservationists began at last to search for common ground between them and local communities and to involve community members in managing land and resources. New patterns began to be set for the continent's future "development."

One widely known example is the ADMADE project in and around Zambia's South Luangwa National Park, where local "village scouts" were recruited, trained, and paid to combat the poaching in which many of them had previously engaged. Local leaders were empowered to make decisions about how fees paid by hunters and other revenues flowing into the program would be spent for community development. The success of this effort was quickly documented as poaching in the area, previously out of control, rapidly dropped to almost nil.[19] Now more than a decade old, ADMADE has matured and prospered from experience, improved communications, and more reliable supply lines. Each year 700 community residents matriculate at its African College for Community-Based Natural Resource Management, which has become a national as well as a regional force. Zimbabwe's well-known CAMP-FIRE program, a well-designed effort to place management authority for land and resources in the hands of district councils rather than a central authority, is another familiar and generally successful example of community management. Late in the 1990s a successor program called MITI (Managing Our Indigenous Tree Inheritance) was founded by the Southern Alliance for Indigenous Resources, a Zimbabwean non-governmental organization. The program gives local communities, which own the preponderance of the country's forested land, access to commercial bank credit for income-generating enterprises in return for their commitment to protect trees. It is still too early to measure results.

At the World Bank and USAID many trial efforts were launched to link conservation and development activities and to meet human needs while protecting wildlands. African examples of these so-called Integrated Conservation and Development Projects (ICDPs) included a game ranching venture in Burkina Faso, an effort in Tanzania's East Usambara Forest Reserves to end commercial logging and substitute a number of new community-controlled economic development activities,

and a plan to encourage agroforestry and tourism in several forest reserves in Burundi. One place where an integrated community-based
conservation and development strategy has failed to meet its goals is
Korup National Park, which is located in southwestern Cameroon and
bordering regions. Here the WWF and partner agencies have been
working for well over a decade to bring about rural development as well
as protection for the park's chimpanzees, elephants, forest buffalo, and
other important species. Myriad mistakes have been made, including a
near-total failure to perceive the importance and value of traditional
bush-fallow land management systems and vain efforts to improve farm
production on poor soils by means of less-effective models imported
from elsewhere. "It's been a disaster," says one experienced British aid
worker. "Everyone did the wrong things."[20]

In a widely cited study researchers Michael Wells and Katrina Brandon expressed little doubt that those engaging in these early experiments
were on the right track.

> While traditional enforcement will continue to play a critical role—
> and in many cases needs desperately to be strengthened—it is
> inconceivable that networks of protected areas can be maintained
> indefinitely by what amounts, in some cases, to military force. This
> leads to the conclusion that innovative, well designed ICDPs at
> carefully selected sites that constructively address local people–park
> relationships are essential to the conservation of biodiversity and
> thus to sustainable development.[21]

Although their overall assessment was positive, Wells and Brandon
found fault with many particulars of how these ventures were conducted
and of the broader context within which the ventures were operating.
In many instances local people were perceived not as participants but
merely as among the beneficiaries. Nongovernmental organizations
"brought important strengths and experience in conservation but sometimes lacked the expertise needed to design, implement, or evaluate integrated projects with development components." More broadly, these

kinds of projects mean little unless they function as "part of a larger framework" in which the principles they represent receive support at the national level in the form of adequate political, financial, and institutional assistance.

During the 1990s considerable progress was made in reconciling biodiversity conservation with local community needs in Africa. But tensions remain as well. Wildlife biologists and traditional foresters are still being sent out to manage field projects involving complex social engineering challenges. Top-down values endure. The Ghanaian scholar Kojo Sebastian Amanor worries about the persistence of what he calls "ecofascism," which he describes as "the legitimation of oppressive actions against the poor in the name of protecting the environment."[22] Forester Gill Shepherd at the Overseas Development Institute in London says that, at the end of the day, she too harbors a sneaking feeling that all too many conservationists still prefer the wildlife to the local people. Where once the challenge was to get the official development institutions to become more transparent, open, and participatory, she now finds that a new chasm is opening between them and conservation organizations that have proven to be less flexible. "This promises to be the next big battle," she predicts.[23]

Biologist John Terborgh of Princeton University provides ammunition for the conflict. In discussing the merits of community-based conservation as effectively practiced in Kenya's Amboseli National Park, he notes the unusual tolerance of the Maasai cattlemen who interact with the park and its wildlife, then expresses doubt that the concept is very widely replicable.

> Apart from Amboseli, and perhaps a few exceptional places like it, wild animals will have to be protected from people in strictly enforced preserves. In the absence of strong financial incentives, such a separation cannot be expected to come about as an initiative of local people. Where such incentives may exist in the form of revenues from ecotourism, the prospects for successful conservation are good, at least in the short run. But in the long run, I find

depressing the idea that the future survival of nature on earth must rest on ecotourism. One dip in the economy could spell disaster.[24]

LESSONS FROM TANZANIA, NIGER, AND GHANA

For all the weakness and failures in all the sectors described above, though, several examples point to the considerable potential of returning power to local hands as a means of saving African forests and bringing about more-stable and less-autocratic societies. In Tanzania's Duri-Hatemba forest, villagers never dreamed that they might one day be able to control the forest themselves. When outsiders asked, they would argue that activities such as grazing and charcoal making were "indispensable" to their well-being. When they were actually given control in the early 1990s, writes the land tenure and development specialist Elizabeth Wily, "the same leaders and ordinary villagers swiftly argued for discontinuation of any use which they considered damaging," and they vigorously set about to enforce the rules they established.[25]

Another striking example comes from a section of Mgori, a large area of dry (*miombo*) woodland within the Eastern Rift Valley in northern Tanzania. Although German colonialists had promoted settlement in this remote area a century ago, it has remained almost entirely forested. The forestland is used largely for hunting and honey gathering by three tribal groups that live on its edges, some using fire as a way to track game and uncover snakes. New pressures from legal and illegal forms of commercial hunting and logging began to develop in the 1960s and 1970s. By the mid-1980s gradual deterioration of this forest, as for most of the entire nation's forest cover, could be foreseen. It was not clear who owned this land. The regional government could not afford to deploy officials to manage it, and local communities in this instance were not organized to do so.

To address this situation the government's Regional Forestry Programme (RFP), with support from the Swedish government, launched an effort to develop a management plan for the region. The outcome of this effort was a scheme, begun early in the 1990s, to declare Mgori a "forest reserve," from which local people would be largely excluded. They would receive a portion of logging and hunting fees and have access to credit and other government benefits to compensate for their being deprived of their customary access to the forest. Although no effort was made to gather local opinion about these plans, villagers were recruited to mark the boundaries that would lead to an official demarcation.

As the discontent of the villagers rose, the RFP recruited Wily to survey the situation and make recommendations. In her summary paper, "A Case Study in Collaborative Forest Management," dated 1995 with a postscript from 1996, she describes how the situation developed. A quick review persuaded Wily that the plan as drafted was "unlikely to work" because of local opposition and that, conversely, "the forest-local communities themselves, and their associated in-forest hamlets, appear to possess the extent of vested interest required to protect and manage the forest, if given the chance and encouragement to do so."[26] The RFP and the regional Council for the Singida Rural District, in which about half of the Mgori forest is located, agreed to scrap the original plan and design a new one based on the principle of partnership between government officials and local communities. Each of five Mgori forest village regions would demarcate its section of forest and, in cooperation with government, develop rules forbidding destructive activities. Each village would get exclusive rights to use its section of forest—as long as their management continued to be successful and they were able to enforce the rules that had been set.

Implementation of the program began in 1995. One early positive signal was that, in marking boundaries, villages tended to include *more* forest than had previously been demarcated. Village forest committees were established, and young men were recruited to function as *sungu-sungu* (forest guards). Once the actual protection got underway, major problems in governance cropped up in three of the five villages, in each instance because the chosen village chairman had abused his power. In the most flagrant case the chairman allowed one-quarter of the people in his village, including his own relatives, the exclusive right to clear and use forestland. At one point the central forest administration lost heart and took steps to replace the program with a more traditionally authoritarian structure. Common sense prevailed, however, and the program's accomplishments could soon be documented. Hunting by outsiders dropped to virtually zero, and other forbidden activities were said to have been substantially reduced. In a short time, Wily concluded, "Mgori Forest has gone from being an unprotected and unmanaged no-man's land, subject to uncontrolled clearing for shifting cultivation and settlement, to one which is now 'watched over' by more than one hundred local villagers." In summary Wily cited a ten-page letter from local forest officials Edward Massawe and Gervais Lyimo to the national director of forestry, in which they urge him to apply the Mgori principles nationally. In describing their program, these authors said, "We have seen that it works and it saves our Forests. It has taken time and there are many problems but the problems come only because there is a solution, in the people themselves."[27]

Wily could report many positive developments when she returned to the region two years later, in 1999.

> The five villages are managing very well, the forest is flourishing (a recent inventory shows only one felled tree in twenty-five blind permanent sample plots), wildlife is abundant, fires are many fewer, illegal or damaging use much reduced. Also very important, it is now accepted in Government that the respective Village Forest Reserves are owned by the villages. They have had minimal support from the district government authorities, but still have persevered. This is indeed a low-cost, self-reliant approach, quite aside from being effective in protective management.

One village, she continued, is even initiating a "cautious and carefully controlled" timber harvesting system.[28]

Conducting field research in the landlocked Salhelian nation of Niger in 1991 and 1992, Jonathan Otto and Kent Elbow reached similar conclusions about managing the region's dry and fragile woodlands. Although traditional patterns of resource management had not been disrupted during the French colonial period, they found that beginning in 1960 a succession of postindependence rulers "sought to circumvent local elites through new state-controlled structures designed to reach into individual rural communities."[29] What the authors call "enormous efforts" were made to bypass local resource management systems and remove forest and install plantations. These efforts failed, and tensions rose. Then, starting in the early 1980s, national and international fieldworkers began working with local leaders to apply the principles of natural forest management as a substitute for forest clearing. After rules had been worked out and local leadership designated, forest regeneration commenced at heavily used Guesselbodi Forest, only twenty-five kilometers from Niamey, the national capital. Community-based efforts to manage woodcutting and control the access of grazing animals to forest areas were initiated.

Ghana, the former British colony previously known as the Gold Coast, boasts landscapes of great beauty and remarkable biodiversity. Some 730 species of trees and 74 species of bats have been recorded here. It is difficult to generalize about this land, which encompasses several distinct ecosystems that range from moist tropical forests in the south to savanna woodlands in the north, as well as a variety of different cultures. A few examples will demonstrate how close Ghanaians still are to the land.

Forests give Ghanaians a bewildering variety of nontimber benefits ranging from fibers for baskets to resins and gums, gourds, medicines, building materials, and many foodstuffs. Giant snails are an important and preferred part of the national diet, along with small animals called grasscutters and bay duikers. Dental care is widely achieved by means of "chewsticks" carved from trees with cleansing properties and sold in the marketplace; at least 126 tree species are used for this purpose.

Women prefer to wrap produce bought at village markets not in paper or plastic, but in large leaves from several species of common plants from the *Marantaceae* family. The leaves themselves are a marketable commodity.

Anthropologist Julia Falconer of Britain's Department for International Development underscores the importance to village economies of the trade of nontimber forest products in a study she conducted for the World Bank. In many communities leaf collection alone is the "main source of income for the majority of households"; she estimates that a million bundles of these leaves are sold each month at the central market in the capital city of Kumasi.[30] She found that the collection and sale of nontimber products was a strong source of supplementary income for many households in the eight villages she studied, and the principal source of income for most families in two of them. Most of these products that had been traded were collected from within forest reserves, although some could be found in degraded or fallow areas. Falconer's study concludes with a fervent statement about the extreme importance of forests to local people as well as to city dwellers, who depend on the forest products that they buy at the market.

In a land where such values prevail, and where most people are farmers, it is no surprise that local knowledge about plants and animals, and about how to get the most out of ecosystems that were less than bountiful even before they became degraded, is both widespread and deep. Forest areas remained lightly populated for hundreds of years. Perhaps as early as the sixteenth century coastal Ghanaians began migrating into forest frontier areas to plant crops (yams and maize, fruits and vegetables) on small patches of cleared forest enriched by nutrients from the trees and bushes they burned. When the soil became unproductive, the patch was left to fallow and a new area was planted. Control of the land remained in the hands of local chieftains who held court (and still do) sitting on stools that represented authority. Complex tenurial systems emerged in which individual families and villages retained the right to work unoccupied land under the control of the "stool" and to gather forest produce in return for helping to support him. Though the British colonialists never managed to get ownership away from the stools, they instituted sharp changes in land use by using European techniques to clear the forest and obtain the maximum possible yield of timber, and by substituting export-oriented plantation agriculture for the time-honored bush-fallow method of subsistence farming.

Oil palms became dominant in some sections of Ghana, cacao in others. As more and more native trees were removed, the remaining forest became degraded, and cocao production dropped as a result of diseases and stress associated with drier microclimates. Even though the newly imposed systems of land use began to show signs of not working, the colonial rulers continued to try to vest "uncontrolled" or "waste" lands in the Crown as well as regulate the use of the forest. According to one recent report, they condescendingly "saw Africans as 'minors' whose heritage had to be managed in trust for them."[31] The forest department that was founded in 1909 carried forward the European traditions of "scientific" forestry and maximum yield by establishing forest reserves only when they were needed to maintain sufficient moisture in the air to stimulate cocoa production. Like their European bosses, Ghanaian forestry officials came to regard the rural chiefs and people not as sources of traditional knowledge, but as a nuisance.

Under such conditions forests continued to decline at a rapid pace through the end of the colonial period. Postcolonial rulers of the 1950s and 1960s added fuel to the fire with their stubborn adherence to the Soviet central-planning model, which placed limitless faith in science, technology, and central control. Although ownership did not change hands, what had been the "people's forest" became the "state forest," and power for the forestry department, the timber industry, and international trade increased. These entities all but totally replaced the local people as the beneficiaries of policy. The general economic downturn of the 1970s and 1980s was characterized by a continuance of excessive logging and centralization. New policies forbidding local people entry into lands that they had previously controlled further widened the gap between government and local people. By the early 1990s conflict in the form of land invasions, hostage taking, destruction of planted trees and crops, and gunplay had become widespread. With the balance of power now in the hands of the national government and the forestry department, those who disagreed could only "vote with their cutlass." They were able to thwart government rules and policies so effectively that the situation in some rural regions deteriorated sharply.[32]

What was obviously required was a shift in power that would give greater authority to the stools and the local communities, and, starting in 1994 with the promulgation of a new set of government policies, a new era of "collaborative management" was inaugurated. In recognition of the intimate relationship between the two, a new emphasis was placed on creating better conditions for farming in forest regions. A community forestry management unit was established within the forest department to work with local people to protect sacred groves, help manage non-timber forest resources, and integrate forest management into farming systems to the fullest extent possible. The views of people other than foresters were actually solicited. Local people were formally accorded access to forest resources in some reserves for which they previously had to have written permission even to enter. While some timber companies resented the swing in policy that lessened their power, others responded by establishing new and more-equitable relations with local communities. In one region a Danish company and the Danish aid agency were working with local communities and the forestry department not only to grow trees for export but also to cultivate nontimber forest products that can improve the incomes of local people. A portion of logging revenues was being used for community development activities. In other areas local forest action groups began to assist with the implementation of government policies that they helped formulate.

The 1994 policy shift and subsequent further experiments in "collaborative forestry" dramatically improved conditions in the Ghanaian interior. The new policies still leave government in the preeminent position, but a far greater degree of harmony in forest areas has been achieved. Outbreaks of violence and sabotage have lessened, and new legislation in 1997 and 1998 accelerated the national progress toward decentralization, equity, and far more participatory forms of making the policies that affect the patchwork "forest-farm mosaic" to which the country was reduced. It is too early to tell whether what is left of the Ghanaian forest will regenerate as a result of these changes. The introduction of community-based forest management is, however, already "making a difference," says Pippa Bird of DFID, which has been heavily involved in planning and carrying out the policy shift.

Other international observers agree that Ghana represents a model for all sub-Saharan Africa, and indeed new and less centralized forest policies in many countries are beginning to follow its example. The World Commission on Forests and Sustainable Development noted progress in several West African nations including Togo, Benin, Mali, and Ivory Coast. Despite the bloody attack that Rwandan Hutu guerillas recently mounted against hapless tourists in a Ugandan encampment, Uganda is said to have made great progress in the direction of establishing an ecotourism industry that offers tangible benefits to local communities and eases the pressure on forests. Bird heralds postapartheid South Africa as another nation that is making rapid strides at several levels with the assistance of a "great" DFID program. In Tanzania, the success of the village forest reserves in Mgori Forest and numerous other communities resulted in 1998 in a dramatic change in national policy: local communities now have the authority to manage all "unreserved" forest and woodland areas and to co-manage reserved woodlands. Although government officials are having difficulty adapting to the new balance of power, Wily reports that "Tanzania is well on the way."

Optimism about Africa is widely considered to be foolhardy, but there is considerable evidence that the outlook for the continent's forests and many of its rural regions is, at least, far brighter than one would imagine from reading the many recent doomsday forecasts of widespread political, economic, and social breakdown across much of the developing world. So durable are the traditions of community forest stewardship in many parts of Africa that government failure can be a blessing. In the village of Mofindor in Sierra Leone, government policy dating from the 1940s called for the introduction of exotic crops and exotic shade trees to cover them. So fragile were the government's agricultural extension services that these plants never arrived, and local farmers continued to protect and plant indigenous shade trees. These trees have grown to form canopies harboring many species of birds and animals and continue to supply traditional foods and medicines. This microecosystem would have perished if the government program had worked.

Even at the worst of the recent Rwanda genocide, with scores of thousands of refugees encamped at the edges of forests and collecting enormous quantities of fuelwood from this periphery, local people were remarkably successful in their efforts to protect the integrity of the forests. This example, to top what this chapter has already said about the resilience and quality of local peoples' ability to manage forests and control access, suggests that over the longer term the influences of colonialism might be a mere blip in the long history of the continent's human occupation as traditional patterns reassert themselves. "The traditional knowledge is still there," says Shepherd. "It never got lost."[33]

Here one must take care to consider the effects of fast-rising populations. The indigenous systems that worked thirty years ago in a Malawi with 12 million people, says Bird, might not apply to today's Malawi, with almost triple that number.[34] Population forecasters say that in all likelihood rapid urbanization will take over in Africa as it has elsewhere on the planet. Even if the overall figures rise as dramatically as the U.N. calculations cited above suggest, however, Kenya's David Western guesses that rural populations in Africa will level off at numbers that are no more than one-third higher than present levels.[35] Given the historical record and the considerable evidence that environmental degradation is far from an inevitable consequence of population growth, research such as that of Fairhead and Leach and Ghana's Amanor offers convincing reasons to think that rural Africans and their forests can cope with a population increase of this relatively modest dimension.

In Africa, as elsewhere, the new interest in genuine forms of local participation is at last beginning to take hold among donor agencies, providing new incentives for positive actions by national governments. Mostly, though, hope lies in the fact that in Africa both colonialism and the postcolonial era of gross corruption and central planning lasted a relatively short time—too short for the older and generally better traditions to become completely lost. The remaining and major question is how durable the swing toward more participatory and democratic forms of national governance will be, and how widespread they will become. Corruption and disregard for the interests of the civil society will surely remain prominent factors in many parts of Africa, but the recent evidence of how effective the new policies can be might encourage even some of the kleptocrats to bend a little.

CHAPTER 7

Learning from Latin America

In 1990 the Group of 7 (G7) leaders, representing the United States and six of the world's other principal industrial nations—Britain, France, West Germany, Italy, Japan, and Canada—gathered in Houston for their annual meeting. West German chancellor Helmut Kohl arrived with a keen interest in coming away with a strong environmental commitment from the group that would assuage his country's pesky Green Party as well as civil-society environmentalists. He proposed agreement on targets and timetables to reduce carbon emissions and to slow the rate of global warming. But George Bush, still heavily influenced by powerful American energy and automotive interests, balked. As an alternative Kohl suggested that the group do something to help save the forests of the Amazon. After a perfunctory phone call to Brazil's president—then Fernando Collor de Mello—to solicit his concurrence, the G7 announced the creation of the collective effort that has become known as the "Pilot Program to Conserve the Brazilian Rain Forest," or PPG7.

The deforestation of Brazil's rainforest began to accelerate after the country's military coup in 1964. A succession of general-presidents expressed confidence that "opening up" the Amazon would bring prosperity to all of Brazil, and they advanced a series of what turned out to be mostly misguided efforts to make this happen. Starting late in the 1960s road and dam building, colonization schemes, and hefty subsidies for cattle ranching began to degrade the rainforest ecosystem.[1] Many of these projects received support from the World Bank, the Inter-American Development Bank, the European Union, and bilateral aid donors. Notable among these projects were the ill-conceived Polonoroeste colonization and road-building scheme, which brought rapid deforestation to Rondônia (then a territory), and the subsequent Grande Carajás effort to design an elaborate set of economic development linkages around the world's largest iron ore mine and to build a railroad to transfer the ore to the port of São Luís in northern Brazil.

The backlash began quietly, with scientists complaining that the Amazonian rainforest ecosystem is largely fragile and not capable of supporting viable cattle ranches, let alone intensive plantation agriculture. Human rights groups and those concerned with the welfare of indigenous people began complaining about their often bloody mistreatment at the hands of newcomers, who included itinerant gold miners, settlers, and military detachments that were deployed far into the interior to protect Brazil's borders from foreign invasions. The reaction gained momentum in 1983, when a coalition of environmental organizations met in Washington and agreed to begin a "cooperative campaign to force changes in the way the multilateral development banks" make and implement their lending decisions. The coalition included not only traditional groups such as the National Wildlife Federation, which has a large, well-established membership, but also newer environmental research and action organizations such as the Natural Resources Defense Council and the Environmental Policy Institute.[2] The coalition's initial targets were Central American loans for "hamburger connection" cattle ranching that turned forests into scrubland and support for the Polonoroeste scheme. The World Bank admitted errors and pledged reform. A subsequent target was financing made by the Inter-American Development Bank for the extension of the highway from the state of Rondônia into the even more remote state of Acre.

By the late 1980s, with the military removed from power and democracy restored, a number of associations of indigenous Brazilians had joined the struggle. The National Council of Rubber Tappers, founded in the territory of Acre by Chico Mendes, had attracted worldwide attention for its spirited protests both in Brazil and abroad. In December 1988 Mendes was gunned down in the backyard of his own house in the town of Xapurí by the son of a cattle rancher. The murder occurred at a time when the cutting, burning, and pillaging of the Amazon forests were accelerating, and the news of Mendes's death was met with outrage the world over, along with fervent appeals for new and more sensitive approaches to Amazonian occupation and development.

Some 90 percent of the Brazilian rainforest was still more or less intact in 1990, and its overall condition was far better than that of the ravaged woodlands of countries like India and the Philippines. Still, 1990 was a ripe moment. The world's principal industrial nations had the opportunity to manifest concern for the Brazilian environment at a moment when worldwide interest in the Earth Summit, which would take place in Rio de Janeiro in 1992, was mounting. They could say not just that they were acting to protect the forest and the region's people, but that they were helping to control global warming as well. The fires that raged in Amazonia in 1987 led to unusually heavy carbon emissions, and Brazil was subsequently ranked in the World Resources Institute's "greenhouse index" as the world's third largest source of atmospheric carbon—right behind the United States and the former Soviet Union.[3] Slowing carbon emissions from Amazonia would be cheaper and more convenient than tackling the problem more forcibly at home.

PILOT PROGRAM TAKES SHAPE

In the aftermath of the Houston meeting, G7 representatives met with Brazilian and European officials to draw up a detailed action plan. At the end of 1991 the Pilot Program to Conserve the Brazilian Rain Forest (now defined as including not only the Amazon region but also Brazil's

Atlantic Forest, a once magnificent coastal forest of which no more than tiny fragments remain) and its details were formally announced. The G7 members plus the Netherlands agreed jointly to feed $50 million into a rainforest trust fund to finance some aspects of the program; an additional $200 million would be allocated to related bilateral projects to be arranged separately. The total $250 million was far and away the largest package ever developed for rainforest protection. Ironically, the G7 asked the World Bank, which had been so heavily involved in Amazonian degradation during previous decades, to undertake the responsibility of managing this entire rehabilitation.

In Brazil, meanwhile, some critics expressed the fear that the entire program would lead to a loss of Brazilian sovereignty and the "internationalization" of the nation's territory. Foreign ministry officials, reflecting a long history of this sort of concern, were especially vocal. Another faction, led by SEMAM, the secretariat for the environment, and a group of nongovernmental organizations, saw the program as a means of halting the decline of the Amazon and manifesting Brazil's commitment to the Earth Summit objectives. They saw the nationalist objections as a means of achieving Brazilian participation in drawing up the detailed plan for the program and a strong hand in its implementation as well. What emerged from the negotiations between Brazil and the G7 was a broad design for a program of outright grants—not the usual World Bank loans—keyed to a series of overall objectives. The participants agreed that the Amazon forest could be developed sustainably and its biodiversity preserved, that its contribution to greenhouse gas emissions could be reduced, and that the program could become a trend-setting model for environmental partnership between industrial and developing countries. Specific components of the comprehensive program were defined:

- A series of small-scale "demonstration projects" would be designed and carried out by local communities. None would cost more than $300,000 over the life of the project. Decision-making authority for the allocation of funds would remain in the hands of government officials. A coalition of some 300 nongovernmental organizations called the Grupo de Trabalho Amazonico, or Amazon Working Group (GTA), would work closely both with the government and with local communities in implementing this aspect of the program and would itself receive funding for this purpose.

· An equally participatory effort would be made to establish a series of extractive reserves of the sort that Mendes had worked to create in Acre and to test their social, economic, and environmental effectiveness.

· To protect the interests of Brazil's remaining indigenous peoples, the long-lagging program to identify and legalize their land claims would be jump-started. Protection for some 121 Amazonian areas was set as a goal.

· Efforts to achieve the sustainable management of forest resources, and of the Amazon region's 4 million hectares of very fertile alluvial floodplain, would receive support.

· A network of "rainforest corridors," linking officially protected areas and private and indigenous lands, would be established to protect the region's spectacular biodiversity.

· Deforestation and forest burning would be carefully monitored and controlled in selected areas.

· The region's two principal scientific research stations, the Museu Paraense Emílio Goeldi in Belém, near the mouth of the Amazon, and the National Institute of Amazon Research (INPA) in Manaus, more than two thousand kilometers upstream, would be strengthened.

· All of the foregoing efforts would undergo various forms of "monitoring and analysis" from Brazilian and international observers.

It was not until 1992 that the bank began actively working with donor countries and the Brazilians to prepare specific projects in these categories. No proposals were approved until 1994, and it was only in 1995 that PPG7 funds actually began to flow. As of mid-1999, well after the program had officially completed its first phase, some of its components were still only barely beginning to function. The very fact that it remained the largest program in Brazil for Amazonian conservation and development made it especially vulnerable to widespread criticisms about bureaucratic delays and the failure to achieve disbursements at anywhere close to the promised levels. What was more, said a 1999 report signed by the National Council of Rubber Tappers, the GTA, and several other prominent Brazilian nongovernmental organizations, the problem the PPG7 was designed to fix had only gotten worse.

> Deforestation in the Amazon has not only increased but in 1995 reached the highest rate yet recorded. It is also clear that the deforestation rate is influenced basically by the weather and economic cycles, there being no indication that the environmental policies of the government affect the process. And—worse—recent research has identified new processes of destruction potentially much faster than deforestation. Ground fires, aggravated by selective timber extraction and by El Niño events, assail immense areas of forest, leaving them increasingly vulnerable to greater destruction. It is now calculated that for every hectare of virgin forest cut down and burned, at least one other hectare is burned by ground fires and/ or degraded by selective timber extraction. Last year, in Roraima state, the largest forest fire on record in the Amazon occurred—and it included high, dense tropical forest. The PPG7 has been utterly innocuous in relation to the deforestation rate and fires.[4]

What is significant about the PPG7, however, is that the success of its various components has varied directly according to the degree of local participation involved. Some top-down subprojects involving coordinated actions from official agencies and cooperation between national and international organizations were still floundering almost a decade after Houston. Little progress has been made on an ambitious effort to designate Amazonian zones for economic development and for biodiversity protection that would provide the basis for the natural resource management increment and the establishment of rainforest corridors. As of mid-1999 only 17 percent of the funds committed to the program had actually been disbursed. Despite Brazilian president Fernando Henrique Cardoso's brave 1998 pledge to set aside 10 percent of Brazil's forests for protection, the country continued to lack a coherent or coordinated approach to managing Amazonia. Meanwhile, the bottom-up elements involving civil-society representatives have become the program's most successful and the quickest to get off the mark, prompting some to say sadly that PPG7 has missed the opportunity to be more productive overall by failing to build the principles of local and civil participation into its broader strategies.

For a century Brazilian law has specified that while indigenous lands belong to the federal government, Amazonian people have the right to use them and their resources. Such lands spread across some 82 million hectares, or about 17 percent of the basin as legally defined. As of 1995, when the PPG7's indigenous lands subproject began to function, only half of the 556 areas recognized by the National Indian Foundation as being "indigenous" had been demarcated and subjected to other formalities required for legal ownership by the communities. With $22 million in resources as of 1998, PPG7 set out to "regularize" 121 such parcels and otherwise "enhance the well-being of indigenous people and promote the conservation of their natural resources."[5] A high degree of local participation was built into the design of the project, whose consultative commission (an advisory body) has as many indigenous members as it has government officials. The work of demarcation was conducted in what is frequently described as a "highly participatory" manner, with the National Indian Foundation using PPG7 resources to teach the indigenous communities how to do the cumbersome paperwork themselves. By the end of 1997, despite a formidable array of legal and bureaucratic obstacles, 17 of the 121 areas were close to being fully legalized and fieldwork was underway in 33 others.

During the 1980s the rubber tapper Mendes and his colleagues worked tirelessly to achieve protection for lands used by traditional communities to harvest such natural resources as rubber and Brazil nuts. In 1989, after Mendes's death, the Brazilian government recognized the concept of "extractive reserves" as a means of conserving forest landscapes and keeping farmers and ranchers out. The PPG7's Extractive Reserves (RESEX) project, once again designed from the outset as a participatory co-management venture, sought to complete the legal formalities that would award rights to traditional users in four extractive-reserve areas—two in Mendes's home state of Acre. The RESEX staff and nongovernmental organizations were also working with the local communities to increase their technical skills and thus the likelihood of achieving sustainable use of the resources they harvest. As in the instance of the indigenous lands project, RESEX was being guided by an advisory body composed equally of government and local people who participated enthusiastically. In mid-1998, as the RESEX effort neared the end of its first phase, a team of World Bank and European Union officials reviewed the entire program and visited the two Acre reserves. The project's implementation, reported the team, was "very satisfactory, with notable progress made toward finalizing land use concessions to inhabitants of two of the reserves and the completion of development plans for the four reserves."[6]

PPG7's most advanced component and principal achievement is the Demonstration Projects, or PD/A in the program's alphabet soup of acronyms. This unit was launched in 1995 when a secretariat was established in Brasília and began to undertake the task of reviewing requests for small grants to support local ventures in such fields as managing aquatic resources, forests, and the environment and reviving degraded areas, while addressing human and social needs. By the end of 1998, 548 proposals had been received, and 97 had been approved, at a cost to PD/A of $13.5 million. All but one of the grants went to a civil-society organization rather than to a unit of government. The decision-making authority itself was divided equally between public officials and representatives of nongovernmental organizations. It is far too early to tell whether a significant number of the demonstration projects will achieve the nirvana of environmentally sustainable development. But even the anthropologist Stephan Schwartzman of the Washington-based Environmental Defense, one of the fiercest critics anywhere of development planning in Brazil, praised the PD/A. "It's working well," he said in 1999. "They've been able to move the money."[7]

One chief reason for the success of this venture is that from the outset prospective beneficiaries had a hand in designing it. In 1992 a number of nongovernmental organizations working in Amazonia joined to form the GTA. In 1999 this entity, with substantial increments of PPG7 support, had fourteen field offices and a major secretariat in Brasília. A similar group called the Rede Mata Atlântica, or Atlantic Forest Network (RMA), a coalition of 120 private groups, was functioning equally well in the coastal states that had remnant Atlantic Forest patches that are also included in the PPG7 program. Both Amazonian organizations were heavily involved in the intensive planning that preceded the initial round of grant making. They also interacted heavily with local communities as they prepared project proposals for PD/A consideration. One measure of their success was the high concentration of approved projects in areas where they were the most active. At both ends of the spectrum, then, the Demonstration Projects are honoring their own dictum that the stable and continuous participation of society is the "key" to forest conservation and sustained development.[8]

A review held late in 1998 resulted in a clear identification of some of the program's shortcomings and some of the lessons that had been learned. Anthony Anderson, a former Ford Foundation program officer who coordinated the program, listed some of them in a short paper. Agroforestry methods that incorporate natural processes including pest control, it was found, tended to work better than did ones where expensive and labor-intensive artificial systems were introduced. Diversity of crops proved to be good insurance against the failure of a single one. Market considerations must be thought through from the outset. Technical solutions will work only if farmers are willing to use them: in the Amazonian state of Pará, technocrats introduced a machine that would grind up slash and eliminate the need to burn it, but they backed off when they learned that farmers expressed worry that the gadgets would be expensive and hard to maintain. While such thoughts, generated in the context of the decentralized and pluralistic PD/A planning and review process, are hardly revolutionary, it is far less likely that they would have emerged in such sharp focus in a planning session involving bureaucrats in Washington or Brussels or Brasília. These findings reveal an encouraging degree of official commitment to the idea that local communities are integral to the process of sustainable development. "It's the most Rio-like thing since Rio," exulted Twig Johnson, a former USAID official who later ran the Latin American section of the WWF-US and served on PPG7's International Advisory Group. The "strength" and importance of PPG7 is found in the organization's active search for local participation and in the fact that the community that benefits is wider than that in more traditional development models, as the Dutch analyst Ans Kolk notes.[9]

THE LESSONS OF MAMIRAUÁ

The Brazilian Amazon offers other encouraging examples of how local participation can bring stability to regions that would without it be doomed to steady decline. A case in point is a large, sparsely populated swampy area, called Lago Mamirauá, in the western state of Amazonas (map 11). Mamirauá is located in the fertile zone called *várzea*, where the forests are flooded under as much as fifteen meters of water for almost half the year and many fish species feed on fruit falling from the trees into the water. It is home to many species of plants and animals that are endemic, giving the area extraordinary ecological importance. Chief among the species that are found nowhere else are two monkeys, the white oukari and the blackish squirrel monkey.

In 1990, when the Amazonas state government declared Mamirauá to be an "ecological station," 5,000 inhabitants, mostly *caboclos*, lived in the area, occupying sixty small settlements within and on its borders.

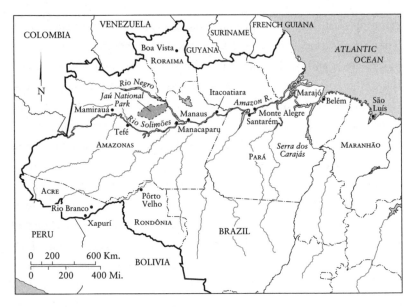

Map 11. The Brazilian Amazon.

Fishing, farming during the dry season, and harvesting timber provided a subsistence-level living. In the 1970s Catholic priests of the liberal *comunidades de base* movement had entered the region in the absence of any other authority; they had been working there ever since and providing the diverse local population with a sense of structure and common purpose that later was to prove highly useful.

Had a top-down approach to managing this region been pursued, the results would have been predictable, with a scenario following a well-trodden course: The government decrees the reserve, but without staff or budget to monitor or manage it the region becomes yet another "paper park" to which access is in fact free and open not only to local people but to migrants who are entering Amazonia in rising numbers and to powerful commercial interests. With no one in charge, the region's aquatic resources, which include manatees, caimans, freshwater turtles, and 290 fish species, are relentlessly pursued by commercial fishermen who supply the markets in the fast-growing nearby town

of Tefé, as well as larger Amazonian cities such as Manaus, Itacoati-
ara, and Manacaparu. Harvesting of the delicious pirarucu, a large fish
that can weigh as much as 200 pounds, quickly reduces the population
of this prized and economically important species to the point of extinction. Biologically important species, including the black caiman,
the turtles, the manatees, and the two endemic monkeys, vanish. Uncontrolled logging, easier in the *várzea* because during the wet season
logs can be floated rather than dragged out, soon depletes the region
of the small number of high-value tree species. Soon the region becomes little more than a wasteland, stripped of resources and good for
little but seasonal farming. Most of the rural people move on to attack
a new area.

Those who began to develop a management plan for the reserve soon
after the reserve's designation decided to pursue a different course. Scientists, led by the primatologist Márcio Ayres, senior conservation zo-
ologist at Wildlife Conservation International, who had done his own
doctoral fieldwork at Mamirauá during the mid-1980s, naturally made
their principal goal the study and preservation of the reserve's biodiversity. At the same time, however, following a preliminary survey of
socioeconomic conditions and of the fishery, the Brazilian government
agency responsible for the reserve also resolved to use "an integrated
approach involving community participation" in the development of a
management plan. From the outset, the key to the reserve's successful
establishment was "the cooperation of the local communities," as an
early planning document noted.

> This will be the first project in Brazil that attempts to integrate the
> conservation of biodiversity with the interests of people living
> within a protected area. The importance to subsistence and livelihood
> of the natural resources that the reserve harbors gives the local
> people a direct interest in protecting them over the long term from
> outside commercial exploitation. The communities have already
> taken the initiative to close some of the lakes to fishing although
> they have no legal basis for doing this and the beneficial impact

of doing so is not scientifically demonstrated. They are in favor of the creation of the reserve and are impatient to see it established.[10]

During this period an "extension team" worked to "stimulate community organization" so that the local people could be "properly represented in reserve management and decision making." In 1993 the project hired two inhabitants of the reserve to act as community assistants to mediate between the communities and project officials and equipped them with a boat. Radio linkages were established. The people organized their own political structure to interact with the reserve, the Sociedade Civil Mamirauá, and in 1993 began annual three-day general assemblies to discuss issues and set rules. Local people were not fully empowered to enforce rules governing fishing and other activities within the reserve, but volunteer rangers could inform the authorities of infractions by intruding commercial fishermen who could damage local interests. The effort had quick success. The percentage of the fish sold in the Tefé market that had come from within the ecological station dropped from 20 percent in 1991 to 6.8 percent in 1995, and local people generated fast-growing revenues from resources that were being harvested sustainably.[11]

In 1996, after four years of research by scholars and extension workers, the management plan was published. It institutionalized the General Assembly of Mamirauá Ecological Station Users as "the principal jurisdictional body for user decisions" and a body capable of providing "highly relevant assistance" to the overall project coordinator.[12] Very significantly, 1996 was also the year that Amazonas state reclassified the region as a "sustainable development reserve"—the first such anywhere in Brazil. The general assembly divided the region into zones for permanent settlement, sustainable use, and total conservation that were adopted by the management of the ecological station. Stiff rules regarding hunting, fishing, and timber harvesting, approved in advance by the general assembly, were incorporated into the plan. So were proposed new rules. All aspects of the program incorporated large increments of community participation. In the years since 1996, community leaders have imposed increasingly tough restrictions on their own behavior; one group even banned caiman hunting, a common although illegal practice in the region, on the grounds that commercial fishermen could use this as a justification to enter the region.

Not all is well at Mamiraúa. The project was launched not by social engineers but by scientists who had much to learn about the interpersonal and intercommunity relations of a people spread thinly across a vast area. Infighting within the communities, where many conflicting interests gather, has often been intense, said Isabel Braga, a biologist working at the World Bank who was involved with the project from its inception. "There's always someone who breaks the rules." This includes some local fishermen as well as those from outside who seek access to the lake's aquatic resources. Only very recently have new social science teams working within the project been able to make progress on social relations in the region. They are working only in the project's core area: people in some one hundred communities on the periphery have yet to be touched in any sense by the project, says Braga. She expresses caution about not overselling a project that has yet to achieve many of its goals.[13]

Braga quickly adds that, for all its deficiencies, the concept put into practice at Mamiraúa is "the only way to go." In the late 1990s the region was enjoying better administration than was almost any other region in the Brazilian Amazon, even though the federal and state governments had a limited presence there. Humans and the nonhuman resources, including the trees that feed the fish and the people, were faring far better than they had before the region's *caboclo* population came to share the responsibility for its management. Mamiraúa's example also helps make a broader statement about the extent to which the Brazilian Amazon is a far more resilient landscape, one that people can use if they do so with respect, than many scientists once considered it. Biologist Christopher Uhl, a longtime student of Amazonia and one whose research demonstrates that even its badly degraded eastern extremity, let alone the far more intact *várzeas* in the west, has recuperative powers that were underappreciated until recent years. He believes firmly in the wisdom and power of local knowledge and argues that "the transformation of public lands into 'working' forests managed by local people" is a strategy that "might stabilize the Amazon frontier more effectively than any other measure."[14] Linking such used and locally managed sustainable development reserves with others that are more fully protected, thus forming extensive "biological corridors," is a leading mantra for the PPG7 as well as for Conservation International and other leading environmental organizations. On paper at least, Mamirauá is now thus linked with the adjacent Jaú National Park and several smaller areas to form a huge, 5.8 million-hectare protected forest zone—the largest such tract anywhere in the world. The PPG7 intends, moreover, to incorporate these lands into an even larger protected zone to be called the Central Amazonian Corridor.

ELSEWHERE

The people of Mamirauá are managing a landscape, not trees. What makes the project work is not that they have inherited traditions of working together as a community, as in the case of many indigenous peoples, but rather the knowledge and skills that they possess as individuals—and the considerable amount of technical help they are receiving from outside. This is not to say that Latin America is without examples of successful community forestry as more precisely defined (map 12). In Bolivia's subtropical lowlands, some 7,000 indigenous people known as Chiquitanos inhabit a biologically diverse but generally infertile region called Lomerio. Thickly forested and remote Lomerio has been under pressure as a result of irrational management during the colonial and postcolonial eras by ranchers, rubber planters, and, more recently, logging companies with concessions from the government.

Although in the late 1990s the Chiquitanos still did not fully own the ancestral forestlands that the current national constitution rather

CARIBBEAN SEA

ATLANTIC
OCEAN

N

VENEZUELA

Chocó

Bogotá

GUYANA

FRENCH GUIANA

SURINAME

COLOMBIA

Quito

ECUADOR

Yanesha

BRAZIL

Lima

PERU

La Paz

Lomerío

Brasília

Santa Cruz

BOLIVIA

PARAGUAY

Rio de Janeiro

CHILE

PACIFIC
OCEAN

URUGUAY

ARGENTINA

ATLANTIC
OCEAN

Forested areas

0   800 Km.

0   500 Mi.

Map 12.   South America.

vaguely allocates to them, they have established user rights. And since 1986 the thirty-five communities and small settlements in the region, united into an indigenous organization called the Centro Intercomunal Campesino del Oriente de Lomerio (Inter-Communal Headquarters of the Communities of Eastern Lomerio, or CICOL), have been collectively operating what has been called "the only ongoing project of sustainable forest management in Bolivia."[15]

As loggers systematically degraded their lands, the Chiquitanos became ever harder pressed. During the 1980s, with the assistance of a local group known as Apoyo para Comunidades Occidentales Boliviamas, or APCOB (Support Project for Indigenous Peasants in Eastern Bolivia), the Chiquitanos succeeded in driving them away. Then, with APCOB's technical assistance and financial aid from the Dutch government, the Chiquitanos founded CICOL and set about managing the use of their own lands, which consist of some 340,000 mostly forested hectares. They inventoried their resources and developed a management plan, using as its basis a Dutch silvicultural system that had been developed in Suriname. They reforested cedar and other valuable species that had been overexploited. They established tree nurseries and agroforestry plantations. They built a mill and began to sell their lumber. They worked hard to improve their technical skills and place the project on a sound economic footing.

The Chiquitanos faced major obstacles. Wood from Lomerio must be hauled over the Andes to reach the market, and thus it cannot be priced competitively. The Chiquitanos lack a kiln and must air-dry their wood. The relationship between CICOL and APCOB is such that, even though the Chiquitanos run their own show locally, financial and other aspects of the project's organization are said to be in urgent need of improvement. Still, they struggled forward and in 1994, despite the hazards of transportation and the increasing scarcity of supply, they managed to harvest fifty truckloads of prized cedar and get this wood to the marketplace. The mill was employing thirty-two salaried workers from the indigenous community even though it was functioning at far below its capacity, and fifty officially accredited indigenous forest guards patrolled the region.[16]

The project shifted gears in 1994, when Sylvania Forestry, a U.S. company that specializes in buying and marketing wood certified as having been sustainably harvested, began buying Lomerio wood. Sylvania executive Bob Simeone, a seasoned forester with long experience working with indigenous woodsmen in Latin America, convinced the Chiquitanos that they should develop markets for their more abundant wood species rather than continue to rely primarily on cedar. Patiently Simeone worked to develop U.S. markets for the Lomerio wood, offering the promise of on-time delivery and excellent quality ("they cut a nice straight board") as justification for higher prices than competitors offered. Lomerio wood now ends up as boardwalk in many U.S. cities, and it is used for outdoor furniture. In 1998 Sylvania was buying just about everything the Chiquitanos could produce, and the company was paying twice the price they would have received on the local market.

Much about the project remains fragile, and its future is uncertain, as Simeone notes: "APCOB is too paternalistic, and the local people just do not have a sense of responsibility. There's no organizational structure that really functions. The delays with money and bureaucracy are terrible. Direct communication between us and them would eliminate about 80 percent of the problems we have, but it seems there's no way to achieve that. This project will only really work well if it becomes fully autonomous."[17] Production, in fact, stopped in 1999–2000. Lomerio may hardly be the "model" community forestry project that some observers hail it as, but Simeone agreed that it has fundamental importance. The Chiquitanos were indeed using their resources sustainably— "Certification is no problem," said Simeone—while getting a good price for their wood, continually improving their technical skills (if not their organizational skills), and living better. One lesson of Lomerio, said

Graciela Zolezzi, subdirector of APCOB, is that "forestry managed through indigenous people can be successful even with little government commitment."[18]

COMMUNITY TIMBER
PRODUCTION IN MEXICO

"Mexican community forestry," says David Barton Bray, "is the face of the future in community forestry." What he means, he adds, is that the emphasis of Mexican communities on commercial timber production, rather than on harvesting nontimber products, requires higher levels of skill and organization that foresters in other developing countries will have to learn if they too enter the commercial marketplace for wood products. Bray, a former representative in Mexico of the Washington-based Inter-American Foundation, later became head of environmental studies at Florida International University. He has long been a keen student of community forestry in Mexico and an enthusiast about the accomplishments of Mexico's indigenous foresters and the potential they have. Mexico still has about 50 million hectares, or 25 percent, of its national territory in closed temperate or tropical forest, the largest concentrations being in the country's southern regions. These forests remain home to some 17 million people, including indigenous residents such as the Mayans of the Yucatán Peninsula and the Zapotecs of Oaxaca state in the south-central region (map 13). Tropical deforestation reached a rate of some 500,000 hectares a year in the 1980s, Bray reports. Although the 1990s saw a reduction in this rate, the nation's remaining tropical forests could be reduced to isolated patches by 2050, thus endangering the chief means of subsistence for many millions of people.[19]

The nation's forests and forest-dwelling people remained relatively untouched until late in the nineteenth century, when capitalistic Mexican administrations opened Mexican forestlands to foreign concessionaires. They trampled on both land and people in their eagerness to

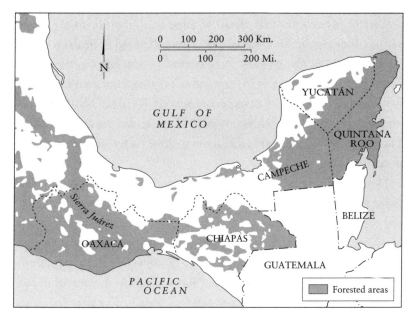

Map 13.   Southern Mexico.

export hardwoods to the United States and other markets. These incursions sparked a strong movement to reaffirm the rights of the country's long-abused indigenous communities. During the Mexican Revolution, which began in 1910 and ended ten years later, the peasantry struck out against the foreigners, taking back land by force. Postrevolutionary administrations continued the nationalistic revolt against the foreign control of Mexican land by seizing and redistributing foreign holdings.

One result of the agrarian reform programs undertaken by the Mexican government after the revolution was the establishment of *ejidos*, or communal land tenure arrangements. By the early 1990s reform policies had placed the ownership of no less than 70 percent of all Mexico's temperate and tropical forestlands and some 40 percent of timber production in the hands of some 7,000 to 9,000 local communities scattered throughout the country.[20] In terms of tenurial rights the indigenous peoples of Mexico were far ahead of those in all the other developing nations discussed in this volume, who were still mired in battles to wrest the ownership of forests away from central governments in the 1990s. Some *ejidos* began trying to harvest and sell timber from their lands, and they tried to expand the commercial market for their nontimber resources, which include chicle, honey, allspice, and medicinal plants. They also used agroforestry techniques to grow such shade-loving crops as vanilla beans.

Despite holding legal title to the forests and their resources, however, the *ejidos* were far from safe. Revolutionary fervor faded at mid-century, and regardless of legalities, the Mexican government again began disregarding indigenous rights and handing out logging concessions to private and parastatal organizations. Just as damaging to local interests were government-imposed bans that forbade access to forestlands and resources to traditionally forest-dependent people. The bans led to severe conflicts between local people and forest police. Such a ban in Chiapas state—instated late in the 1980s, after most of Mexico had moved on to wiser forest policies—was one of the factors leading to severe polarization in local communities and the creation of the Zapatista National Liberation Army. The ban did little to halt the inexorable deforestation as ranching and government-sponsored colonization spread and logging continued. During the 1990s the *ejidos*, with help from nongovernmental organizations, became increasingly well organized and vocal at the national level, prompting policies that offered vigorous alternatives to logging bans. After passage of a new forestry law that strongly favored plantation development over community forestry in 1992, the *ejidos* fought for a different policy. In 1997 a new law was passed that granted provisions that are more favorable to communities. Although this law has helped, the *ejidos* have continued to be buffeted by successions of poorly planned and managed government programs, adverse market conditions in the aftermath of NAFTA trade liberalization in 1994, and the general lack of government support to back their efforts.

What they have accomplished despite these handicaps is consequently quite remarkable. In Oaxaca state's Sierra Juárez, local communities successfully fought off a government effort in 1981 to award a private company called FAPATUX the right in perpetuity to continue unsustainable timber operations in a region that the company had effectively controlled for many years with little regard for local peoples' needs or knowledge. The local communities began to harvest the forests themselves, at first haltingly, since they lacked experience in forest management, but with increasing success. They bought capital equipment, established sawmills, and reinvested earnings from timber and wooden furniture sales in community development projects such as schools and clinics. During the 1990s, even as market conditions turned sour because of post-NAFTA competition from freely traded low-cost imports, they enlisted help from domestic and foreign nongovernmental organizations to make their enterprises more efficient and more competitive. They pay salaries to local workers and one Oaxacan cooperative was even able to organize a pension program for widows.[21]

In the Yucatán Peninsula local communities established an impressive assortment of forestry activities ranging from extracting and processing mahogany to marketing chicle, honey, and allspice. Profits from these activities have been sufficiently high to encourage local communities to fight hard to save their forests rather than convert the land to less profitable uses such as cattle ranching or plantation agriculture. In some instances the communities slapped limits even on swidden agriculture, in which all the people had been engaged.[22] As of the mid-1990s rates of deforestation in the region's larger *ejido* communities were lower and living standards were higher than in surrounding areas. Because it has grown harder for these communities to sell their wood competitively, they began working to develop markets in other sectors where sustainability can be achieved. One such market is for organically grown vanilla beans.

Overall, says Bray, only ten or twenty of the thousands of *ejidos* trying

to manage their forests have been able to operate profitably in the commercial marketplace. But, he adds,

> it is ten or twenty more experiences than most Third World
> countries have. Community forestry in the Yucatán state of Quintana
> Roo sharply braked rampant deforestation in the early 1980s.
> Seventy percent forest cover, one of the highest percentages of forest
> cover anywhere in tropical Mexico, has been retained in the
> central part of the state. These forests harbor species representing
> some 40 percent of the birds, 25 percent of the mammals, and
> 20 percent of the butterflies in Mexico.

Bray is quick to add that "the communities didn't just rise up and make
all this happen." In the 1980s there were "very enlightened people" in
a number of national and international agencies who had "a genuine
vision of promoting participatory community forestry."[23] Today the
bloom is somewhat off the rose. One observer argues that communal
forestry in the Maya region has lost competitiveness because the competition is not fair. He suggests that if Mexico were to subsidize the
ejidos to the same degree that the United States and other competitors
supply forest industries with technical and infrastructure support, there
would be "solid reasons to believe that social forestry can be economically viable" in Quintana Roo and other regions.

BROADER CONSIDERATIONS

Against these modest community successes one must, of course, place a
set of dismaying broader trends in Latin America. Overall, reports scientist Daniel Nepstad of the Woods Hole Research Center in 1999,
Amazonian deforestation rates may be double those reported in conventional Landsat estimates, which highlight forest conversion for farming and ranching but overlook "those forest alterations that reduce tree
cover, but do not eliminate it, such as logging and surface fires in standing forests." In Brazil's northern state of Roraima, which is covered in

part by moist forest that had been considered immune to burning until
the drying effect of El Niño kicked in, some 9,000 square kilometers of
forest were destroyed in 1997 and 1998. Logging crews annually cause
severe damage in more forest that the Roraima fires burned, Nepstad
and his team report, and surface fires—some triggered by the drying
out that logging causes—"burn additional large areas of standing forest."[24]

Such patterns are evident in other tropical regions. Predatory Indonesian and Malaysian logging companies lurk on the periphery of the
region with hard money in their pockets to hand over to ministers in
the governments of weak countries in return for long-term clear-cutting
deals. Such companies have begun operations even in Brazil, acquiring
Brazilian firms despite public outcry. In Guyana logging concessions
covered 60 percent of the country in 1998, according to one report,[25]
and the government was planning to increase logging by 300 percent
over three years despite vigorous opposition from indigenous groups.
Each week Econet, a World Wide Web service of the Institute for
Global Communications in San Francisco, is studded with reports of
such trends and of violations of indigenous peoples' human rights and
territories at the hands of loggers, miners, and marauding soldiers. In
Costa Rica, the world's prime model for sustainable development, 25
percent of the land is well protected. What remains of forest cover on
the remaining 75 percent is fast disappearing. Even when local communities do gain power, things do not always work out right. In 1993
one of the world's most highly touted and best financed community
forestry projects, the Yanesha Forestry Cooperative in the Peruvian Amazon, collapsed because it had grown too big and was suffering marketing difficulties.

If one looks at the situation with a broader perspective, however, one
can find encouraging signals of various sorts. Some governmental officials within Amazonia have become environmental enthusiasts. In the
western Amazon region, for example, state governors have been notably
negligent about protecting forests; one even campaigned holding a

chainsaw. Yet in the Brazilian state of Acre in 1999 the governor and two of his principal lieutenants were ardently green. So were the environment ministers in many national governments. Their ability to change the course of events is limited by their incumbency, however, and it is the nongovernmental sector that has a better chance of leveraging improvements in policy and practice. If there is hope for the forest-dependent people in the region, these are the people most likely to help. Fortunately, the power and influence of nongovernmental organizations have grown mightily in recent years.

During the 1960s and 1970s, when political conditions were harsh in many of the region's principal countries, civil opposition to environmentally destructive governmental actions remained muted. Fear of reprisal was one reason. Another was the lack of a tradition of environmental activism within the region. In Brazil, as in other countries including Peru, Venezuela, and Costa Rica, resident expatriate communities had founded bird-watching societies whose concerns sometimes encompassed protecting habitats for threatened plant and animal species, but seldom reached farther. A few despairing individuals—William Phelps in Venezuela, Felipe Benavides in Peru, José Cándido de Melo Carvalho at the National Museum in Rio de Janeiro—cried in the wilderness, but their voices had little influence.

Awareness gradually began to grow in the 1970s. In several countries brave citizens began to confront hard-line governments on human rights issues, sometimes using the environment as cover. Interest in tropical Latin America among international environmentalists also grew. Up to the mid-1960s the principal transnational actor in this field had been the International Union for the Conservation of Nature and Natural Resources (IUCN), an awkward coalition of governmental and nongovernmental scientists and nature lovers who directed their attention largely to plant and animal species facing extinction. No one had any power. IUCN's leaders, said Max Nicholson of London, one of the movement's founders, "had no contact with heads of government or important ministers. And they had no money. A lot of them were quite hopeless about anything practical."[26] In 1962 the WWF was founded as a high-profile fund-raising adjunct to the IUCN, and later it began conducting its own conservation activities.

Until the mid-1970s the WWF was far more vigorous in Europe and in Africa than in Latin America. Then the biologist Thomas Lovejoy, who had done his doctoral work on Amazonian birds, became program director of the then-tiny WWF-US. With great energy he turned the organization's attention to Latin America and, especially, Amazonia. Almost single-handedly at first, Lovejoy began campaigning in Brasília and elsewhere to save the rainforest and its human and nonhuman inhabitants. He gradually formed partnerships with fledgling local institutions—the Fundação Brasileira para a Conservação da Natureza in Rio de Janeiro, the Fundación Natura in Quito, and the Fundación para la Defensa de la Naturaleza in Venezuela—which later independently made striking contributions to the advancement of environmental thought in their countries.

NEW PUNCH FOR THE NONGOVERNMENTAL ORGANIZATIONS

In those early days much of the international effort in Latin America and Brazil was concentrated on the designation of national parks and protected areas in order to preserve some measure of the biological diversity of the forests and the fragile coastal zone. The Corcovado National Park in Costa Rica, a vast expansion of the Brazilian national parks system, and the creation of several major parks in the tropical Andes marked this period. WWF and others fought hard but without much success to get governments and international donors to provide for the proper management of these areas, lest they remain no more than lines on the map, areas subject to predation by loggers, miners, migrant farmers, and other destructive forces. "Ecosystem management" became a popular rallying cry.

At the same time, conservationists fought hard to get adequate national and international support for scientific research so that the complex workings of tropical ecosystems, especially the rainforest, could be better understood while still relatively intact. Brazil's National Institute of Amazon Research in Manaus and the Museu Paraense Emílio Goeldi in Belém, near the river's mouth, were beneficiaries. So were the scientific and agricultural research institutions in Costa Rica, which were then beginning to exert the leadership they still maintain in their fields. Lovejoy himself launched a benchmark twenty-year scientific study, the Biological Dynamics of Forest Fragments project, which examined the relationship between Amazon deforestation and species attrition. In Costa Rica ecologist Daniel Janzen embarked on an equally prominent effort to study forest regeneration in an arid region called Guanacaste.

Botanist Ghillean T. Prance (then at the New York Botanical Garden and later director of London's Kew Gardens), a few other U.S. and European scientists, and a growing number of Latin American scientists delved deep into the forest. They followed the tracks of Alfred Russel Wallace and other far-ranging European naturalists of the nineteenth century, and they retraced perilous routes far into the interior that the adventurous Harvard University ethnobotanist Richard Evans Schultes and João Murça Pires, his Brazilian colleague, had pioneered in the 1930s and 1940s. This new generation of natural scientists, aware that the precious biodiversity that they were discovering and documenting was fast disappearing as a consequence of mounting human pressures on the land, struggled mightily against illness and other severe hardships to conduct their research in remote and primitive locations.

The Liz Claiborne and Art Ortenberg Foundation reports that for more than a century international conservationists' "chief strategy" in Latin America had been "exclusionary and implicitly misanthropic."[27] Foreign scientists and environmentalists, usually working in sparsely populated rainforest areas, seemed to focus their interest less on people than on the important but isolated work of studying and protecting plants and animals. To this day they are accused of excessive emphasis on animals. What such accusations ignore is that by the 1980s most of the international nongovernmental organizations were coming to regard attention to human needs as an essential component of efforts to preserve wildlife and wildlands. The experimental USAID-supported Wildlands and Human Needs effort launched in the 1980s was the basis for new partnerships between a number of international environmental groups, local citizen groups, and other nongovernmental organizations. The WWF was in the vanguard of these participatory ventures. If relations between the homegrown organizations and the large international groups were not always warm, in most instances effective and workable alliances were formed.

The blunders that the World Bank and the Inter-American Development Bank made in the region during the 1980s gave the domestic and international branches of the environmental nongovernmental organization community their first big chance to work together, with critically important support from the foundation community, toward the clear and fully shared goal of stopping the multilateral development banks from underwriting gross forms of environmental and human rights violations.[28] What was notable about all these efforts was that U.S. and Latin American nongovernmental organizations cooperated on all of these projects: local groups initially guided their U.S. counterparts to the sources of trouble and showed them what was wrong, eyewitnesses from the region testified before the U.S. Congress, Latin American groups generated media coverage within nations that led to international media attention. In the instance of the dispute over the highway to Acre, Chico Mendes and Steve Schwartzman jointly lobbied in Washington and in Miami at an annual meeting of the Inter-Developmental Bank and were principal factors in persuading the bank to suspend its loan for the road. It was the first time the bank had ever taken such an action on environmental grounds. In Acre, the creation of the extractive reserves that PPG7 later worked to strengthen was directly attributable to Mendes's long struggle and the national and international nongovernmental organizations that helped make it a global issue.

By 1989, the WWF was able to report that a

> new conservation movement has come of age over the course of the past decade. Private nonprofit conservation organizations (NGOs) in Latin America . . . have proliferated and have now begun to contribute in crucial ways to sustaining the natural environment of their regions. Evolving in social and economic settings unlike those in which U.S. and European conservation groups arose, these nongovernmental organizations are pioneers. They have broken new ground in their form and style of commitment to conservation.[29]

According to one conservative estimate, WWF said, the number of environmental nongovernmental organizations in Latin America had grown from almost nil in the mid-1970s to more than 230 by 1988. Brazil had listed 2,000 private organizations, Peru 80, the eastern Caribbean over 200.[30] Today, over 500 are concerned just with Brazil's Atlantic Forest.[31]

During the 1990s the trend toward partnerships between governments and nongovernmental organizations accelerated. A major push forward came in the form of the 1992 Earth Summit's emphasis on equity and human rights as indispensable components of sustainable development. International donors and nongovernmental organizations had become more sophisticated in their approaches to local groups and were allocating more money to them. Politically, meanwhile, Latin America was turning away from authoritarian and top-down systems toward more democratic and participatory approaches. Civil society involvement was being preached everywhere. In 1995 Ruth Cardoso, Brazil's first lady, told the Inter-American Development Bank that the very "future of development in Brazil lies in partnerships between state and civil society." Mexican president Ernesto Zedillo said that his country could not escape its current crisis "without enlisting civil society in the effort." Countries began to "mainstream" the process by building the participation of nongovernmental organizations into plans submitted to international donors. Wrote Charles Reilly, adviser on civil society at the Inter-American Development Bank, "Partnerships with government at the national and sub-national level, mobilization of resources from entrepreneurs and the poor themselves, and the decline of state–civil society antagonism is the trendline throughout the region."[32]

At the national level, nongovernmental organizations have become far more integrated into planning and policymaking processes, moving from criticism and advocacy into positions involving cooperation with government, management responsibilities, and involvement in issues that go to the heart of national development policy. In Mexico and elsewhere, former leaders of these groups began winning key government jobs. Within most countries in the region, national environmental planning efforts were launched even before the 1992 Earth Summit. The impetus usually came from nongovernmental organizations. In a number of countries, groups that began by addressing strictly environmental questions began to take on mainstream economic issues with environmental implications. In Costa Rica, Peru, and Ecuador, the Rainforest Alliance and local partners have become deeply involved in planning for environmentally and economically sound production of such important crops as coffee and bananas.

Nongovernmental organizations are reaching in the other direction as well by encouraging governments to include authentic representatives of local communities in planning for development and by learning more from local communities about where the real needs and opportunities lie. In many countries of the region, nongovernmental organizations are encouraging governments to make constructive use of time-honored traditions of communal work in local communities, at tiny fractions of what the cost would be if government employees were involved. They are also doing more and more to increase environmental literacy among the citizens of their countries. Many groups have followed the lead of their international counterparts by recruiting members and thus increasing their political leverage. They have enthusiastically embraced the new computer technologies and are using them effectively to gather and disseminate information. The electronically disseminated Action Alert is becoming as familiar a device in Latin America as it long has been in North America. Throughout the region nongovernmental organizations have been winning legal battles over such issues as access to information, public participation, and the right to complain. Brazil's Instituto Socio-Ambiental operates a freewheeling home page on the Internet that disseminates information on long-suppressed subjects ranging from land rights for indigenous people to establishing legal responsibility for environmental crimes. An "emerging paradigm" throughout Latin America, wrote former World Resources Institute official Aaron Zazueta, "links environmental management, human well-being, and democratic processes."[33]

The stage, in short, is set for an era of more rapid progress in which newly forceful and newly effective coalitions of nongovernmental organizations, working in closer harmony with one another as well as with more responsive, more democratic, and more open-minded governments and international institutions, can hope to begin scoring broader gains. In particular, the timing is right for them to press for the extra national and international backing needed for the experiments of PPG7 and Mamirauá, of Lomerio and the Mexican *ejidos*, to succeed, get replicated, and fulfill their considerable promise.

Early in 1999 a delegation of Amazonian leaders assembled in Washington. Members included José Juarez Leitão dos Santos, the current president of Mendes's rubber tappers' union, Euclides Pereira, general coordinator of the Coordinating Group of the Indigenous Organizations of the Brazilian Amazon, and Claudionor Barbosa da Silva, president of the Grupo de Trabalho Amazonico. They articulately complained of government indifference to the principles and plans of the PPG7, of budget cutbacks attributable to International Monetary Fund demands on Brazil, and of harassment of the usual sort. What was striking was that they were there at all, and getting attention, if not action. "The irony," says Schwartzman, "is that things have never been worse in their region. But never before has the civil movement to tackle the problems been politically stronger or better organized."[34]

PART III

The Way Ahead

CHAPTER 8

Shifting the Balance

Flying northeastward from San José, Costa Rica, we passed two lofty dead volcanoes—Poás, a national park and major tourist destination area, and Turrialba.[1] Then the pilot of our single-engine Cessna Caravan throttled back and we began a gradual descent, over coffee and banana fincas and cattle ranches and the occasional small town, to the edge of the Tortuguero National Park. The park is located on the country's Caribbean shore, near the Nicaraguan border. Below us was a swath of unbroken forest, the crowns of myriad large trees reaching toward us in a splendid succession. Soon we were over water and banking left toward the short airstrip on a narrow band of land between the sea and a river, near the village of Tortuguero (map 14).

As we made our approach we could see on the beach scores of what looked like jeep tracks from the water's edge straight inland to where the sand gave way to scrubby coastal vegetation. Yet no automobile had ever wandered onto this remote shoreline, and no road provided easy access to it. Female green turtles, large reptiles weighing several hundred pounds apiece, had made those tracks. Each year, during the June–September nesting season, they swim here from the high seas, selecting this spot for reasons that remain mysterious to science. Avoiding the daylight hours for security's sake, they clamber ashore each night, using

NICARAGUA

CARIBBEAN
SEA

Guanacaste
National Park

Tortuguero River — Tortuguero

—Tortuguero
National Park

• Limón

⊛ San José

N

PACIFIC
OCEAN

PANAMA

Forested areas

Corcovado
National Park

0   20 40 60 80 Km.

0 10 20 30 40 50 Mi.

Map 14.   Costa Rica.

their flippers to propel themselves ponderously forward over the berm, and select nesting sites at the edge of the beach. There they dig large holes, deposit up to one hundred or more eggs, bury them, then return to the sea. The completion of this ancient ritual comes sixty to eighty days later, when three-inch hatchlings break open the white, golfball–sized eggs, flipper their way to the surface of the beach, then scramble for the relative safety of the sea.

Some of the hatchlings die from the heat or from flipping themselves over on their backs, which makes them helpless. Some succumb to the many predators on the beach: vultures, herons, gulls and other large seabirds, dogs from the village, jaguars and pumas that emerge from the adjacent forest during the hatching season for easy meals. The water provides these little creatures little more security than the land, for many species of fish like to eat them too. One fisherman gutted a crevalle jack and found twenty-two green turtle hatchlings in its stomach. Some eggs never hatch. Maggots and other insects attack the nests, and so do humans, who illegally collect the eggs and sell them at the market in Limón, the nearest large town. Only a few—2 percent—of these captivating little creatures make it to maturity and become breeders themselves. So compelling is the spectacle of the breeding cycle on this beach, where more green turtles congregate each year than anywhere other than one remote Australian location, that it attracts scores of thousands of tourist spectators each season.

I was one such tourist during the record-breaking 1998 season, when as many as 1,000 turtles (some repeaters) came ashore each night at Tortuguero. The plane's *comandante* greased the Cessna onto the tarmac with hardly a squeak of the tires and coasted to the end of the runway. There awaiting me were several staff members of the U.S.-based Caribbean Conservation Corporation (CCC), which since 1959 has been patrolling Tortuguero's beaches to protect and study the turtles. Included were Roxana Silman, CCC's determined manager in Costa Rica, Fredy Piedra, manager of its research station a short way down the beach from the airstrip, and Sebastian Troeng, a young Swedish turtle biologist who was spending his third season at Tortuguero and his second as the facility's research coordinator. Escorted by this group, I sped up the Tortuguero River aboard CCC's well-equipped, outboard-powered *Dona Lavinia.*

En route to the research station over glassy water, we passed many riverfront lodges. Some of those who visit here simply come to relax in hammocks in the balmy tropical air. Some enjoy boat trips into the narrow canals off the river's main channel, where a profusion of wildlife—howler and spider monkeys, many spectacular birds including colorful toucans and aracaris and the turkey-sized great currasow, large iguanas and snakes—can readily be seen in their magnificent, half-flooded forest habitat. For most of the tourists, however, the prime attraction of Tortuguero is to walk the beaches at night, with a local man as guide, to witness the enthralling spectacle of the turtles nesting.

Over several days, as a member of CCC's board of directors, I had a privileged opportunity to witness the work underway at the biological station, and to evaluate the meaning of tourism to the Tortuguero region. Here are some excerpts from my logbook:

Friday, 9/28/98. I put away my stuff at the Mawamba Lodge, then took the short walk down the powdery gray sand beach to the green-painted buildings of the biological station. There I found Rob, a young Canadian, and Andy, a self-styled "immigrant biologist from the United States." They had both come to Tortuguero to work as volunteers to band and document birds for the Redwood Center in northern California. "Sorry we can't spend much time with you," said Rob. "We're kind of busy right now." It had rained the previous night, for the first time in several weeks, and the aftermath was a sudden flush of migrant birds from the north. From mist nets placed near the compound they had already extracted, bagged, measured, weighed, and banded a couple of dozen birds. Included were warblers, vireos, flycatchers, and a profusion of thrushes— Swainson's, gray-cheeked, veery. They were also catching the occasional local bird, and without warning handed me one of these— a species of hummingbird called the rufous-tailed bronzy—and suggested I hold it for a while. Apprehensive that I would crush it, I was also enchanted by the feel of this soft, warm, and virtually weightless creature, which seemed to relax when properly grasped back-down and held gently but firmly. I opened my hand and the bird drilled off into the woods. The biologists went about their work with quiet precision, bird in one hand, pencil in the other as they recorded data on sheets that would end up in California to go on the computer. Feathers flew off one gray-cheeked thrush while it was being measured. "It's a way they react to being stressed," said Rob.

After an hour with the bird banders I returned to the lodge and

sat under a thatched gazebo by the river, watching the busy traffic of
tourist-laden outboards passing to and fro. A barefaced tiger heron
settled on a nearby perch and commenced fishing. Near me, relaxing
on hammocks, were Mike and Jennifer, a Canadian honeymoon
couple. Adorably enthusiastic, they told me the wonders of the
wildlife watching they had done. Later I walked down the beach, past
the Biological Station, to the scruffy and poor-looking village of
Tortuguero. Prominent there was a recycling effort to replace the
former littering, and a plaza in front of a pink-painted little shopping
complex that featured two large plastic Disney-type bird figures,
calculated by one local booster to be a tourist attraction. Also several
stores, restaurants, one resort and several beds-and-breakfasts, and
two nightclubs. Swarms of children, one knot of men drinking rum.
"Ruben" was advertising guide services on a small billboard. In
the absence of cars, the prevailing modes of transportation are boats,
of which many were drawn up on the river side of town, or foot.

Sebastian came by to fix a rendezvous for me to go out turtle
tagging with him. He could not stop talking about the fantastic
season that was still in progress. Blond, amiable, rail-thin, tireless,
British-educated, he spoke in that vaguely Cockney accent that
has become fashionable among young upper class British: "We've
'ad more tur'les than in any year since they started counting in
1971. And poaching for eggs and meat is way down. The government
changed and, after *La Nación* ran a major ah'icle about it, the new
president ordered his environment minister to crack down. The
pahk gaads have become far be'er equipped to confront the bad
people from Limón with their AK-47's, and they're busting people
left and right. It's great time to be paht of CCC."

Saturday, 9/26. Last night, dark, no moon, Sebastian and Emma, a
young British volunteer en route to a doctorate in turtle biology,
took me out tagging. We walked the beach to an area so marked by
transverse turtle tracks that it looked almost like a corduroy road.
Earlier in the season, Sebastian said, it had been so busy that turtles
were literally bumping into each other and nesting so close together
that the nests all but blended together. Feeling the tracks with

their toes, Sebastian and Emma could tell instantly which was an "up" (turtle moving toward the nesting site) and which a "down" (turtle returning to the water after laying eggs). An "up" with no corresponding "down" meant a turtle on the beach either preparing a nest, laying eggs, covering the nest, or beginning her return to the water.

During the evening we encountered a dozen or so turtles on the beach. They are wary before and after they lay their eggs: we spooked one while she was moving back to the water and she reversed direction and headed back for the woods. Sebastian and Emma gently lifted her and pointed her back toward the sea. In a tangle of tree roots and vegetation, where one turtle was preparing to lay eggs, I was invited to be the counter. Darning a rubber glove in my left hand and a counter on a right-hand finger, I lay on my stomach and reached *far* down into the cavity under the turtle's rear end. Dimly lit by Sebastian's little red light (the turtles flinch when bright white light hits them), the eggs came out at a prodigious rate. I counted 111 of them before the turtle signaled that she was through by beginning to agitate her rear flippers to cover the eggs with sand. Concurrently the researchers were feeling under the turtle's front flippers to look for a tag and if found record its number, or attach a tag to an animal that had none already attached.

While moving on the beach in the darkness, the turtles appeared as dim pale oblongs in slow motion. Tour groups were moving about too. It was too dark to distinguish human characteristics: a shadow getting bigger indicated someone moving toward you. Sebastian was polite and informative with their groups and the guides from the village. Just being on the beach, he said, was a good way of seeing to it that the guides followed the rules and of warding off poachers. We walked for hours. Blisters on my heels from new sneakers forced me to abandon them and walk barefoot. No matter. It was exhilarating.

This afternoon, after we had toured the canals by boat and seen many interesting monkeys and birds, I returned to the beach where Sebastian, Emma, and another Brit volunteer were excavating old nests, full of broken eggs, from which hatchlings had recently departed. At one site an exploratory feel with a pole revealed a nest, and a handful of sand contained a healthy, energetically wriggling hatchling that had belatedly made its way to the surface. Sebastian inspected the little creature, then reburied it in the sand so that it could make its perilous dash for the sea under cover of darkness. The team also found eggs in which embryos had never formed, dead embryos including a set of twins, and a small number of insect-predated eggs.

9/29/98. At the CCC board meeting yesterday, Sebastian gave a fine turtle presentation that included some arithmetic about the merits of turtle (hence forest) conservation versus exploitation. A guide gets $5 a head for a turtle walk, or $50 for the usual group of ten. The meat of one turtle, on the other hand, fetches only $40 at the faraway market. Ecotourism is about all that supports this isolated local economy, and there is tension about this. For the short term, it supplies most local jobs—tour guides, boat drivers, workers at the lodges. The lodges themselves require capital that helps the banks, and so on. But as usual, another world is approaching as farming drives a wedge through the forest, even though it is supposedly parkland, that brings cattle and subsistence agriculture— and grievous biodiversity losses—ever closer to Tortuguero and the beach. A proposed road through the forest would dramatically quicken the rate of illegal logging and deforestation while at the same time offering what many villagers want: better access to markets and health services. The challenge for a commission now studying the matter, which includes local community representatives as well as the CCC's Silman, is to accommodate these aspirations and at the same time maintain the healthy ecotourism ecosystem that now exists.

Up at 0445 this morning in hopes of seeing a full-fledged hatch just before daybreak. No luck, although we did find two hatchlings on the sand, flipped onto their backs and tired from struggling fruitlessly to right themselves. We did this for them and they made their way as best they could, through the cliffs and valleys of many human footprints, to the edge of the sea. Then came gentle waves, and abruptly they were gone in the foam.

A remarkable couple, Guy and Maria Angela Marcovaldi, has replicated CCC's success in Tortuguero with a national project along the larger part of Brazil's sweeping coastline. Their Projeto Tamar, which started as a small turtle monitoring and raising station at the remote Praia Forte on the northeast coast, later became a much heralded and prize-winning national effort to provide comprehensive education about coastal and marine environments as well as a program to monitor and protect sea turtles. Maintaining the conditions that offer such opportunities requires a deliberate effort and the kind of consultation with local people that reveals the importance of environmental projects to their well-being. It requires the elaboration of a national strategy for protecting natural areas and basing much of the economic development scenario on environmental considerations.

FLIES IN THE OINTMENT

At a meeting in Washington a few days after my return from Tortuguero, I heard Costa Rica's president, Miguel Angel Rodriguez, forcibly make this case for his country. Only high-tech industry, on the model of a successful Intel plant now exporting $2 billion worth of products a year, ranks ahead of the related roles of ecotourism and forest protection in the vision he described for his country's future. "We have been able to use our nature for business," he said. "Eight percent of our gross national product comes from ecotourism, and the way we get the tourism is by taking care of our nature."[2] In his talk he outlined a number of strategies apart from direct tourism that the country employs to generate income for private landholders so that they will keep and not destroy their forest properties. He did not articulate the reverse: that when a developing country fails to target priorities such as those he has established, unregulated agricultural frontiers will almost inevitably continue to advance into forestlands and local people will suffer. In this scenario Tortuguero's tour guides and boat drivers and hotel workers would in all likelihood become subsistence farmers struggling to survive.

Rodriguez emphasized the virtues of privatization and decentralization, and thus struck at the heart of this book's message. In its earlier chapters, we showed how in many countries the shift to state management and away from local hands, accompanied by the ascendancy of large-scale commercial logging, are major reasons why global deforestation rates have accelerated in recent decades. Consequently the importance of restoring the balance between these interests—reestablishing and spreading the concept of at least partial local ownership and control over forests and adjacent landscapes—is becoming increasingly imperative.

That said, we should hastily add some qualifiers, for no analysis of global forest degradation reveals simple answers or stark truths etched in black or white. Applying the concept of community-based management will not always result in forests that are better than those produced by state control. Nor will common property regimes, in and of themselves, necessarily provide more equity or protect more forest than systems that protect individual property rights. Conflicts between neighboring villages, gender inequities, and simple misunderstandings often inhibit the ability of local institutions to assume management rights and responsibilities. Such groups are not automatically capable of, or even interested in, managing forests for sustainable use. Success will often require help from other social actors. Even when governments or donors attempt in good faith to set rules or policies to increase local participation, power sometimes falls into the hands of local elements who have no greater interest than the state does in protecting the forest. And if governments simply confer responsibilities while withholding rights and access to benefits, the result may be tension rather than progress.

Other difficulties occur because the local officials of federal departments and private concessionaires often disregard policies calling for community empowerment and fail to transfer real management authority. Mainstream bureaucrats in government forestry departments often prove inflexible and unwilling to share power. Many forest officers continue to see their role as defenders of the forest from local people. States more readily grant property rights to communities when they do not conflict with private commercial interests or when the forest is already logged or degraded. The better the forest is, the more difficult it is for local communities to get hold of it.

Despite the strides forward that have been made, only a tiny fraction of all the world's forests has yet come under community management. Even in India, after more than two decades of growing national commitment to the idea, local communities currently share control of no more than 1.5 percent of the nation's forest territory. With only a small portion of all the world's forests now being managed sustainably for timber production, the promising concept of local forest management has far to go before it begins to stem the tide of overall forest decline. The very idea of sustainable use, as we shall see in this and subsequent chapters, is hotly debated. Some consider the phrase an oxymoron. But if shortcomings such as these increase the difficulty of achieving progress toward effective community empowerment, they only emphasize the importance of the struggle and the magnitude of the stakes.

WAYS TO CHANGE

No change is more essential than for states to delegate legal control of forest ecosystems, and much of the responsibility for their protection and use, to local forest-dependent communities or individuals within them. The specifics of how this shift can best be accomplished vary from country to country and are affected by legal and constitutional intricacies, cultures and traditions, and the reasons why previous arrangements failed to arrest the forest's deterioration. Behind it all lies one fundamental point: when governments surrender tenure—defined in one authoritative paper as what "determines who can (and can't) do what with the property in question and under which circumstances they can (or

can't) do it"³—the result is seldom the kind of misuse of land and resources that biologist Garrett Hardin describes in his often-cited "Trag
edy of the Commons" essay.

Hardin claims that individuals attempting to maximize their own
good will prevail over other individuals seeking rational management of
a common resource, and that the population explosion will exacerbate
the problem immeasurably.⁴ Researcher Gill Shepherd disagrees and
argues that Hardin misses a key point: that population growth is more
a function of declining death rates than of increasing birth rates. In the
Bay region of southern Somalia, Shepherd and her colleagues discovered
while doing fieldwork in the late 1980s, local trees could either support
a local economy for the long term or supply charcoal for the nearby city
of Mogadishu for a short while—but not both. Government agencies
lacked the manpower and local people the authority to deal with widespread charcoal burning. Villagers were defending their trees with bows
and arrows, but the resource was inexorably vanishing. What the case
illustrates, Shepherd concludes, is both that lands held in common *can*
be successfully managed, and that "the real tragedy comes when the
commons are thrown open and unrestricted exploitation allowed."⁵
Reallocating tenure to the community level often restores order.

Recognizing community-based rights and granting state rights to local resource users are acts that move far beyond the boundaries of politics as usual. In countries as disparate as Brazil and Papua New Guinea,
regional and local politicians, when compared to their national counterparts, have proven to be even less responsible and even more short-
sighted as forest stewards. Careful selection of local heirs to power is
important. The more that governments do to make sure that they are
investing power in appropriate local hands, and not simply extending
the range of their own power and influence, the more likely it is that
the goal of arresting forest losses will be achieved. Nepal's community
forestry program, which took off only after the state stopped empowering *panchayats*, the local political units, and delved deeper to support
"forest user groups" within communities, is only one example.

Governments need also to establish a solid legal framework for community empowerment. Counterproductive laws that regard nature as an enemy, encouraging deforestation by declaring forested lands to be "idle," empty, or *territorium nullius*, and therefore subject to tax or tenurial inequities, remain in force in many countries. Some regimes award land tenure rights on the basis of demonstrated use—that is, forest clearing. The beginning of forest wisdom is to repeal such laws where they exist and to substitute or strengthen ones that promote the conservation and sustainable management of forest ecosystems. New arrangements that empower local communities need sufficient flexibility to encompass situations where community management cannot or will not work, and where smallholders of individual property rights are also important forest stewards capable of taking on responsibility for forest management. Europe's twelve million smallholder forest stewards are an example. Even in countries where common property regimes are likely to be more effective safeguards, the Western idea that private individual rights are the key to responsible forest use continues to be exclusively upheld. In such instances, a better legal balance between these two forces needs to be struck.

In many societies, tree tenure and land tenure are traditionally separate matters: the person or group controlling the land may or may not control the trees on it, and vice versa. State owners who yield user rights to local communities, while remaining respectful of these customs, need to make sure that the rights conferred apply not only to land, but to trees and other forest resources as well, and they need to help communities market those resources. If the expansion of areas to protect wildlife and preserve biodiversity and genetic resources is contemplated, failure is almost a certainty if decisions are reached without the full participation of local communities and if the new rules ignore the needs of traditional human users of the forest.

Conferring tenurial rights on local communities is one *sine qua non* in the development of new decentralized approaches to forest management. No catalog of needed reforms would be complete without a call for better education and training both for community leaders and for government officials. In the future, sound forest management at the village level will benefit from relatively complex but useful new technologies and procedures that range from GIS mapping systems to PRA assessments. Access to the Internet, and knowing how to take advantage of its capabilities, can put community groups far closer to the cutting edge than they otherwise would be. Mastering these skills requires new kinds of training in technical areas as well as in planning, meeting facilitation, administration and financial management, conflict resolution, and consensus building. The development of training programs specifically designed for community leaders remains a top priority.

Training centers can often serve to bridge the gaps between nongovernmental organizations, government officials, and communities. The Regional Community Forestry Training Center (RECOFTC) at Kasetsart University in Bangkok, which not only trains community leaders but also sensitizes government officials in rural districts to citizen concerns, has established a solid reputation for its ability to improve relations between government agencies and nongovernmental organizations. It is a model that merits replication elsewhere in the developing world. A similar program could usefully become part of the new Andean Center for Sustainable Development, which was created in 1998 by Manuel Rodriguez Becerra of Colombia, a distinguished professor and environmental leader. Other Latin American and African locations also beckon.

Fortifying the system of multidisciplinary research and training centers for forest management will have an important secondary effect: greater and much needed interaction and information sharing between local communities and state agencies, as well as among donors, international nongovernmental organizations, and international researchers. Too much knowledge, once acquired, remains confined within the discipline or institution where it originated. Even within institutions frequent staff and policy shifts render it difficult for outsiders to get a sense of what is or is not happening. The waste is huge. The wheel gets reinvented far too often, at a time when financial resources are scarce. Just as important as the new knowledge created at the new centers is its cross-cultural dissemination. Creating better communications channels is yet another task for the enlightened state.

These proposals come over and above the essential need, which cannot be overstated, for basic capacity building in forestry and agroforestry techniques. Specialized new education and training centers cannot substitute for the conventional colleges or agencies where most field foresters will continue to receive their training. These often neglected institutions, many of which still preach the outmoded doctrines of "scientific" or "social" forestry and in some instances fail to discriminate between temperate and tropical circumstances, need increased support to improve and broaden their curricula and leadership abilities.

Governments need also to redirect the attention of their "forest police" away from local people and toward the illegal loggers whose destructive actions underlie most forest problems. Beyond controlling corruption, national governments can do much to curb the wasteful and highly inefficient forms of logging that the least responsible logging companies practice. They can improve the situation through serious efforts to hold logging corporations accountable when these companies do not submit the comprehensive long-term forest management plans that are called for in their concession contracts. Governments can adjust stumpage fees and other levies as long as they concurrently establish policies that prevent the private sector from responding to these higher assessments by extracting at faster rates, and they can restructure fiscal policies in ways that would discourage wanton logging.

On the positive side, opportunities for state cooperation with more responsible segments of private industry also beckon. To date, the record of interaction between forest communities and forest industries is mixed, ranging from thinly disguised exploitation (hiring local people to guard industrial teak plantations for a pittance) to far more positive situations where poor rural people win significant transfers of income.

In Brazil and Mexico mutually beneficial partnerships between corporations and communities or individuals owning and managing small forest tracts are at work. These latter examples should become far more prevalent, and policy shifts can help. Consumer and government incentives should reward private sector logging companies for adhering to independent third-party certification procedures. Codes of conduct should also govern the effects of their activities on the people and wildlife that share their space. Responsibly conducted, clear and transparent social and environmental impact assessments should precede logging activities in such regions.

In countries with forest management systems designed more for subsistence or for environmental protection than for economic development, commercial community forestry is now more often seen as a desirable goal. Private sector logging companies should seek opportunities to establish commercial partnerships with local community organizations, providing sustainable small-scale community-based commercial logging efforts with technical, business, and marketing expertise in return for a share of economic returns. Governments and international donors should foster such relationships, offering incentives to both sides.

Beyond the tactical task of making existing loggers more responsible and more responsive to community needs lies the larger question of the overall role of commercial logging in national development. Many tropical nations need to conduct comprehensive exercises to determine how much logging should be allowed, and where this logging should take place. While the situation of course varies from country to country, many of them, Brazil for example, have broad options as to how much of their remaining primary forest cover should be placed under protection and how much should be opened for limited logging or even full-throttle development. These decisions relate closely to economic considerations about the role of wood and wood products in the present and future national economy, and to the need for closely reasoned judgements about whether to encourage domestic and international investors to establish plantations of fast-growing tree species on unproductive or already degraded portions of the national landscape.

THE PLANTATION QUESTION

Here we run into a zone of heavy crossfire among those interested in promoting environmentally sound development. Defenders see technologically advanced plantation forestry, producing yields far higher than those that can be achieved in natural surroundings, as a means of saving most of the world's remaining primary forests while also supplying demand for forest products. Some environmentalists tolerate plantation proliferation on the grounds that it will happen whether or not they like it, that it offers an opportunity to get guilt money from pulpwood growers, and that combinations of plantation lands and protected forest areas can create corridors for wildlife and biodiversity conservation.

Others point to multiple dangers. They point out that some plantation trees hog water and have toxic properties that jeopardize other forms of life. The uniformity of plantations lacks the habitat characteristics that many species require, they contend, and plantations have less biomass and therefore sequester less carbon than the natural forest. Earlier in this century, Henry Ford II failed in two efforts to establish rubber tree plantations in Amazonia. The trees were destroyed by blight, which would not have spread across the natural forest with anything like its ferocity in attacking a monoculture. Similar disasters have befallen other tree plantations in many different parts of the world, and they have occurred often enough that many environmentalists think, conventionally, that plantation monocultures frequently will not work in tropical forest regions, and that their establishment will result in all the evils of outright deforestation with few positive consequences other than to supply resources for people living far away.

The recent book *Pulping the South*, a blistering and detailed attack by Ricardo Carrere and Larry Lohmann on the fast-growing industry of wood pulp production, has an answer for every argument in defense of plantations that the industry puts forth. Plantation harvests do not relieve pressure on the natural forests, the book's authors argue; the plantations are often subsidized by logging revenues, and they drive migrant settlers deeper into other forests, "setting off a chain reaction of further impoverishment and forest destruction." Plantations do not add trees; they are merely "a continuation of deforestation by other means." The "global" need for ever more paper does not outweigh the need for healthy "local" environments. Tree planters will if possible avoid degraded lands good for no other purpose, preferring well-watered land "suitable for superior biological growth rates" that small farmers or agroforesters could also ably use. If plantation trees store carbon and inhibit global warming, they have far less biomass and thus less storage capacity per unit of space than natural forests. It is the responsibility of the rich industrial north and not the poor developing south to curb greenhouse emissions. It is the companies and not the countries that profit from tree plantations, and the amount of local employment they provide is minimal. "In a world thronged with naked emperors," the authors conclude, "paper industry figures claiming sustainable environmental benefits for large-scale monoculture pulpwood plantations are more notable than most for their sartorial minimalism."[6]

As do many environmentalists, the authors of *Pulping the South* defend the idea that if used properly, wood is a renewable resource that can be sustainably harvested if proper controls are applied to the harvesters. Even though practically no logging operations are conducted in what can be described as a sustainable manner, no matter how that slippery adjective is defined, the concept of "sustainable forest management" (SFM) has many adherents. Few scientists would argue that sustainable forest management, standing alone, can protect biodiversity or save natural forests. Many, however, noting the impracticalities of reliance solely on protection, feel that sustainable forest management can be a useful tool for conservation. Noting that "the stage is set for the Amazon basin to become the new center for tropical timber extraction," several Amazonia-based researchers regard sustainable forest management as "one viable and conservation-friendly option to complement an overall conservation strategy."[7] Gary S. Hartshorn, executive director of the Organization for Tropical Studies at Duke University, feels that "improved and enlightened uses" of unprotected tropical forests are the only alternative to their destruction and conversion to farmland and is cited as offering several project examples of how "SFM can be compatible with conservation."[8] The WWF's Forests for Life campaign is built around the idea that the best hope for forests lies in a combination of protection and sustainable management in adjacent buffer zones.

The WWF, however, is quick to add that "markets will not promote the development of sustainable forestry without government and consumer recognition and support for the environmental value of forests." In a paper suggesting environmentalist responses to the fast-growing private sector presence in Latin America, WWF fuzzily proposes that sustainable forest management can best be promoted "through market-based policies that directly address private sector needs."[9] The primatologist Russell Mittermeier, president of the influential Conservation International, suggests an alternative approach. In an article in *Science*, he and several co-authors expressed little hope that sustainable management will carry the day since, for private investors, "reaping a one-time harvest of ancient trees is simply more profitable than managing for future harvests."[10]

Although these authors advocate further attention to sustainable forest management in the form of "carefully monitored experiments," they attach far greater importance to two alternatives that strike them as more promising. One is to "make protection an industry," seeking to achieve economic parity with tree harvesting by such means as eco-tourism development, expanded programs of scientific research that bring dollars to poor countries, and new forms of compensation for carbon sequestration. The other affects forests that are currently outside protected areas.

If our goal is to conserve biodiversity in the context of commercial timber production, then we should focus on meaningful efforts to set aside pristine areas within logging concessions, and retire concessions that have been lightly logged in the past—an option available on millions of hectares on every tropical continent. If our aim is to help meet future global wood demand, then the obvious step is to fast-track the transition to plantations in areas that have already been deforested.[11]

Conservation International thus joins other pragmatists in advocating a strategy that calls on the environmental community to cooperate with the more responsible tree growers, Brazil's Aracruz Celulose for example, rather than confront them. Tree plantations adjacent to natural forests can help consolidate corridors for wildlife and biodiversity, Mittermeier says. They contribute to carbon sequestration while also giving time and space for natural forests to regenerate—which, in the tropics, they often do with remarkable speed.[12]

Another indefatigable proponent of the plantation idea is the forester John Spears, a former World Bank official who has long had a prominent voice in the ongoing forest policy dialogue. He advocated this scenario for wood production during his incumbency as executive director of the independent World Commission on Forests and Sustainable Development (WCFSD) and later as a principal force within the World Bank–World Wildlife Fund Alliance:

· A trend toward intensification of forest management could have
a significant impact on future industrial roundwood (IRW)
supply. It could plausibly lead to a situation where by year 2050
all of global IRW demand could be produced from about
20 percent of today's global forest area.

· From both social and conservation perspectives that could have
positive implications since, to the extent that current threats
to forests can be contained, it would be possible to manage
80 percent of the world's forests for the benefit of local communities

and for the benefit of their both local and global environmental and other benefits.

Such a scenario, Spears continues, could lead to a "great restoration" in which, over the next half-century, global forest losses might be stemmed and a possible increase in total forest area achieved.[13]

In January 2000 a distinguished group of forest experts gathered in Washington to discuss the "global vision" that Spears has posited. One highly vocal participant, Marcus Colchester of the Forest Peoples Programme in England, spoke with passion about the negative effects of modern forestry and farming practices on indigenous communities in developing countries. Many others found reason to support at least part of the Spears hypothesis. Some participants underscored the dramatic increases in yields that can be achieved by means of intensive management; others predicted flat or even falling future demand for commercially harvested timber as consumers recycle more wood or turn to alternative materials. Still others said that agricultural intensification would lead to the reforestation of large amounts of today's cropland. While many of the most promising sites for intensive management projects are to be found in the developed world, especially the southern United States, analysts also designated many locations in the Southern Hemisphere as attractive for plantations. Brazil, Chile, Argentina, and Oceania are principal among the developing regions where the plantation movement has already gathered momentum. I left the meeting with the sense that most of the experts there would recommend to government officials (and aid donors) that they build the plantation "vision" into their planning and policies on the grounds that it is happening anyway, mostly in ways beyond their ability or willingness to control.

SHIFTING THE BALANCE

Such is the range of professional advice available to national governments as they weigh the question of how to arrange national landscapes.

Economically viable protection mechanisms, experiments in sustainable forest management, and an emphasis on tree plantations may all warrant placement in some national strategies, or in regional strategies in countries as geographically diverse as Brazil, India, and China, where no one policy or system will be right for the entire nation. Beyond the specifics of managing the forest sector, a broader task for states is to rearrange their bureaucracies and to adjust how they make policies affecting forests in ways that will give forests and the forest-dependent a better competitive advantage vis-à-vis competing interests. Independence and greater visibility for forest agencies, too often buried within agriculture departments that are oriented toward the goal of "production" rather than of maintaining the integrity of forest ecosystems, would result in policies and strategies that are more sensitive to the health of forests.

The problem, however, is broader than this. Even if forest departments have more strength, the fact will remain that forest issues tend too often to be considered by foresters whose concern is classical forestry—the planting, management, and harvesting of trees. What is required is not just better forest management by foresters. It is an integrated approach to planning for rural development in which forests are assessed for all their uses and services, not just for their potential as suppliers of timber, and in which authentic community-based institutions with traditions of forest stewardship are fully involved.

CHAPTER 9

Helping from Afar

How can the international community lead developing nations toward better forest policies? How can faraway people and institutions encourage weak and often corrupt national governments to delegate power to local people, for their sake and that of the standing forest? It depends. On the political side, the dreary history of the intergovernmental forest debate suggests little hope for the future. A recent independent initiative, the World Commission on Forests and Sustainable Development (WCFSD), did a thorough and frank job of analyzing the importance of forests and the causes and consequences of their disappearance, but after three years of expensive deliberations it failed to produce policy recommendations with any real bite to them.

On the economic side, those who donate aid and those who distribute it have largely ceased to be part of the problem, as they were well into the 1990s, when their programs encouraged the degradation and destruction of the world's forests. Today's innovative donor-driven programs have formed new relationships with national governments, nongovernmental organizations, and intended beneficiaries. The formation of these partnerships suggests a far greater will to lead the world toward a new perception of forests than what is visible on the political horizon. What is lacking among the donors, keen as they are to bring about

change, is sensitivity and the ability to make it happen. The community
of international nongovernmental organizations has, meanwhile, become an influential and powerful instrument. The budget of the World
Wide Fund for Nature, as the worldwide WWF organization is known,
now exceeds that of the Nairobi-based United Nations Environment
Program.[1] This chapter scans this broad horizon.

POLITICS: THE DELEGATES DRONE ON

There is little reason to suppose that the deliberations sponsored by the
United Nations will in the future be any more useful to the cause of
community forestry than they have been in the past. Nongovernmental
groups, especially the World Conservation Union's Working Group on
Community Involvement in Forest Management, energetically lobbied
the official delegates to the Intergovernmental Panel on Forests and its
successor, the Intergovernmental Forum on Forests, seeking to place
language in official documents that would help local communities gain
leverage. Indigenous people joined with human rights groups and the
WWF in a campaign to get the panel to pay more attention to questions
of traditional, customary, and management rights for forest-dwelling
people. Although these efforts made an impression on the officials, the
panel failed for legal and financial reasons to come forward with recommendations with any real heft to them.

The delegates were prepared to talk for or against only one thing: a
global forests treaty and the money that might flow from such a treaty.
For reasons outlined in chapter 2, the United States, which pushed hard
for a global forests pact as a principal product of the 1992 Earth Summit,
was firmly opposed by 2000. Environmental organizations in the United
States, which were among those urging Washington to remain posi-
tioned against the convention, tended to think that it is better to have
no convention than the weak one that would result from an exhaustive
United Nations negotiation. This is precisely the reason why some tim-
ber-producing nations such as Malaysia, Indonesia, and Papua New

Guinea have been in favor of a U.N. agreement. Some relatively powerful forces, including Canada and the European Union, support a convention, and many world leaders feel that there is no viable alternative to a legally binding treaty.

The preponderance of the relatively poor Group of 77 developing countries remained uninterested in a treaty without financial muscle, and the industrial countries were clearly not willing to provide the necessary funds. Without assertive leadership from the United States, the convention idea will go nowhere. There has been no hint of a shift in the U.S. position on the subject, which is that a new treaty would be unlikely to achieve any major objective for forests since other countries are not ready to negotiate a meaningful convention. As of late 1998 other nations that had previously supported the convention idea also seemed to be drifting away from it. Without U.S. backing for this or any other compelling idea regarding the world's forests, what seems likely is that the U.N. dialogue will soon be reduced to occasional mentions at meetings of the Commission on Sustainable Development (CSD) and even less frequent references at future General Assemblies.

Why this bleak future beckons, some people think, is that those who sit on the national delegations still largely view forests as crops to be harvested. "The underlying purpose of all this is to keep the world safe for production forestry," said Bill Mankin, director of an initiative called the Global Forest Policy Project, which is sponsored by several environmental nongovernmental organizations. Official views tend to reflect not the values of the broad civil society, but those of narrow interests such as timber companies and manufacturers of pulp and paper and corrupt government officials. In search of an independent vision, a group of nonofficial international leaders, which was convened soon after the 1992 Earth Summit at the request of the Inter-Action Council of Former Heads of State, began informal discussions about how the deep splits in opinion about forest policy might be reconciled. In 1995 this body, the WCFSD, began its deliberations with funding from the European Union and several governments including those of Sweden and the Netherlands. Headed by Ola Ullsten, former prime minister of Sweden, and Emil Salim, former environment minister of Indonesia, the commission comprised twenty-three members from as many countries and a small secretariat. Its model was the well-known World Commission on Environment and Development, which was headed by Gro Harlem Brundtland, Norway's prime minister; in 1987 this commission issued the influential report titled *Our Common Future*, a pioneer statement that provided the classic definition of sustainable development and set forth a detailed agenda for how to achieve it.[2]

The WCFSD convened a series of regional hearings in Jakarta, Winnipeg, San José, Yaounde, and St. Petersburg; at least one of us (the authors of this book), attended each of these regional sessions. Hundreds of witnesses from a rich diversity of backgrounds gave "testimony" at these gatherings, each of which lasted for several days. Field trips gave the commissioners good opportunities to gain insights from within the forest rather than from a dais in a hotel ballroom. Some of these excursions, such as the one to a "showcase village" in Indonesia's East Kalimantan that was arranged and paid for in 1996 by Suharto confidant Bob Hasan, were rigged to give the commissioners a favorable impression of industrial forestry's effects on local communities. In contrast, a well-organized program of excursions to several areas inhabited by indigenous people in Canada, where local community forest management is as hot a subject as it is in the tropics, offered a vivid appreciation of the spirituality of these First Nations and of their respect for living things and nature as a whole. Even in the formal sessions the members of the commission heard many statements from members of the public and from invited panelists or "experts" about the urgent need for new approaches and new criteria for forest policymaking.

From the outset the commission emphasized that "very high priority should be given to ensuring that improved mechanisms are put into place for involving local communities, NGOs, and the private sector in policy dialogue and in the implementation of forest development and conservation programs."[3] In closed sessions during the regional hearings and at one week-long plenary gathering convened exclusively to consider the text of the final report, a number of commission members argued heatedly for a heavy emphasis in its text on community empowerment and decentralized forest management. Notable among these were Kamla Chowdhry, the spirited professor from India, and Angela Cropper, a Trinidadian who was then a senior manager at the United Nations Development Program. Others involved were less concerned with the welfare of local communities than with pressing for measures to protect the landscape and safeguard the environmental services that forests provide. Still others saw the commission as a stalking horse to promote the idea of a forests convention. Another group wanted the commission to champion the spread of intensive plantation forestry to grow pulpwood, as widely practiced in the southeast United States and in some developing countries.

Even though there was no consensus among the commission members about major issues such as these, nor even much of an effort to achieve one, the drafting of the WCFSD report began in the fall of 1996. It finally appeared in print in the spring of 1999. Several factors contributed to the delay. A principal one was that, even after three years of deliberations at a cost of more than $4 million, the full commission was largely unable to agree on what it wanted to say that would be fresh and incisive. Proposals for specific steps constituting an "action plan" seemed invariably to drift off into banalities, and the idea of including an action plan in the final document was ultimately rejected. After a prolonged debate that took place far later in the process than it should have, the commissioners firmly resolved to be neither for nor against a forests convention. "I don't understand what we're doing here," one wearied commission member complained after yet another interminable plenary, line-by-line drafting session. "I don't see that we are saying anything that the Intergovernmental Panel on Forests hasn't already said."[4]

When finally issued, the report, *Our Forests, Our Future*, outclassed the official rhetoric in its brave assertions that national governments had mismanaged their forests and that sharp changes in timber concession policy were urgently required. It labeled the corruption of government officials by timber interests as a major cause of forest decline. It called for a comprehensive set of measures that would lead the world and individual countries toward systems of forest management that would extend far beyond the confines of traditional "forestry" and would reflect not narrow sectoral interests but the broader public interest. Recognizing the considerable contribution to forest protection and management that local communities had already made, the report strongly advocated "the removal of obstacles to release the great potential of communities to make an even more significant contribution to planting new and rehabilitating degraded forest stands."[5] Unfortunately, after crisply defining the crisis and declaring the need for radical new approaches that would do much to bring local communities onto the playing field, the report's recommendations did little more than prescribe the superimposition of new levels of bureaucracy over useful increments of work that had been already well launched elsewhere by nongovernmental organizations.

The "umbrella" organization the commission said it wanted to create would be called "Forestrust International," which, like the World Conservation Union, would open its membership not only to governments but also to nongovernmental organizations, local communities, and individual citizens. Its "overall purpose" would be to "catalyze, encourage, facilitate, and support communities in organizing themselves in relevant localized activities."[6] Under the Forestrust umbrella would be a freewheeling forest ombudsman, an award program, an information-gathering "Forest Watch" entity, and a "Forest Management Council" to coordinate and harmonize technical aspects of trade in wood and wood products. To the extent possible, each of these international entities would be replicated at the national level. In addition the commission challenged governments to form "F15," a grouping of officials and citizens in the fifteen key nations that possess and use the lion's share of all forests, to monitor the forests crisis and press for remedial actions.

Finally, instead of joining many leaders in Europe and the Southern Hemisphere in demanding that the overconsumptive nations of the north pay most of the bill if it expects developing countries to protect their forests for environmental reasons, the commission proposed a complex "Index" to evaluate each nation's forest capital and provide an arithmetical basis for distributing financial responsibilities.

The commission's allegation that "more, not fewer mechanisms" are required if forest management is to improve was not accompanied by suggestions about who might take the lead in creating them and making them effective. Given the dismal history, it is not likely that either national governments or the United Nations will respond to the commission's fire alarm. Several large nongovernmental organizations such as the WWF and the World Conservation Union already had their own major forest initiatives in progress. Currently under development, with leadership from the Washington-based World Resources Institute, is the establishment of an independent "Global Forest Watch" entity (described in more detail later in this chapter) that would monitor the overall state of forest policy and practice. The World Resources Institute was understandably miffed when the commission barely acknowledged this program's existence while announcing its own. Similarly, in announcing its Forest Management Council, the commission paid scant attention to the broad-based Forest Stewardship Council (FSC), which for years has bravely pioneered in the field of establishing criteria for the independent third-party certification of hardwood forests as being sustainably managed.

NEW APPROACHES FOR THE WORLD BANK

Little on either the official political agenda or its unofficial counterpart offers much hope for forests or those who depend on them. Aid agencies created more problems for forests and forest-dependent people than they solved from the 1950s through the 1980s, as described in the previous chapters of this book. During the late 1990s, however, the mood within these agencies swung quite sharply toward sensitive and participatory approaches. Equity and the environment have become important concerns in most forms of bilateral and multilateral development assistance, and at the policy level the idea of local participation has become an organizing principle. "The message is very simple," said James Wolfensohn, president of the World Bank, where advice from the outside has not always been welcome. "Participation works."[7]

The World Bank is hardly the only international aid lender that has discovered the virtues of shifting from trickle-down, growth-based approaches to development assistance to ones in which civil-society beneficiaries are fully involved in planning and implementing projects that are also environmentally far more sensitive than were their forebears. As the World Bank and other multilateral lenders have come to show greater interest in the social and environmental consequences of their investments, they have made more of an effort to incorporate those considerations into their thinking about economic development. It is far from a complete process; some feet are still dragging. Policies fervently iterated at headquarters are not being fully honored in the field. Some local communities are still being badly hurt by what the banks insist constitutes development. Yet even many of those who were once the banks' harshest critics have grudgingly come to respect the major efforts that they are making to break free from their old orthodoxies and fundamentally redefine the business that they are in.

The evolution of the World Bank's forest policy is instructive. Prior to 1978 its "forest sector" loans were almost fully allocated to industrial tree-harvesting activities that promised to bolster short-term economic growth in developing countries. That year a new policy paper showed greater determination within the bank to support "people-oriented forestry" as well, in recognition of the social and environmental damage that deforestation triggers. Yet even what became known as "social forestry" programs funded by the World Bank and other international agencies, wrote Donald A. Gilmour, for many years the World Conservation Union's top forest expert, "often paid only superficial attention to the needs of local people, whose participation was often limited to providing paid (or free) labor."[8]

Meanwhile forest carnage and its adverse consequences continued, and critics of the World Bank fastened on bank-supported activities outside the forest sector as principal reasons. With the bank's role under growing attack by the late 1980s, especially for financing the Brazilian road building and Indonesian transmigration programs mentioned earlier in this book, a new forest sector policy was developed and published in 1991. Although the bank hardly reversed its position on supporting production forestry as a means of stimulating economic growth, it admitted in stronger terms that these achievements often had social and environmental costs attached to them. The bank also admitted that its support for highways, dams, and other nonforestry activities had often harmed forests. Consequently, said the 1991 policy, "the Bank Group will not under any circumstances finance commercial logging in primary tropical moist forests. Financing of infrastructural projects (such as roads, dams, and mines) that may lead to loss of tropical moist forests will be subject to rigorous environmental assessment. . . . A careful assessment of the social issues involved may also be required."[9]

It was not long after 1991 that observers, within the bank as well as outside it, began to question whether, as the global forest situation continued its downward curve, the policy corrections had been sufficient. In 1994 a bank team with representatives of its agriculture, natural resources, and environment departments completed a comprehensive review of what had changed as a result of the 1991 directives and published a report. While it was too early to reach conclusions about how the policy shift had affected the overall course of development in beneficiary countries, the report said, bank lending to the forest sector had more than doubled and the structure of the portfolio had undergone sharp change. Loans for "resource expansion"—the euphemism for production forestry—had dropped from 32 to 23 percent of the total. Lending for "protective and restorative activities" had, meanwhile, risen from 7 to 27 percent, and support to nurture "alternative livelihoods" for forest-dependent people had grown from practically nil to 14 percent. The report also noted the continuance of forest decline since 1991 in tem perate and boreal as well as tropical regions and questioned whether conditioning support "on commitment to sustainable and conservation- oriented forestry" would work in countries where "strongly vested in- terests that benefit from existing policies will resist change."

The team called on the World Bank to make further improvements in the forest sector, including Houdini-like efforts to "reconcile con- servation and utilization" and promote policy and institutional reforms in client nations. The report highlighted as the "top priority" the need to use forest lending to reduce rural poverty, making specific mention of the need to support joint forest management efforts, expand the role of women, and transform forest departments into "agents of sustainable development." Finally and tellingly, the report raised the question of why the relatively small forestry sector should have to bear dispropor- tionate responsibility for anticipating and coping with the consequences of often far larger loans for dams, roads, agribusiness, and other activities that harm forests.[10]

By mid-decade the bank had developed rules that called for environ- mental and social assessments of more and more of its forest-related projects. Guidelines for encouraging local participation in project design and implementation were also promulgated, and the bank's leaders worked with growing conviction to see to it that task managers and other mid-level officials were observing them. Evidence mounted that the bank was doing increasingly less harm to forests as a result of lending in other sectors. In 1997 its president, James Wolfensohn, announced an "alliance" with the WWF. Its ambitious goals were to bring 200 million hectares of production forests under "independently certified sustainable management" by 2005, to achieve "effective management" for 50 million hectares of currently protected forestland, and to bring about "complete protection" for a new 50 million hectares of currently unprotected forests by the same year. Even as these goals were being announced, however, the bank was finding that "nearly 40 percent of forest projects were performing less than satisfactorily" and that while there had been much discussion of "mainstreaming environmental and certain social goals into bank activities, in the case of forests these goals remain unfulfilled at this time."[11]

The concurrent arrival of a couple of red herrings complicated the scene. Private and other interests began pressing the World Bank ever harder to abandon its across-the-board ban on the financial support of logging in primary tropical forests on the grounds that it prevented the bank from pursuing the elusive dream of sustainable forest management. And even as some bank officials were loudly proclaiming the great value of forests for all people, a pair of unreconstructed staff members, Kenneth M. Chomitz and Kanta Kumari, published a paper, "The Domestic Benefits of Tropical Forests: A Critical Review," that questioned even the most sacred of shibboleths about the environmental services that forests provide. The authors cited cases suggesting that deforestation does not increase erosion, sedimentation, and flooding. Their analysis of a well-known case study from the Philippines (mentioned in chapter 1), in which the researchers showed how logging had killed the fishing- and tourism-based economy of a bay on Palawan island,[12] tagged road building and not logging as the reason for the erosion and sedimentation that killed the bay. If better engineering techniques had been used for the roads, they argued, there would have been no problem. Without subsidies, they implied, the Chico Mendes extractive reserves in Brazil could not survive. For these analysts, who attributed no value at all to the nutrition, health, and spiritual benefits that forests give local people, domestic considerations "provide an uncertain rationale" for forest conservation. "The more compelling rationale for preservation," they concluded, "is based on global values" such as carbon sequestration and preserving genetic diversity. The "hopeful converse" they suggested is that it also costs little to preserve forests since the biologically richest of them are often "poorly suited to agriculture because of isolation and poor soils."[13]

Over the longer term the standing forest will offer greater long-term economic benefits than will timber extraction, a point that a former environment minister of Indonesia, Sarwono, tellingly made in a 1998 interview with a BBC television reporter.[14] It is, however, well and broadly understood that from a strictly cash perspective no use of primary tropical forest is now more lucrative than the sale of its timber. At least at the moment, the markets for alternative values—biodiversity, recreation, carbon sequestration—either do not exist or are not competitive. Community-minded observers nonetheless faulted the Chomitz-Kumari study for the narrowness of its perspective and for the extent to which it ignores the nonfinancial benefits that forests offer very poor people. What is disturbing is that, regardless of its weaknesses, some at the World Bank regarded the paper's information as "empirical" evidence that supported the resumption of the bank's support for logging in primary tropical forests.

Buffeted by conflicting views, wondering whether "proactive" rather than "proscriptive" approaches would better promote the cause of sustainable forest management, and stung by allegations that it lacked sincerity in its alleged quest for closer and more-cordial relations with the outside world, the bank in 1998 began elaborating yet another set of forest sector policy reviews highlighting "participatory evaluation processes." The bank's Operations Evaluation Department (OED) would conduct a crash inquiry, raising hard questions about what had happened to bank lending patterns, to countries, and to forests since the installation of the 1991 policy. Another independent assessment would be conducted by a team convened by the bank with the World Conservation Union (IUCN) as its partner and with the involvement of many other nongovernmental organizations. The result would be true transparency and "a full vetting of ideas and strategies," and the effort would be based on the central and important idea that "forest policy has emerged as a defining issue in the development debate with global as well as local dimensions."[15]

Late in 1999 the OED issued a "preliminary" set of findings. They attracted broad attention. As a result of the 1991 policy, overall forest sector loans had increased by 78 percent, and accusations of the bank's association with "wasteful and illegal deforestation and degradation" had gone away. The bank's policy, however, had discouraged risk-taking while having no more than a "negligible" influence on rates of tropical deforestation. Increased lending for such activities as forest conservation and biodiversity protection "were not incorporated in the bank's rural development or poverty alleviation strategies, even though large numbers of poor people and minorities in the developing world rely for their livelihoods on the forest sector." Among the policy shifts recommended in the report were far greater integration between conservation and development strategies and a far sharper focus not just on indigenous communities, but on those individuals—"at least one out of four of all poor"—who depend to some degree on the forest."[16]

NEW DIRECTIONS AT THE REGIONAL BANKS AND BILATERAL AID DONORS

Regional development banks, although well behind the World Bank in making adjustments toward sounder forest policies and greater local participation, began to follow suit. In Asia during the 1990s intemperate forest clearing was bringing increasingly strident reactions from such indigenous groups as Malaysia's Penan and the Dayaks of Kalimantan. The 1992 Earth Summit called for the world's greater attention to such voices. The Manila-based Asian Development Bank (ADB), which since 1977 had been making forestry loans with mixed success, accordingly began to develop new policies with more environmental punch to them. Its 1995 forest policy paper, which stressed "the need to balance the three imperatives of production, protection, and participation," hardly ruled out bank support for plantations and production forestry. The policy did echo the World Bank in barring loans for commercial logging in old-growth forests (which the ADB had never extended anyway), and it stipulated the replacement of "wasteful and destructive practices in second growth forests with those that are sustainable and environmen-

tally sound." It also pledged itself to "actively promote the involvement
of people from a wider cross-section of society in forestry policy formulation and implementation."

Bindu Lohani, ADB's principal environmental officer, admitted in a
1997 interview that "we are still evolving our strategies for participation." On the basis of the bank's previous experience, he added, they
had learned that "trying to regulate forests through prescriptive approaches is not going to work. Forest people are part of the equation
and we need to take their advice. It takes longer, but it works better and
it pays off." Task managers expressed surprise at the success of their
initial experiments with participation, as Bhuvan Bhatnagar, a social development specialist who had been working on a road-building project
in China, noted: "I must admit that I really didn't expect that by spending just $19,500 on a participatory poverty assessment I would see such
clear and significant benefits. And, frankly, I was astonished by the extraordinary ability of poor villagers to assess and analyze their own situation and plan for the future."[17]

In the mid-1990s the Inter-American Development Bank, which for
some years had been conducting environmental reviews of some of its
loans, also moved to strengthen its capabilities in this area. Similar shifts
were taking place among bilateral aid donors. In the mid-1990s Britain's
Department for International Development (DFID), after many years
of rather frosty approaches to the task of distributing the Queen's lar-
gesse, conducted a policy review and consequently shifted in the direction of participation. In describing the change, Pippa Bird, the rural
development policy specialist, cited the Roman poet Horace: "We cannot impose our version of help." She and others felt that the DFID-
supported project to protect the Lago Mamirauá Ecological Reserve in
western Brazil's upper Amazon region (described in chapter 7) was one
of the most effectively participatory of such efforts anywhere. With the
arrival of Tony Blair in 1997, the concept of development assistance
gained greater favor in official London, the DFID's administrator
achieved cabinet rank, and the budget shot upward. Local participation,

in managing forests and elsewhere, formed the centerpiece for the agency's new mission statement.

As for the United States, it is difficult to assemble a clear picture from the muddle of a long-confused development assistance effort. For many years Washington tended to see foreign aid not just as a progressive force for social change but also as a political weapon, to be used in order to maintain the "stability" of nations and regimes in power. The torrents of bilateral aid that flowed from the United States into Brazil after the 1964 military coup, in which a left-leaning elected president was ousted, seemed more directed at containing "communism" than at building a more equitable and less hierarchical nation. To this day those who seek genuine development in poor nations find fault with the high costs of U.S. military and paramilitary assistance to regimes it wants to shore up. In Latin America, quixotic and expensive U.S. efforts to stamp out drug traffic with high-tech machinery, such as the current paramilitary effort that has sent Night Hawk helicopters to hapless Colombia, have distorted bilateral relationships. Problems plaguing the U.S. Agency for International Development (USAID) have included often uninspired leadership and a surfeit of confusing mandates from the U.S. Congress, which rises from its usual apathy about foreign aid only to become meddlesome, and a chronic shortage of funds. Of all donor nations the United States has ranked the lowest in development assistance as a percentage of GNP, and even though various divisions of USAID began working on biodiversity and tropical deforestation as early as the late 1970s, it was only a decade later that top-level administrators began paying more than lip service to environmental considerations. Since USAID's decision making is decentralized, its performance in any individual country bears a direct relationship to the competence and interests of that country's mission director.

All that said, USAID's progress during the 1990s has placed it in the vanguard among donor agencies in supporting community forestry initiatives and strengthening local organizations, as well as in pushing recalcitrant national governments in the direction of institutional reform. In the Philippines, the local USAID mission has been a staunch partner of the Institute of Environmental Science for Social Change, the fierce defender of local peoples' rights (described in chapter 1). USAID was one of the leaders in efforts to invigorate Nepal's long-dormant joint forest management program. In those and other countries, our research has revealed that concern for the environment and concern for local stewardship have emerged as major USAID priorities.

The Organization for Economic Cooperation and Development (OECD), which works out of premises near Paris's Place de l'Etoile that splendidly isolate its staff from the issues they address, is a rich nations' club seeking orderly economic progress for member and nonmember nations alike. Its Development Assistance Committee (DAC) carefully monitors the flows of official aid from industrial nations and publishes a detailed annual report providing the details. Remarkably, in recent years the concept of "people-centered, participatory development" has become prominent in DAC rhetoric; it was noted in the 1997 *Development Cooperation* annual report as an "important paradigm shift with some quite radical implications for the practice of development cooperation."[18] The report goes on to say all the right general things about how to apply this new paradigm, using such expressions as "democratic processes," "transparency," "gender equality," "environmental sustainability," "integration with local institutions," and "operationalizing stakeholder participation in development activities." It is notable that, even if their language is stilted, such a remote and stuffy institution as the DAC should have caught the tenor of the times.

FURTHER NEEDS

In 1996 and 1997 we convened an e-mail conference with a worldwide group of some forty experts in forestry and forest policy to review the question of what further steps the international community could take to improve its approaches to the forest problem. Most of the ideas that won the group's consensus involve international donor policies and practices. While the group clearly recognized the powerful role of private corporations in today's global economy, there was also the feeling that donors in many respects could exercise leadership by pioneering new approaches and new kinds of partnerships that would encourage more powerful forces to do the same. The beginning of the answer, the group agreed, would be for the development banks to complete the shifts in philosophy and direction on which they have embarked. Despite the brave rhetoric of recent years and the evidence of tangible change, most participants felt that these institutions have not yet fully abandoned the autocratic, secretive, and top-down manner of thinking to which they had long been accustomed. They have yet to fully stop making unilateral decisions about how money should be spent, planning ways to spend it that conform to their own institutional requirements rather than to the needs of the intended beneficiaries, and expecting positive results to occur at regular quarterly intervals. They need to become far more open-ended, flexible, and more responsive to local needs; they need to work at a smaller scale and issue smaller grant increments.

Making such shifts would involve further revision in how the donors allocate responsibilities in planning for rural development. Gone are the days when positive outcomes are likely to be achieved, if they ever were achieved, as the result of expensive visits by large delegations of donor Ph.D.'s to hapless villages deep in the interior of poor countries. By and large, our group felt, donors should stay out of microplanning at the local level, leaving this task in the hands of community-based institutions, well-intentioned intermediary nongovernmental organizations (if available), or properly motivated government institutions. Even at this level, where representatives of these smaller agencies will usually need to participate in planning and modeling exercises, it is important for local people to play the leading roles in envisioning their future and the pathways to progress. In instances of disagreement about what needs to be done, Socratic approaches to the debate are likely to be more productive than dogmatic ones. Transparency, in the implementation of projects as well as in their design, is a characteristic of fundamental importance. Since the good projects that are developed by participatory and transparent procedures often take far longer to emerge than do projects that are simply willed into being, donors are well advised not to act precipitously with regard either to planning or to funding. Ten-year project cycles will often be more appropriate than the more customary two- or three-year time frames.

Moving in such directions will compel the big donors to do far more of their work in the capitals than out in the field. In their past dealings with often corrupt officials in government ministries, they often set conditions to their loans and grants, stating that the next loan or increment would not be forthcoming unless the country had done something that the lender had wanted it to do. Our review group felt that aid agencies should continue to seek opportunities to apply such conditions, especially ones having to do with devolution, equity, and local participation. When they are imposed, it was stressed, they should be responsive to the just demands of local civil-society groups and progressive government agencies. Conditions have often failed to prevent donor funds from being badly used and projects from failing, and they have sometimes backfired, bringing accusations that the donors lack sensitivity to recipient needs and cultures. When this sort of friction seems likely, aid agencies are advised to apply the principle of selectivity, wherein the donor clearly establishes the ground rules for support in advance and negotiates detailed agreements only with those countries that agree to them.

Donors, as they say they know, need to be very careful about underwriting commercial logging projects in inhabited but little disturbed natural forest areas. Our group did not rule out the possibility that donors will find opportunities to invest in productive and sustainable community-based logging or agroforestry activities. Through several new experimental mechanisms multilateral donors have already begun to demonstrate the effectiveness of financing smaller-scale development efforts. Microcredit facilities, such as those now functioning well in many cities and towns, can usefully be extended via the private sector to individuals, small user groups, and local communities whose subsistence depends on harvesting forest resources and selling or trading them. In negotiating community forestry deals, the donors need to try hard to establish whether their own task managers are observing their stated policies regarding local participation. Then the donors need to make sure that their funds do not get short-circuited in the capital or fall into the hands of corrupt local politicians, but instead actually reach the community-based and community-supportive institutions for which they are intended.

International donors can do little directly to generate internal domestic support for changes in land tenure and property rights that would benefit local communities. They can help by being selective about supporting individual land-titling efforts, usually limiting these to urban peripheries, and often by encouraging the formation of community land trusts as alternatives to individual registrations. They can also back national-level research and policy advocacy efforts to remove the legal constraints to, and create legal incentives for, sustainable community-based forest management. They should emphasize the development of public interest environmental law institutions that focus on the problems, potentials, and aspirations of rural resource users, including forest-dependent communities. In many parts of the developing world, nongovernmental organizations are following the U.S. example in using and changing the law as a means of achieving environmental progress. This trend requires the maximum possible encouragement. Experimentation with more decentralized forest tenure and management systems will also benefit from donor-supported practices that reduce the risks to civil servants of relinquishing control.

Good information is an essential prerequisite to direct actions that will support community-based forest management, and here there are many useful roles for the international community of donors, researchers, and scholars. In collecting data it is important to achieve understanding both of bioregional conditions and of the sociopolitical situation. One model for this sort of data collection is the International Forestry Resources and Institutions (IFRI) program at Indiana University. After extensive field testing of its detailed, collaborative, and comprehensive research strategy, IFRI established in-country research centers in Bolivia, Nepal, and Uganda. Sustained long-term funding is required to maintain these centers. Similar new centers are required in other critical regions. Among other information collectors whose work requires additional support are the Center for International Forestry Research in Bogor, Indonesia, the FAO's Forests, Trees, and People Program, the Environment and Policy Institute at the East-West Center in Honolulu, the International Institute for Sustainable Development, and the Overseas Development Institute in London.

More field research is badly needed. Academic researchers should particularly be funded to analyze the economic benefits of local forest management, to develop criteria and indicators for success in sustainable local forest management, and to review the effects of international trade policies and distortions on forest-dependent communities. Another important area of research is the assessment of the environmental or ecological trade-offs from community forestry as compared to "scientific" conservation approaches. Moreover, anecdotal evidence shows that community forestry does guarantee more social and economic benefits to the local people, but that more empirical data is needed to strengthen the case and counter arguments such as the insensitive hypothesis about the domestic value of tropical forests advanced by Chomitz and Kumari.

The links between power and communications skills grow ever stronger. As the costs of computer technology and associated services decline and the benefits of reaching out increase, it becomes ever more important for donors to equip nongovernmental organizations (especially at the community level) with appropriate skills and hardware. For grassroots-level organizations a computer is a more valuable possession than a small tract of marginal land. At the other end of the communications spectrum, the World Bank and other aid agencies still too often edit out large portions of the most useful material in their extensive internal reports, then send the rest to the public information office. The need for secrecy is not apparent. There is, conversely, a great need for far more information about the donors' own experience with participatory forest management projects. Publication of such materials in local as well as mainstream languages would be helpful. The wondrous efficiency of the Internet greatly eases the task of distributing this information.

At the broadest level, it will still be desirable for the donors to put a full stop to the nonforest activities that still contribute, at some times in some places, to the forest problem. Forests absolutely must be fully considered in donor assessments of structural adjustment efforts and contemplated support for dam, road, mining, or agribusiness projects. Proposed new directions for World Bank loans to the forest sector offer reasons for encouragement, but what remains to be seen is how willing the staff will be to, first, dismantle bureaucratic rigidities and truly integrate forest lending into its overall strategies to alleviate poverty; second, work effectively with private partners; and, third, bring alive its newly stated goal of improving national governance. Planning for forests and agriculture needs far more careful coordination at the FAO. Designated as the U.N. agency responsible for forests, FAO is overwhelmingly biased toward agriculture. It needs to emphasize the forest sector (especially community forestry and its Forests, Trees, and People Program) to a far greater extent. Forest communities should help plan not just forestry activities but also agricultural and other rural development projects that will affect the forest.

NONGOVERNMENTAL ORGANIZATIONS IN THE SPOTLIGHT

In all of the foregoing, national and international nongovernmental organizations have become the increasingly visible, strong, and useful observers, critics, and partners of donors and villagers alike. As late as the 1970s there was virtually no such thing as organized opposition to the accelerating forest decline perpetuated by deliberate government actions, aid donor practices, and the practices of almost totally unregulated private industries. Thousands of citizen-led environmental organizations have since sprung up, and 1,400 made it to the 1992 Earth Summit to participate in the lively "NGO Forum," which paralleled the official proceedings. These organizations are not just protesting. They are helping to make and change national laws and policies, sitting with government representatives on official delegations at national meetings, and actively working to improve the system. They have constructively blurred the lines between environmental concern and concern for human welfare and economic development.

After the 1972 Stockholm Conference on the Human Environment advanced the refreshing idea that economic and environmental progress could be achieved together, the international environmental community began taking greater interest in addressing human concerns as well as protection for other species. The WWF program titled Wildlands and Human Needs, launched early in the 1980s with support from USAID, the Moriah Foundation, and several other private donors, was an early manifestation of this new idea. Highly participatory activities were launched, with varying degrees of success, in such places as the southeast coast of St. Lucia, the national parks of Zambia, and village communities bordering Thailand's Khao Yai National Park. Although opposed by fundraisers who worried that helping poor people as well as plants and animals would muddle the WWF message, and criticized by evaluators who correctly reported that WWF biologists were not necessarily good social engineers, the principles of local participation and concern for human well-being have more than survived: at the WWF and in many other quarters, they have become gospel.

A growing number of other U.S.-based environmental groups—among them The Nature Conservancy, Conservation International, the World Resources Institute, the National Wildlife Federation, the National Audubon Society, and the Natural Resources Defense Council—were by the mid-1980s active internationally. Motivated primarily by a will to halt environmental decline and to strengthen the world's system of parks and protected areas, these organizations also began to compete against each other for the attention of donors and the public. Sometimes the partnerships they forged with local nongovernmental organizations seemed designed more for public relations purposes at home than to strengthen environmental movements in target countries. Nonetheless many of the still small and struggling local organizations have found ways to play the international organizations and donors off against each other, and they have rapidly grown in strength and sophistication.

Washington-based nongovernmental organizations have become intimately involved not only in the affairs of the United Nations and its agencies but also in those of the formerly standoffish World Bank and, especially, the Global Environment Facility (GEF), a fund that the bank manages in partnership with the United Nations Environment Program and the United Nations Development Program. By no means do all nongovernmental organizations feel that the process of reform within the bank is complete. Commenting on a recent independent analysis of the GEF, economist Korinna Horta of the Environmental Defense Fund recently wrote:

> The bank continues to prepare detailed development strategies for entire countries without consideration of their environmental implications. Worse, the evaluation finds that in many cases the GEF may represent a perverse incentive. It quotes a leading World Bank official, who states that regular financial assistance for investments in renewable energy and conservation may have actually declined, since bank staff now look to the GEF to deal with such matters.[19]

Rather than sit on the sidelines and take potshots at the World Bank, however, even skeptics within nongovernmental organizations are more willing to enter the bank's newly opened doorways and work shoulder-to-shoulder with bank officials in efforts to discuss and improve the bank's policies, practices, and operations. Much of this work is aimed at making the GEF more effective. Nongovernmental organizations not only want direct mid-sized grants through the GEF but also seek modifications in the bank's cumbersome financial management procedures, which are designed for large loans to governments. Such changes would expedite the flow of GEF funds to small but urgently needed environmental projects. Nongovernmental organizations have been exercising leadership in lobbying for new monies for the GEF even though this fund has been something of a disappointment to date.[20]

Beyond the effort to improve the GEF and shift its focus beyond the mainstream business practices of the World Bank, nongovernmental organizations have also made their way toward the heart of bank affairs. Representatives from organizations the world over have been deeply involved in the bank's most recent review of its forest sector strategy. The WWF is the bank's equal partner in the ambitious Alliance for Forest Conservation and Sustainable Use, whose overall goal is to achieve protection for no less than 10 percent of each of the world's principal forest types. In 1998 World Bank president Wolfensohn convened an ad hoc panel of leading private sector industrialists, who discussed ways to bring sustainable management to the forests they control; significantly, the leaders of nongovernmental organizations as well as corporate chief executives were seated around the table. Biologist Thomas Lovejoy, for many years a fixture at the WWF and later at the Smithsonian Institution, more recently began working part-time at the World Bank as a principal environmental adviser. One of his major concerns, he says, is to do his utmost to persuade the bank to formulate a *forests* policy rather than a *forestry* policy.[21]

While improving relations with official aid givers, nongovernmental organizations have also begun to pay far greater attention to private corporations. While official development assistance remains flat and far below the 1 percent of GNP once envisioned, the infusion of private capital has soared as the international business community has seen increasing promise in the many newly liberated economies across the developing world. A challenge for the new century, equivalent to that once posed by the multinational development banks, has become to push the flourishing private sector business community toward improving its own environmental standards—or persuade its leaders that better environmental stewardship will help the bottom line.

Great hope rests with "joint implementation," a carbon sequestration scheme in which polluting companies can trade the right to domestic carbon dioxide emissions if they help save forests that store carbon elsewhere. The idea emerged from the 1992 Earth Summit in Rio de Janeiro, and it has become a striking example of the interaction between corporations and nongovernmental organizations. The Nature Conservancy and its local partners are among the organizations that have worked hard to broker such trades with U.S. firms. The nongovernmental organizations reserve the right to judge whether the site to be protected contains sufficient biodiversity to make the grade. Participating companies regard these transactions as investments, not tax-deductible write-offs.

The Mexico-based Forest Stewardship Council has become the leader in pressing to get forest-products companies to commit themselves to environmentally responsible methods of wood harvesting. Along with "buyers' groups" in a number of countries, the council also seeks to build consumer demand for products from well-managed forests. Many nongovernmental organizations seek ways to approach the problem of supply not simply by increasing it but by reducing demand, asking the consumers of wood and wood products to switch to alternative materials or to reuse or recycle more wood. A highly promising initiative is the World Resources Institute's Global Forest Watch, which monitors forest cover, forest condition, and major development activities in key forest nations. By early 2000, working with a diverse assortment of seventy-five local partners, the institute had already launched Global Forest Watch activities in four countries, and plans call for the program to encompass twenty-one countries, containing 75 percent of all the world's forests, by the end of 2005. Promoting transparency and accountability are principal goals of this effort, and so is decentralization. Nigel Sizer, former forest policy director at the institute, sees the initiative as a clear and promising alternative to the babble produced by the U.N. agencies. "Forests cannot be cared for through edicts from globetrotting diplomats and experts," he wrote. "Instead, the U.N. agencies should encourage partnerships with dynamic civil society and community-led initiatives that can protect and manage forests for future generations."[22]

While learning to work more effectively with the private sector as well as with other elements of society, nongovernmental organizations have also improved their ability to relate better to each other. Thanks in large measure to the success of the campaign to reform the policies of the multinational development banks (described in chapter 7), relations between local and international nongovernmental organizations have become more cooperative and less marked by suspicion and hostility. Today each side tends to be more aware of and sensitive to the other's needs. Local organizations educate their northern counterparts as to local realities. Domestic organizations enhance the credibility of projects and improve access to government and private sector leaders. International organizations, meanwhile, supply new technologies, training, planning, communications and management skills, and scientific expertise. They also help put grant proposals into formats to which international donors are accustomed.

Conflict continues over how scarce funds are allocated, with local nongovernmental organizations preferring to get support directly rather than have it channeled through international intermediaries. International organizations, on the other hand, claim that there is still much they can do to help the local organizations gain power and become more professional. With staff deployed in the field, international groups are also able to help donors make discerning selections of local partners and grantees. An equilibrium has emerged in which each side has learned to build on the strengths and capabilities of the other.

If nongovernmental organizations generally have become increasingly effective as bridges between forest communities, national governments, and international agencies, demonstrating their growing ability to work both at the grassroots level and in the international arena, they too need to refine their skills. Too many development-oriented organizations harbor old-fashioned links between development and security and still lack sensitivity to economic-environmental linkages and the importance of the new connections between environmental stability and human rights. Environmental groups still often send out field biologists to organize complex social engineering projects that require extra training in development and management techniques. The representatives of developing nations often criticize international and northern nongovernmental organizations for placing their own needs above those of the clientele they are there to assist; these tendencies must be curbed, and training once again can help. Conservation groups are still widely accused of too often favoring strict protection for nature over the needs of local people.

A vast challenge lies ahead for environmental organizations in their quest for sustainable forms of development. National governments, and many within the international community, will continue to resist these improvements for the sake of heedless, anti-environmental "growth." Still, the important political and economic power shift that has taken place has given the nongovernmental organizations their best chance ever to arrest environmental decline and shift the world on new courses toward environmentally sound economic progress. Donors have done much to adjust to the need for far more careful thought about the ever closer relationship between the economic and the environmental consequences of what they do. If the funds available to them are tiny relative to those available to private business, they can still exercise leadership and show the way. If there is hope, it lies in the useful interactions between these communities and their beneficiaries at the local level, rather than in the droning deliberations of an international political system that seldom gets to the point.

CHAPTER 10

Future Imperatives

Jesse Ausubel, director of the Program for the Human Environment at The Rockefeller University in New York City, sees hope in the global trend toward what he calls precision agriculture. The cropland needed to feed a single person was more than one acre in 1950, he calculates. Now the figure is only about half an acre. "If during the next sixty or seventy years the world farmer reaches the average yield of today's U.S. corn grower," he reckons, "10 billion people will need only half of to-day's cropland. The land spared exceeds Amazonia. . . . In other words, if innovation and diffusion continue as usual, feeding people will not stress habitat for nature."[1]

Ausubel estimates that by 2050 shrinking cropland requirements will make a huge positive contribution to the planet's stability, liberating 100 million hectares of land for reforestation. He finds other reasons for optimism. The human population growth rate is down. Total per capita water use is down. Future U.S. demand for wood products will weaken thanks to recycling and competition from other materials. Prices may even fall, reducing the incentive to log. Overall, he finds, more and more countries will in the future replicate the experience of the United States, where forest losses peaked a century ago and a strong comeback (in size, if not quality) has more recently occurred. "Our vision," Ausubel concludes, "should be the *expansion* of the forest estate."[2]

The biologist George Woodwell, director and president of the Woods Hole Research Center in Massachusetts, holds less sanguine views. He sees ample signs of "progressive failure" as the "human enterprise" fills the earth, and he considers "the harvest of residual forests for profits from timber" to be a persistent form of exploitation requiring major readjustments in the management of human affairs. "The destruction of forests, even if the land is left as forestland to recover through succession, is always impoverishing," he writes. "Where is the largest public interest? It is not difficult to define it. It does not lie in timbering and mining concessions imposed from outside at the expense of forest dwellers, no matter a long history of disenfranchisement. Nor is there any overriding law that says all primary forests must be harvested for profit." No one, he continues, is "telling the poor how to be rich enough to buy the products of industrialized agriculture or fix the ills of agricultural poisons."[3]

Even if Ausubel's optimism for the long term proves to be justified, at least for developed parts of the planet, the severe stresses that Woodwell highlights are also bound to occur in many regions during the interim, especially within the nations of the equatorial belt that are the concern of this book. These are the areas where the highest population growth rates and the highest forest loss rates persist, where sound governance and competent management from central authorities are the hardest to come by, where the temptation to cash in now is the greatest. What is required to save what is left of the forests of such nations, we conclude, goes deeper than the technical promise of "precision agriculture" or the spread of high-yielding tree monocultures. Helpful as such innovations may eventually become, they are not likely to do much for present generations of poor people who depend on forests that in many places continue to recede from their grasp.

Many developing countries will need to double their food production by 2020 if they are to feed burgeoning populations. In such places further forest conversion for agriculture is inevitable. Past patterns of agricultural growth in developing countries provide scant reason for encouragement. Most successful breakthroughs have occurred in well-endowed agroecological zones and have involved intensive use of irrigation water and of fertilizers and pesticides. The Green Revolution, which has enabled many developing countries to feed themselves since the mid-1960s, has been limited largely to irrigated rice and wheat-growing regions. Agriculture based on the intensive use of modern inputs easily lends itself to mismanagement, with dire consequences for the environment, particularly when managed by small farmers with little technical knowledge. Unlike developed countries with agricultural surpluses, most developing countries cannot simply switch to low-input farming systems because they cannot afford the associated reduction in yields. If India were to return to pre–Green Revolution technologies, for instance, it is said that close to half the current population would go hungry. The way out is strewn with hazards.

For all the talk of sustainable forestry, as it is said to be practiced commercially in places like Sweden and North America, evidence mounts that many loggers in such places still function just barely within the law and beyond the grasp of regulators. According to the Maine Forest Service, for example, entirely uncontrolled "liquidation harvesting" is occurring from one end of the state to the other. Practitioners leave just enough timber standing to avoid being labeled as illegal clear-cutters while removing virtually all harvestable timber to make a quick dollar and leaving the land open for development. The Natural Resources Council of Maine reported that "there are serious problems in Maine's forests that threaten the future of Maine's people, economy, and environment." The report concluded, "Not a pretty picture."[4] But it is far prettier than those presented by the fully despoiled landscapes in many parts of Madagascar, El Salvador, Indonesia's Kalimantan island, or any other poor country where migratory loggers find politicians an easy mark. Suriname, alas, is only an exception.

Countering Ausubel's forecast of flattening demand for industrial wood products in the developed world is the prospect of increased consumption within developing countries. By 2020, although opinions vary as to the exact figure, global demand seems likely to grow from the present level of 1.6 million cubic meters a year to about 2.4 billion cubic meters a year.[5] Production from temperate forests and from industrial wood plantations in developing countries will meet rising portions of this demand, but for all the theoretical advantages associated with the movement of industrial forestry into the Southern Hemisphere, practical problems remain. Tighter rules, incentives, and financial and technical support could minimize the damage and concentrate the plantations on agricultural wastelands or cut-over degraded forests rather than in areas that retain high biodiversity values. Such a tidy outcome is hardly likely in countries that will continue to be plagued by weak and corrupt governance. Some of the new tree plantations will inevitably replace natural forests, which will be cut and burned, and some portion of the demand will be met, often illegally, by slashing yet deeper into the natural forest. Amazonian forests will continue to recede as frontiers for ranching and agricultural monocultures continue their advance, and the same fate awaits much of the Indonesian forest, which was widely burned again in 2000 to make way for palm oil plantations. "Given current trends," says researcher Gary Bull, "most industrial logging by mainstream industry in forest undisturbed by man will have halted by 2030."[6] For those who are forest dependent, that means three long decades of further displacement.

Current world consumption of fuelwood accounts for more than half of all wood production. Projecting the future of this demand is not easy. "In many countries, notably western and sub-Saharan Africa," says a World Resources Institute analysis, "fuelwood consumption exceeds the average replenishment of trees by 30 to 200 percent."[7] As household collectors (usually women and children) need to walk ever farther in search of wood to burn, usage becomes more sparing. Many people have turned to burning agricultural residues in place of wood. New and more efficient kinds of wood-burning stoves have become available, and they can be widely distributed at no great cost. The old legend of the egg frying on the sidewalk during summer heat waves comes alive with the appearance of new and efficient stoves that use only solar energy. Agro-forestry systems that produce fuelwood as a byproduct can be encouraged. For all that, however, it seems certain that rural well-being in many parts of the world will indefinitely continue to rely heavily on access to ever scarcer supplies of fuelwood that are harvested unsustainably from traditional sources.

Against these unrelenting sources of pressure on tropical land and forests is arrayed the battery of official institutions that are meant to cope with them. Once again, reasons for hope are in short supply. As Woodwell says, not only do governments fail to control the activities of loggers, miners, ranchers, and others who damage the world's forests; they are often active partners in the destructive enterprises, whether overtly or behind the scenes. Management of parks and protected areas is often slipshod and insufficiently concerned with the needs and skills of local people. In many lands "forest police" continue to harass community forest managers. Many new foresters, says Tashi Wangchuck of Bhutan, a recent graduate of the Yale University School of Forestry and Environmental Studies, are still being trained to believe in the virtues of establishing "strict nature reserves" and denying local people access to the fullest extent possible.[8]

As we have pointed out, no agency of the United Nations seems capable of winning the attention or funds required to stop the hemorrhage in the world's forestlands. Even though the World Bank and other donor agencies have been struggling toward reform and are currently emphasizing forest protection over forest production far more than in the past, their "first imperative," as the prominent Australian forester Neil Byron puts it, remains to justify their existence and expansion by "transacting business," too often in ways far behind the cutting edge.[9] Still today the banks shovel out the money faster than they can fully measure its results or check to see that policies dutifully proclaimed at headquarters are actually being adhered to in the field. Claiming to be overwhelmed by the rapid growth of private sector capital, they say modestly that they have little influence anymore. Many of them still have far to go in making up for their past omissions and counterproductive past practices, and they are missing many opportunities for innovative leadership.

Many observers are persuaded that approaches involving only public officials are categorically doomed to failure. They fear that economic remedies will be no more than Band-Aids and that the political discussions will inconclusively dither on while tropical deforestation and global forest degradation continue. They warn, ever more shrilly, that government officials backed by powerful special interests, often facing severe constitutional impediments to action, will not ever be likely to commit either their own nations or the world to new systems of forest controls and priorities that truly represent the interests of civil society. For substantive improvement to take place, it is ever more widely believed, the civil society itself will have to take the lead.

In this regard, a notable and hopeful feature of the official policy dialogue in recent years has been the influence of nongovernmental organizations within it. These organizations are far from without their own shortcomings, but as we have emphasized in these pages, they have grown fast in sophistication as well as in power and they are increasingly effective as representatives of the civil society vis-à-vis the official institutions. Especially important is the extent to which nongovernmental organizations in poor countries are now serving as bridges between national governments and the local communities that form civil society's bedrock. The Indonesian Environmental Forum and the Peru-based Coordinadora de las Organizaciones Indígenas de la Cuenca Amazónica (COICA) in Amazonia are examples. Thousands upon thousands of other increasingly competent organizations in the Southern Hemisphere, many five years old or less and many supported by creative private donors such as the Ford and MacArthur Foundations and the Rockefeller philanthropies, deal with environmental, human rights, sustainable development, and anticorruption issues. Collectively these

groups are helping governments—if they are at all willing to yield power
to local people—to place responsibility for forest management in the
right hands rather than those of local politicians who are not any more
likely than their national counterparts to improve things.

Empowering local communities hardly guarantees an easy ride toward stable forests. Friction will prevail in instances where local people
are totally denied traditional access to forests that are designated as parks
or protected areas. Even if honest and authentic community representatives gain control and local officials show sympathy, there is no guarantee that the forest will be saved. "There are indeed convincing examples of sustainable use of forests by traditional societies," says the
British forester and professor J.E.M. Arnold, a veteran with decades of
fieldwork in Asia under his belt. "But it defies one to know how, in the
modern world, communities can re-create the religious and mytholog-
ical constraints that have been so effective in the past in dissuading
individual transgression." Population growth imposes mounting pressure on forests that mature slowly, he continues, and he has yet to see
an example of "consistently strong and uncorrupt community leadership
over the necessary time period." Community ownership and management can only work, he concludes, if the advice and, "where necessary,
the authority, of forest specialists" is available and heeded.[10]

Touché. But even if Arnold's warning is warranted in places, the
general failure of other forest management systems leaves the world
with no better a bet than community empowerment. We do not recommend abandoning all other kinds of efforts to save forests. This approach will always remain one of many pathways toward improvement.
In our judgement, however, it is both the most neglected, at the moment, and the most likely to achieve positive results. This was our hypothesis when we began the research for this book in 1994. Although
our views have become more nuanced, nothing in our subsequent travels, experiences, readings, or conversations shakes our fundamental conviction about this. Witnessing the wisdom and skills of uneducated local
people with few possessions has, if anything, reinforced them. So has

the evidence we have accumulated of official apathy, neglect, and inadequacy.

For all the forces arrayed on the side of the status quo, changing circumstances in a variety of respects favor the dispersal of forest power. As developing countries industrialize, traditional timber tycoons are losing political clout to other, faster-growing, business power centers. Logging king Bob Hasan of Indonesia may have been the last of his ilk. With little or no commercial timber left to harvest in countries such as the Philippines, Nigeria, and Thailand—countries that have become net importers of wood products—many newer avenues for economic development are seen as more promising. More accurate measurement technologies, available to anyone, are showing with ever greater precision the adverse economic and environmental consequences of deforestation. The glare of increased media attention has highlighted many instances of policy failure and corruption, evidence of a new need for governments and companies to be more prudent than before about their attitude toward forests and more open to new ideas and new approaches. "Today it is simply not possible for companies to get away with bad corporate practice and not expect some coverage in the media, " says Pippa Bird.[11]

While large development agencies are still dragging their feet and are often unable to put policy fully into practice, they have long since articulated their underlying belief in participation and in the inclusion of the civil society. The task now is making it work. Progress has been made in this regard as well. "Of course there is some resistance," says Bird. "The old business of the old dog and new spots. But a shift really has happened. There's been a revolution at DFID in the past five years, and it's not just that the Labour government has more interest in us. It all started well before Tony Blair. It's a completely different place now. We know how to do local participation on the ground. We really do."[12]

In Bangkok in 1997 I attended a gathering of 183 people from twenty-nine countries for a program called "Community Forestry at a Crossroads," which had been convened by the Regional Community

Forestry Training Center at Kasetsart University. The distinguished international group included ubiquitous Ford Foundation representatives, World Conservation Union forestry coordinator Donald A. Gilmour, and such country experts as Kaji Shrestha from Nepal and the articulate Mahdu Sarin, a professor from India. Most delegates felt that over the past decade growing sophistication had been achieved in their circles about what makes communal forms of managing forests at the local or village level work or not work. They reviewed the techniques of group dynamics, data collection, and information dissemination that can make this form of governance an improvement over the top-down mechanisms that had long prevailed.

The idea had won growing acceptance in official circles as the "most legitimate form of land management," said Gilmour, and it was well on its way to becoming national policy in many countries even though this shift would weaken the power of many government people. The question now was not whether community forestry will survive, it was whether governments would "expropriate" the concept, as Sarin put it, and turn it into "just another government program," enhancing the power of local power elites, or a peoples' movement that would offer broad benefits for most people.[13]

Arnold is of course right in expressing fears about the effects of population pressures on some forests, but politics is more often the reason why underprivileged people get forced out onto unproductive land, argues Gill Shepherd. "In more promising situations," she said, "higher population density may in fact be accompanied by *increased* tree cover, as contiguous farms and increasingly remote forest force farmers to invest in highly productive hedgerows and on-farm tree planting of various kinds."[14] No matter at what level the human population stops growing, moreover, there is no doubt that the demographic transition to lower population growth rates favors even tropical forests and forest-dependent local communities.

Subsistence farming will far from disappear. Indeed, this book's ideas and recommendations are largely targeted to the world's neediest rural people. Yet the demographic shift toward cities can also be helpful. Two Amazonian cities now have seven-figure populations; the region's population will soon be 70 percent urban. With the environmental problems of Amazonia becoming ever more ones of slums and shanties as well as of forest cutting and burning and of advancing agricultural frontiers, the chances of saving the preponderance of its remaining primary forest have improved somewhat. They will improve further if national and local officials follow the route so well and wisely taken in Acre's Mamirauá region. If David Western's prophesy is true, and Africa's rural populations increase by no more than 50 percent, the task of managing rural and forest sectors will greatly ease.

For nations endowed with the kinds of forests that attract hikers or ecotourists, recreational travel represents a growing economic opportunity. Travel is now the world's biggest industry, and what is broadly defined as ecotourism is a dynamic portion of it. Some of the nations that have tried to cash in have suffered. One example is Nepal. Visitors there have grown in numbers from 2,000 in 1970 to some 300,000 in the late 1990s, and the adverse environmental consequences are sadly visible everywhere. In contrast is Belize, a small country that has profited wisely from making tourism the biggest single factor in the national economy. Another positive example is Bhutan, where limited numbers of visitors are still greeted as "guests of the people" and pay $200 a day for the privilege. Launched only in 1971, when the country suddenly felt its first need to earn foreign exchange, the tourism industry ranked sixth in the national economy in 1999, and it was the top foreign exchange earner. Change is everywhere in this remote and beautiful Himalayan land, but the pace of tourism has increased gradually. Tourists here stay on the main trails and pay for their upkeep. Bhutan's experience compares favorably with that of Nepal, which faced a "sudden onslaught" of tourism, and it bodes well for the future of the kingdom's well-forested national parks. Local people are allowed access to resources that seem likely to stay around for a while.[15]

Local participation in managing forests not only saves trees; it also leads to improved human rights for many people, especially women, and to fairer and more equitable societies. Those who exploit the forests unsustainably have no sense of history, no sense of place, no sense of where the public interest lies. One cannot expect forest policies to change sharply in favor of the public interest in countries that do not have a more general concern for equity, openness, and participation. Even in countries that do have those tendencies, strong forces will continue to oppose policy reform. Nonetheless, we have an unprecedented opportunity to score gains for forests across the globe. Perception of the threats that environmental degradation poses to humanity and the planet has sharpened, and the strength of citizen-driven campaigns to protect the world's natural resources, including its forests, is growing rapidly. The people have their best chance in centuries to get their forests back.

NOTES

INTRODUCTION

1. Nigel Sizer, with Lars Laestadius, Marta Miranda, and Michael Totten, "Drawing the Line? Toward a New Policy Agenda for the World's Forests," unpublished draft issues paper (Washington, D.C.: World Resources Institute, 1999), 7.

2. Mark Poffenberger and Betsy McGean, eds., *Upland Philippine Communities: Guardians of the Final Forest Frontiers* (Berkeley: Center for Southeast Asia Studies, University of California, 1993), 35.

CHAPTER 1. FOREST USE AND MISUSE

1. Nigel Sizer, with Lars Laestadius, Marta Miranda, and Michael Totten, "Drawing the Line? Toward a New Policy Agenda for the World's Forests," unpublished draft issues paper (Washington, D.C.: World Resources Institute, 1999), 3.

2. The United Nations Conference on Environment and Development, *Agenda 21: Programme of Action for Sustainable Development* (New York: United Nations, 1992), para. 11.1.

3. Sizer et al., "Drawing the Line?" 3.

4. Nancy Lee Peluso, *Rich Forests, Poor People: Resource Control and Resistance in Java* (Berkeley: University of California Press, 1992), 36.

5. These and many other examples can be drawn from John Perlin, *A Forest Journey* (Cambridge, Mass.: Harvard University Press, 1989), 282.

6. Peluso, *Rich Forests*, 36.

7. Betty J. Meggers, *Amazonia: Man and Culture in a Counterfeit Paradise* (Chicago: Aldine-Atherton Inc., 1971).

8. Roger D. Stone, *Dreams of Amazonia* (New York: Viking, 1985), 64.

9. Anna Roosevelt, personal communication, August 1996.

10. William M. Denevan, ed., *The Native Population of the Americas in 1592* (Madison: University of Wisconsin Press, 1976), 289.

11. Roosevelt, personal communication.

12. Gregor Hodgson and John A. Dixon, *Logging vs. Fisheries and Tourism in Palawan: An Environmental and Economic Analysis*, East-West Environment and Policy Institute Occasional Paper 7 (Honolulu: East-West Center, 1988).

13. Worldwatch Institute, *Worldwatch Briefing on the Yangtze Flood* (Washington, D.C.: Worldwatch Institute, 1998), 1.

14. See chapter 5, p. 146, for details.

15. Stephanie Fried and Stephan Schwartzman, *Rainforest Fires in Indonesia and Brazil: The U.S. Link* (New York: Environmental Defense Fund, 1998), 2.

16. Very detailed coverage of these points is available in Emily Matthews, Richard Payne, Mark Rohweder, and Siobhan Murray, *Pilot Analysis of Global Ecosystems: Forest Ecosystems* (Washington, D.C.: World Resources Institute, 2000).

17. World Bank–World Wildlife Fund Alliance for Forest Conservation and Sustainable Use, *1999 Annual Report* (Washington, D.C.: Alliance for Forest Conservation and Sustainable Use, 2000), 6.

18. Walter Reid, personal communication, January 2001.

19. Edward O. Wilson, ed., *Biodiversity* (Washington, D.C.: National Academy Press, 1988).

20. H. N. Kamara, *Firewood Energy in Sierra Leone: Production, Marketing, and Household Use Patterns* (Hamburg: Verlag Weltarchiv, 1986).

21. Kojo Sebastian Amanor, *Managing Trees in the Farming System: The Perspectives of Farmers* (Kumasi, Ghana: Planning Branch, Forestry Department, 1996), 93.

22. Gill Shepherd, *Restoring the Landscape: Proposals for a Participatory Ap-*

proach to Managing the Darwda Escarpment (London: Overseas Development Institute, 1995).

23. Martha Honey, *Ecotourism and Sustainable Development: Who Owns Paradise?* (Washington, D.C.: Island Press, 1999), 9.

24. D. A. Gilmour, "Conservation and Development: Seeking the Linkages," in *Community Development and Conservation of Forest Biodiversity through Community Forestry* (Bangkok: Regional Community Forestry Training Center, 1994).

25. Jim MacNeill, unpublished speech to the Organization for Economic Cooperation and Development, Paris, August 1997.

CHAPTER 2.
WHY TROPICAL FORESTS DECLINE

1. Stephan Schwartzman, *Brazilian Forest Policy in the Collor Government* (Washington, D.C.: Environmental Defense Fund, 1991), 4.

2. Gill Shepherd, "The Reality of the Commons," in *Forest Policies, Forest Politics*, ed. Gill Shepherd (London: Overseas Development Institute, 1992), 80.

3. Louise Fortmann, "Taking Claims: Discursive Strategies in Contesting Property," *World Development* 23, no. 6 (1995): 1053.

4. Korinna Horta, "The Last Big Rush for the Green Gold: The Plundering of Cameroon's Rainforests," *The Ecologist*, May-June 1991.

5. "Borneo's Forest Fire Catastrophe Spreads," *London Sunday Times*, 28 September 1997.

6. Asia Pacific Action Group, "The Barnett Report: A Summary of the Report of the Commission of Inquiry into Aspects of the Timber Industry in Papua New Guinea," unpublished report, 1990; for the quote see World Commission on Forests and Sustainable Development, *Our Forests, Our Future* (London: Cambridge University Press, 1999), 55.

7. "Suriname's Example," *New York Times*, 21 June 1998, p. 14.

8. World Bank and the WWF Alliance, *Annual Report* (1999), 26.

9. Robin Broad, with John Cavanaugh, *Plundering Paradise: The Struggle for the Environment in the Philippines* (Berkeley: University of California Press, 1993), 45.

10. Nigel Sizer and Richard Rice, *Backs to the Wall in Suriname: Forest Policy in a Country in Crisis* (Washington, D.C.: World Resources Institute, 1995), 1.

11. George M. Woodwell, personal communication, December 1996.

12. Tade Akim Aima and Ademela T-Salau, eds., The Challenge of Sustainable Development in Nigeria (Ibadan: Nigerian Environmental Study/Action Team, 1992), 80.

13. World Bank, "Review of Implementation of the Forest Sector Policy," unpublished paper, December 1994, p. 8.

14. These are the principal conclusions drawn from *Forest Politics* (London: Earthscan Publications Ltd., 1996), a comprehensive analysis by David Humphreys.

15. Kheryn Klubnikin, personal communication, June 1999.

16. D. A. Gilmour and R. J. Fisher, "Evolution in Community Forestry: Contesting Forest Resources," in *Community Forestry at a Crossroads* (Bangkok: Regional Community Forestry Training Center, 1997), 17.

17. Royal Forest Department-Thailand/DANCED, "Upper Nan Watershed Management Project, Stakeholder Workshops (Virum, Denmark: Ramboll 1996), 16.

18. Pinkaew Laungaramsri, "Reconstructing Nature: Community Forest Management and Its Challenge to Forest Management in Thailand," unpublished paper presented at the international seminar, "Community Forestry at a Crossroads," Regional Community Forestry Training Center, Bangkok, July 1997.

CHAPTER 3. THE ROAD TO BENDUM

1. This chapter was written by Roger D. Stone.

2. Peter Walpole, personal communication, 1997. All citations of Walpole in this chapter are from conversations with him in the Philippines during my two-week visit in July and August of that year.

3. Owen J. Lynch and Kirk Talbott, *Balancing Acts: Community-Based Forest Management and National Law in Asia and the Pacific* (Washington, D.C.: World Resources Institute, 1995), 44.

4. Robin Broad, with John Cavanaugh, *Plundering Paradise: The Struggle for the Environment in the Philippines* (Berkeley: University of California Press, 1993), 52.

5. J. C. Westoby, Forest Industries in the Attack on Underdevelopment in the State of Food and Agriculture (Rome: FAO, 1962).

6. Juan M. Pulhin, "Community Forestry: Paradoxes and Perspectives in Development Practice," unpublished doctoral thesis, Australian National University, Canberra, 1996, unpaginated.

7. Broad and Cavanaugh, *Plundering Paradise*, 32.

8. Pulhin, *Community Forestry*.

9. Datu Nestor, letter to the Indonesian secretary of environment and natural resources, 1994.

10. Datu Nestor, letter to Victor Ramos, Indonesian secretary of environment and natural resources, 1997.

11. Robin Broad, "The Poor and the Environment: Friends or Foes?" *World Development* 22, no. 6 (1994), 814.

12. One hectare, a unit in the internationally used metric system, equals 2.2 acres.

13. Victoria M. Sabban, *Community Forestry and Decentralization Policies: Reflections on Experiences from the Philippines* (Manila: Social Development Research Center, De La Salle University, 1997).

14. World Bank, "The Forest Sector," policy paper (Washington, D.C.: World Bank, 1991), 66.

15. André McCloskey, interview with Molly Kux, USAID Asia staff member, 1995.

16. Roger D. Stone attended this meeting. For further information on the Mangyan see Peter Walpole, ed., *Upland Philippine Communities: Securing Cultural and Environmental Stability* (Quezon City: Environmental Research Division, Manila Observatory, 1994).

17. Pulhin, *Community Forestry*.

CHAPTER 4. VILLAGE FORESTS IN INDIA

1. This chapter was written by Claudia D'Andrea.

2. World Bank, *India: Madhya Pradesh Forestry Project* (Washington, D.C.: World Bank, South Asia Department II, Agricultural Operations Division, 1995).

3. Mark Poffenberger and Betsy McGean, *Village Voices, Forest Choices: Joint Forest Management in India* (Delhi: Oxford University Press, 1996), 23, 57.

4. Poffenberger and McGean, *Village Voices*, 2.

5. Mark Poffenberger, with Prodyut Battacharya, Arvind Khare, Ajay Roi,

S. B. Roy, Neera Singh, Kundan Singh, *Grassroots Forest Protection: Eastern Indian Experience*s. Asia Forest Network Research Report No.7, March 1996.

6. Poffenberger and McGean, *Village Voices*, 17–18.

7. Poffenberger and McGean, *Village Voices*, 86–94.

8. Poffenberger and McGean, *Village Voices*, 324–326.

9. Poffenberger et al., *Grassroots Forest Protection*.

10. Government of India, "Circular on Joint Forest Management," official document of the Government of India, issued by the Principal Chief Conservator of Forests for India, June 1990.

11. Kamla Chowdhry, personal communication, 4 February 1996.

12. Syed Rizvi, personal communication, 5 February 1996.

13. Rizvi, personal communication.

14. Anonymous, personal communication, 7 February 1996.

15. Prodyut Battacharya, personal communication, February 1996.

16. D. P. Singh, personal communication, 8 February 1996.

17. Anonymous MPFP task officer, personal communication, 8 February 1996.

18. Anonymous MPFP task officer, personal communication.

19. M. K. Singh, personal communication, 8 February 1996.

20. Prodyut Battacharya, personal communication, 10 February 1996.

21. O. N. Kaul, personal communication, 1 February 1996.

22. Bakshish Singh, personal communication, 12 February 1996.

23. Bakshish Singh, personal communication.

24. Neera Singh, personal communication, 4 December 1996.

25. Sankharsan Hota, personal communication, 4 December 1996.

26. Sankharsan Hota, personal communication, 8 December 1996.

27. Shashi Kant, Neera Singh, and Kundan Singh, *Community Based Forest Management Systems (Case Studies from Orissa)*(Bhopal: Indian Institute of Forest Management, 1991).

28. Kant, Singh, and Singh, *Community Based Forest Management Systems*.

29. Govindo, personal communication, 10 December 1996.

30. Saktrugana Buhana, personal communication, 10 December 1996.

31. Neera Singh, personal communication, 12 December 1996.

32. Prateep Nayak, personal communication, 12 December 1996.

33. Giri Rao, personal communication, 13 December 1996.

34. Anonymous, personal communication, 6 December 1996.

35. Neera and Kundan Singh, personal communication, 14 December 1996.

36. Sarthak Pal, personal communication, 15 December 1996.

37. Manoj Pattanaik, personal communication, 15 December 1996.

38. Pattanaik, personal communication.

39. Kant, Singh, and Singh, *Community Based Forest Management Systems.*

40. Nancy Peluso, *Rich Forests, Poor People* (Berkeley: University of California Press, 1992), 242.

CHAPTER 5. CONSERVATION IN INDONESIA

1. This chapter was written by Claudia D'Andrea.

2. Mark Collins, Jeffrey Sayer, and Timothy Whitmore, *The Conservation Atlas of the Tropical Forests Southeast Asia and the Pacific* (New York: Simon and Schuster, 1991).

3. World Bank Staff, *Indonesia: Kerinci-Seblat Integrated Conservation and Development Project* (Washington, D.C.: World Bank, 1995).

4. Erwin, personal communication, 18 February 1996.

5. Aaron G. Bruner, Raymond E. Gullison, Richard E. Rice, Gustavo A. B. da Fonseca, "Effectiveness of Parks in Protecting Tropical Biodiversity," *Science* 291, no. 5 (2001): 125.

6. Jeffrey Sayer, "Preface," in *World Heritage Forests: World Heritage Convention as a Mechanism for Conserving Tropical Forest Biodiversity*, ed. Center for International Forest Research, UNESCO, and Government of Indonesia (Bogor: CIFOR, 1999), 1.

7. Owen Lynch and Kirk Talbott, *Balancing Acts: Community-Based Forest Management and National Law in Asia and the Pacific* (Washington, D.C.: World Resources Institute, 1995), 1.

8. Lynch and Talbott, *Balancing Acts*, 21–22.

9. Lynch and Talbott, *Balancing Acts*, 112–113.

10. Louise Fortmann, "Locality and Custom: Non-aboriginal Claims to Customary Usufructary Rights as a Source of Rural Protest," *Journal of Rural Studies* 6, no. 2 (1990): 195.

11. Lynch and Talbott, *Balancing Acts*, 40.

12. Mark Poffenberger, ed., *Communities and Forest Management in Southeast Asia: A Regional Profile of the Working Group on Community Involvement in Forest Management* (Gland, Switzerland: IUCN, 1998), 141–142.

13. Peter Ashton, "Towards a Regional Forest Classification for the Humid Tropics of Asia," in *Vegetation Science in Forestry*, ed. E. O. Box et al. (Netherlands: Kluwer Academic Publishers, 1995), 453–464.

14. World Bank Staff, *Indonesia: Kerinci Seblat.*

15. Asmeen Kahn, personal communication, 27 February 1996.

16. Nuhalis Fadhli, personal communication, 2 March 1996.

17. Wawan, personal communication, 2 March 1996.

18. Firdaus, personal communication, 3 March 1996.

19. Damsir, personal communication, 3 March 1996.

20. Damsir, personal communication.

21. Desrizal Alira, personal communication, 4 March 1996.

22. Wun, personal communication, 3 March 1996.

23. Anonymous, personal communication, 5 March 1996.

24. Anonymous, personal communication.

25. Agus Purnomo, personal communication, 8 March 1996.

26. Purnomo, personal communication.

27. Peluso, *Rich Forests, Poor People*, 5.

28. Peluso, *Rich Forests, Poor People*, 238–239.

29. Peluso, *Rich Forests, Poor People*, 238–239.

30. Claudia D'Andrea, "Damar Forest Gardens, Krui District, Indonesia," in *Communities and Forest Management in Southeast Asia: A Regional Profile of the Working Group on Community Involvement in Forest Management*, ed. Mark Poffenberger (Gland, Switzerland: IUCN, 1998), 75.

31. LATIN, *Studi Banding Lampung Barat, Krui, dan Jambi Selatan, Kubu* (Bogor: Lembaga Alam Tropis Indonesia, 1996); and E. Torquebiau, "Man-made Dipterocarp Forest in Sumatra," *Agroforestry Systems* 2 (1984): 107.

32. Poffenberger, *Communities and Forest Management*, 76.

33. Mustafa, personal communication, 31 July 1997.

34. Mustafa, personal communication.

35. Poffenberger, *Communities and Forest Management*, 1.

36. Genevieve Michon and Hubert de Foresta, "The Indonesian Agro-forest

Model." In *Conserving Biodiversity Outside Protected Areas: The Role of Traditional Ecosystems*, ed. P. Halladay and D. A. Gilmour (Gland, Switzerland: IUCN, 1995).

37. Hubert de Foresta and Genevieve Michon, "The Agroforest Alternative to Imperata Grasslands: When Smallholder Agriculture and Forestry Reach Sustainability," *Agroforestry Systems* 36 (1997): 105.

38. David Kaimowitz, "Oil Palm Displaces Forests and Smallholders in Indonesia," CIFOR email news release, 20 April 1998.

39. Mustafa, personal communication.

40. Poffenberger, *Communities and Forest Management*, 78.

41. Abdul Hakim Garuda Nusantara, "Kajian Hukum Surat Keputusan Menteri Kehutanan No. 47 Tentang Kawasan Dengan Tujuan Istimewa," in *Komuniti Forestri: Menguak Evolusi Pemikiran Komuniti Forestri*, ed. Dani Wahyu Munggoro. Seri 1, Tahun 1, March 1998.

42. Margot Cohen, with Murray Hiebert, "Where There's Smoke: Spread of Indonesian Oil-Palm Plantations Fuels the Haze," *Far Eastern Economic Review*, 2 October 1997: 17.

43. Peter Dauvergne, "The Political Economy of Indonesia's 1998 Forest Fire," *Australian Journal of International Affairs*, 52, no. 1: 14.

44. Fred Stolle and Thomas P. Tomich, "The 1997–98 Fire Event in Indonesia," *Nature and Resources* 33, no. 3 (1999): 22.

45. Dauvergne, "The Political Economy of Indonesia's 1998 Forest Fire," 16.

46. Arief Wicaksono, personal communication, 20 July 1999.

47. Stolle and Tomich, "The 1997–98 Fire Event in Indonesia," 23.

48. Stolle and Tomich, "The 1997–98 Fire Event in Indonesia," 29.

49. "Eight-Year Jail Sentence Sought for Bob Hasan," *Jakarta Post*, 19 January 2001, p. 1. See also Christopher M. Barr, "Bob Hasan, the Rise of AP-KINDO, and the Shifting Dynamics of Control in Indonesia's Timber Sector," *Indonesia* 65 (1998).

50. Nilai, personal communication, 12 July 1997.

51. Nonda, personal communication, 12 July 1997.

52. Nilai, personal communication, 24 August 1998.

53. Nonda, personal communication, 24 August 1998.

54. Poffenberger, *Communities and Forest Management*, 81.

CHAPTER 6. AFRICA'S CORNUCOPIA
AND SCORPION

1. The reference was, or course, principally to the North African region that they knew best. In this chapter the Africa that we describe, unless otherwise noted, is its sub-Saharan portion.

2. This chapter was written by Roger D. Stone.

3. Peter Veit, Adolfo Mascarenhas, and Okeyeame Ampadu-Agyei, *"Lessons from the Ground Up: African Development That Works"* (Washington, D.C.: World Resources Institute, 1995), 1.

4. Jennifer Whitaker, *How Can Africa Survive?* (New York: Harper & Row, 1988), 127.

5. Jonathan S. Adams and Thomas O. McShane, *The Myth of Wild Africa* (New York: W. W. Norton, 1992), 239.

6. Chun K. Lai and Asmeen Khan, "Forest Policy in the Sahel," in *Forest Policies, Forest Politics*, ed. Gill Shepherd (London: Overseas Development Institute, 1992), 30.

7. Clement Dorm-Adzobu, Okeyeame Ampadu-Agyel, and Peter G. Veit, *Religious Beliefs and Environmental Protection: The Malshegu Sacred Grove in Northern Ghana* (Nairobi: Center for International Development and Environment, World Resources Institute, 1991).

8. Thomas Pakenham, *The Scramble for Africa* (New York: Random House, 1991); Adam Hochschild, *King Leopold's Ghost* (New York: Houghton Mifflin, 1998).

9. Whitaker, *How Can Africa Survive?* 41.

10. See James Scott, *Seeing Like a State* (New Haven: Yale University Press, 1998), 223.

11. See Paul Richards, *Fighting for the Rainforest: Youth and Resources in Sierra Leone* (Oxford: James Currey, 1996), 164.

12. James Fairhead and Melissa Leach, *Misreading the African Landscape: Society and Ecology in a Forest-Savanna Mosaic* (Cambridge: Cambridge University Press, 1996), 24.

13. Fairhead and Leach, *Misreading the African Landscape*, 24.

14. World Commission on Forests and Sustainable Development, *Our Forests, Our Future* (London: Cambridge University Press, 1999), 9.

15. Data collected from *World Resources 1998–99* (New York: Oxford University Press, 1998), 244.

16. James Fairhead and Melissa Leach, *Reframing Deforestation* (London and New York: Routledge, 1998), xiv.

17. Fairhead and Leach, *Misreading the African Landscape*, 3.

18. Fairhead and Leach, *Misreading the African Landscape*, 267.

19. A full description of this program is to be found in Roger D. Stone's book *The Nature of Development* (New York: Alfred A. Knopf, 1992), 174. Newer information came from a January 2000 interview with project director Dale Lewis, in Washington, D.C.

20. Pippa Bird, personal communication, New York, February 1999.

21. Michael Wells and Katrina Brandon, *People and Parks: Linking Protected Area Management with Local Communities* (Washington, D.C.: The World Bank, 1992), xi.

22. Kojo Sebastian Amanor, *The New Frontier: Farmers' Response to Land Degradation, A West African Study* (London: Zed Books Ltd., 1994), 170.

23. Gill Shepherd, personal communication, April 1998.

24. John Terborgh, "Trouble in Paradise," book review in the *New York Review of Books*, 18 Feb. 1999, p. 33.

25. Elizabeth Wily, *Villagers as Forest Managers and Governments: Learning to Let Go* (London: International Institute for Environment and Development, 1997).

26. Elizabeth Wily, "A Case Study in Collaborative Forest Management," unpublished paper, 1995–1996.

27. Edward Massawe and Gervais Lyimo, "Joint Village Forest Management: The Solution to Save Our Forests," September 1996. Cited in Wily, *Villagers as Forest Managers.*

28. Elizabeth Wily, personal communication, March 1999.

29. Jonathan Otto and Kent Elbow, "Profile of Natural Policy: Natural Forest Management in Niger," in *Natural Connections: Perspectives in Community-Based Conservation*, ed. David Western and R. Michael Wright (Washington, D.C.: Island Press, 1994), 238.

30. Data cited here are from Julia Falconer's study, "Non-timber Forest Products in Southern Ghana," a summary report published in London in 1992 by the Overseas Development Agency, the predecessor to the current DFID.

31. This citation, and much of the information in this summary of changing forest use in Ghana, comes from *Falling Into Place*, a summary report written by six Ghanaian authors—Nii Ashey Kotey, Johnny Francois, J. G. K. Owusu, Raphael Yeboah, Kojo S. Amanor, and Lawrence Antwi—and published in London 1998 by the International Institute for Environment and Development; see p. 9.

32. Kotey et al., *Falling Into Place*, 49.

33. Shepherd, personal communication.

34. Pippa Bird, personal communication, New York, February 1999.

35. David Western, "Vision of the Future: The New Focus of Conservation," in *Natural Connections: Perspectives in Community-Based Conservation*, ed. David Western and R. Michael Wright (Washington, D.C.: Island Press, 1994), 549.

CHAPTER 7. LEARNING FROM LATIN AMERICA

1. Roger D. Stone's book *Dreams of Amazonia* (New York: Viking Press, 1985; New York: Penguin Books, 1986, 1993) provides a succinct overview of how Brazilian and international policies failed environmentally and in large part economically during those years.

2. Barbara J. Bramble and Gareth Porter, "NGOs and the Making of U.S. Policy," in *The International Politics of the Environment*, ed. Andrew and Benedict Kingsbury (New York: Oxford University Press, 1992), 328.

3. The figures were published in the World Resources Institute's *World Resources 1990–91* (Washington, D.C.: World Resources Institute, 1990), 345.

4. "The G7 Pilot Program and Brazil's Forests: The End of the Illusion and the Hour of Truth," unpublished paper written and signed by the National Council of Rubber Tappers, the Amazon Working Group (GTA), the Coordinating Body of the Indigenous Organizations of the Brazilian Amazon, the Confederation of Agricultural Workers, and the Brazilian Network on Multilateral Financial Institutions, March 1999, p. 2.

5. PPG7, *The Pilot Program to Conserve the Brazilian Rain Forest* (Washington, D.C.: PPG7, 1998), 27. This publication, as well as periodic *Pilot Program Update* newsletters, are the sources for much of the data used in this section of our work.

6. *Pilot Program Update* 6, no. 2 (1998): 2.

7. Stephan Schwartzman, personal communication, Washington, D.C., March 1999.

8. *The PD/A: A Contribution for the Intelligent Use of Tropical Forests* (Brasília: Ministerio do Meio Ambiente, dos Recursos Hídricos e da Amazônia Legal, 1998), 16.

9. Ans Kolk, "From Conflict to Cooperation: International Policies to Protect the Brazilian Amazon," *World Development* 26, no. 8 (1998): 1489.

10. "Lago Mamirauá Ecological Reserve Project," project memorandum (London: Overseas Development Agency, 1992), 10.

11. *Mamirauá Ecological Station Management Plan* (Tefé: Sociedade Civil Mamirauá, 1996), 38.

12. *Mamirauá Ecological Station Management Plan*, 38.

13. Isabel Braga, personal communication, March 1999.

14. Christopher Uhl, personal communication, September 1997.

15. Amado Olivera V., "Forestry Project of the Indigenous Chiquitano Communities of Lomerio," unpublished report, 1996.

16. Olivera V., "Forestry Project."

17. Bob Simeone, personal communication, 1999.

18. Zolezzi made a presentation on the Lomerio project at a forum on community involvement in forest management that was organized by the World Conservation Union (IUCN) on the occasion of the September 1996 meeting in Geneva of the United Nations Intergovernmental Panel on Forests.

19. David Barton Bray, personal communication, July 1997.

20. David Barton Bray, personal communication, January 2001.

21. David Barton Bray, "The Struggle for the Forest: Conservation and Development in the Sierra Juárez," *Grassroots Development* 15, no. 3 (1991), 18.

22. David Barton Bray, "Optimal Arrangements for Sustainability: Mexican Community Forestry and Its Global Significance," draft paper, July 1996.

23. Bray, "Optimal Arrangements for Sustainability."

24. Daniel C. Nepstad et al., *Large Scale Impoverishment of Amazonian Forests by Logging and Fire* (Woods Hole, Mass.: Woods Hole Research Center, 1999), 2.

25. "Support Needed to Protest Increased Logging in Guyana," posting authored by "grbarry@students.wisc.edu" at igc.org/igc/econet, 15 April 1998.

26. Nicholson is quoted in Roger D. Stone, *The Nature of Development* (New York: Alfred A. Knopf, 1992), 61.

27. *The View from Airlie: Community Based Conservation in Perspective* (New York: Liz Claiborne and Art Ortenberg Foundation, 1992), 2.

28. Key foundation supporters of the MDB Campaign, without whose assistance it would not have happened, included the John D. and Catherine T. MacArthur Foundation, the W. Alton Jones Foundation, the C. S. Mott Foundation, and the Moriah Foundation. More recently the Wallace Global Fund joined in.

29. Lisa Fernandez, *Private Conservation Groups on the Rise in Latin America and the Caribbean*, World Wildlife Fund Letter No. 1 (Washington, D.C.: World Wildlife Fund, 1989), 2.

30. Lisa Fernandez, "Private Conservation Groups on the Rise in Latin America and the Caribbean," *WWF Letter*, 1989, no. 1, p. 2.

31. Russell Mittermeier, personal communication, September 1998.

32. Charles A. Reilly, "Complementing States and Markets: The Inter-American Development Bank and Civil Society," paper presented to the North-South Center Conference on "Multilateral Approaches to Peacemaking and Democratization in the Hemisphere," Miami, April 1996.

33. Aaron Zazueta, *Environmental Challenges in Latin America: Building Organizational Capacities* (Washington, D.C.: World Resources Institute's Center for International Development and Environment, 1994).

34. Stephan Schwartzman, personal communication, May 1999.

CHAPTER 8. SHIFTING THE BALANCE

1. The chapter was written by Roger D. Stone.

2. Miguel Angel Rodriguez, remarks to the Council on Foreign Relations, Washington, D.C., 2 October 1998.

3. Owen J. Lynch and Janis B. Alcorn, "Tenurial Rights and Community-based Conservation," in *Natural Connections: Perspectives in Community-Based Conservation*, ed. David Western and R. Michael Wright (Washington, D.C.: Island Press, 1994), 373.

4. Garrett Hardin, "The Tragedy of the Commons," *Science* 162 (1968).

5. Gill Shepherd, "The Reality of the Commons: Answering Hardin from Somalia," in *Forest Policies, Forest Politics*, ed. Gill Shepherd (London: Overseas Development Institute, 1992), 74.

6. Ricardo Carrere and Larry Lohmann, *Pulping the South: Industrial Tree Plantations and The World Paper Economy* (London: Zed Books Ltd., 1996), 144.

7. Claude Gascon Rita Mesquita, and Niro Higuchi, letter to *Science* 281, 4 Sept. 1998.

8. Gascon, Mesquita, and Higuchi, letter to *Science*.

9. Pamela Stedman-Edwards, Pamela Hathaway, Konrad von Moltke, and Gonzalo Castro, *The Private Sector in Latin America: Implications for the Environment and Sustainable Development* (Washington, D.C.: World Wildlife Fund, 1997), 49.

10. Ian A. Bowles, R. E. Rice, R. A. Mittermeier, and G. A. B. da Fonseca, "Logging and Tropical Forest Conservation," *Science* 280, 19 June 1998.

11. Bowles, Rice, Mittermeier, and da Fonseca, "Logging and Tropical Forest Conservation."

12. Russell Mittermeier, personal communication, September 1998.

13. John Spears, "Global Vision Research Project Briefing Paper for the Project Steering Committee," unpublished paper, 2000, p. 3; John Spears, personal communication, January 2000.

CHAPTER 9. HELPING FROM AFAR

1. The largest national chapter of the organization, that of the United States, calls itself the World Wildlife Fund, as the entire worldwide movement was once titled. It refused to go along when Prince Philip of the United Kingdom, as chairman of the international organization, insisted on shifting to the cumbersome new name. Both groups use the WWF acronym and conduct joint activities in many places.

2. World Commission on Environment and Development, *Our Common Future* (Oxford: Oxford University Press, 1987).

3. *World Commission on Forests and Sustainable Development: Proposed Work Program* (Woods Hole, Mass.: Woods Hole Research Center, 1995), 21.

4. Manuel Rodriguez Becerra, personal communication, October 1997.

5. World Commission on Forests and Sustainable Development, *Our Forests, Our Future* (Cambridge: Cambridge University Press, 1999), 58.

6. World Commission on Forests and Sustainable Development, *Our Forests, Our Future*, 76.

7. Wolfensohn is cited in *Environment Matters,* a World Bank periodical, summer 1996, p. 18.

8. D. A. Gilmour and R. J. Fischer, "Evolution in Community Forestry: Contesting Forest Resources," in *Community Forestry at a Crossroads,* RE-COFTC Report No. 16 (Bangkok: Regional Community Forestry Training Center, 1998), 30.

9. World Bank, *The Forest Sector* (Washington, D.C.: World Bank, 1991), 19.

10. World Bank, "Review of Implementation of the Forest Sector Policy," unpublished paper (Washington, D.C.: World Bank, 1994), ix.

11. World Bank, "Initiating Memorandum for the Forest Policy Implementation Review and Strategy," unpublished paper (Washington, D.C.: World Bank, 1998), 2 and 4.

12. Gregor Hodgson and John A. Dixon, *Logging versus Fisheries and Tourism in Palawan: An Environmental and Economic Analysis* (Honolulu: East-West Center, 1988).

13. Kenneth M. Chomitz and Kanta Kumari, "The Domestic Benefits of Tropical Forests: A Critical Review," *Research Observer* 13, no. 1 (1998): 20 and 28.

14. Interview in "Kings of the Jungle," a 1998 BBC World News documentary.

15. World Bank Operations Evaluation Department, "Forests and the World Bank: An OED Review," unpublished paper, 1998.

16. World Bank Operations Evaluation Department, *A Review of the World Bank's 1991 Forest Policy and Its Implementation,* preliminary report (Washington, D.C.: World Bank Operations Evaluation Division, 1999), xi.

17. Bhuvan Batnagar, "Participatory Poverty Assessment in the People's Republic of China," *ADB Review* 30, no. 2 (1998).

18. OECD Development Assistance Committee, *Development Cooperation 1997* (Paris: Organization for Cooperation and Development, 1998), 17.

19. Korinna Horta, *Band-Aid for a Battered Planet: Evaluating the Global Environment Facility* (New York: Environmental Defense Fund, 1998).

20. Gareth Porter, Raymond Clemenson, Waafis Ofosu-Amaah, and Michael Philips, *Study of the GEF's Overall Performance* (Washington, D.C.: Global Environment Facility, 1998).

21. Thomas C. Lovejoy, personal communication, December 1998.

22. Nigel Sizer, "Forests Can be Saved Only By Communities, Not By Treaties," op-ed article, *The Guardian*, 16 Feb. 2000.

CHAPTER 10. FUTURE IMPERATIVES

1. Jesse H. Ausubel, "Five Worthy Ways to Spend Large Amounts of Money for Research on Environment and Resources," address to the San Diego Science and Technology Council, La Jolla, Calif., 9 December 1998.

2. Jesse H. Ausubel, remarks made at the meeting of the Council on Foreign Relations, Washington, D.C., 20–21 January 2000.

3. George M. Woodwell, "Whither the Public Interest?," unpublished submission to the World Commission on Forests and Sustainable Development, 1997, p. 3.

4. Report posted at www.maineenvironment.org/nwoods, 1 November 2000.

5. Sten Nilsson, *Do We Have Enough Forests?* Occasional Paper No. 5 (Laxenburg, Austria: International Institute for Applied Systems Analysis, 1996), 12.

6. Gary Bull, "Macro Trends in Fibre Supply," unpublished paper prepared for the Council on Foreign Relations, 1999, p. 5.

7. Nigel Sizer, with Lars Laestadius, Marta Miranda, and Michael Totten, "Drawing the Line? Toward a New Policy Agenda for the World's Forests," unpublished draft issues paper for the World Resources Institute, 1999, p. 15.

8. Tashi Wangchuck, personal communication, May 1999.

9. Neil Byron, "International Development Assistance in Forestry and Land Management," draft paper, undated.

10. J. E. M. Arnold, personal communication, November 1996.

11. Pippa Bird, personal communication, February 1999.

12. Bird, personal communication.

13. Donald A. Gilmour and Mahda Sarin, statements made during sessions of the seminar "Community Forestry at a Crossroads," Bangkok, July 1997.

14. Gill Shepherd, *Forest Policies, Forest Politics* (London: Overseas Development Institute, 1992), 8.

15. Data presented by Om Pradhan, Bhutan's ambassador to the United Nations, at the Mountainfilm festival, Telluride, Colorado, May 1999.

FURTHER READING

Foresters, economists, sociologists, anthropologists, geographers, journalists, and all manner of students and professors have tried their hand at studying the dynamics of local and indigenous communities in forest settings. Between the covers of this volume is evidence that participation works. Why and how it works remains something of a mystery, and how to arrange for it to work better still is a formidable challenge. What follows, culled from a vast library of offerings, is an annotated selection of works that all cast useful light on the matter.

J. E. M. Arnold, of Oxford University, is author or co-author of many studies of community forestry. See *Managing Forests as Common Property* (London: Overseas Development Institute, 1997) for thumbnail sketches of how well or poorly governments of key countries have fared in their efforts to support or encourage community forestry initiatives.

William C. Ascher's *Communities and Sustainable Forestry in Developing Countries* (San Francisco: Institute for Contemporary Studies Press, 1995) was prime reading for us as we began our research and is highly recommended. The book does not compare community empowerment with other ways to protect forests, but the author, a professor of public policy, does outline a set of "basic design principles for community forestry management," which are drawn from his extensive experience, especially in Latin America.

David Barton Bray spent many years as Mexico representative for the Inter-American Foundation before he assumed his present position as dean of environmental studies at Florida International University. Among the many articles he has written on Mexican community forestry, a good overview is "Peasant Organizations and the Permanent Reconstruction of Nature: Grassroots Sustainable Development in Rural Mexico," *Journal of Environment & Development* 4, no. 2 (1995): 185–204.

Plundering Paradise: The Struggle for the Environment in the Philippines (Berkeley: University of California Press, 1993), by Robin Broad with John Cavanaugh, is not just about forests. Illegal and grossly unsustainable forms of logging, which result in miseries for countless villagers, play a central role in this absorbing tale of environmental mismanagement.

Neil Byron, who has held various academic and government positions in Australia and at the Center for International Forestry Research (CIFOR) in Bogor, Indonesia, has written with caustic wisdom about the forces that bear on tropical forest peoples. He and co-author J. E. M. Arnold relate the specifics of their dependence to the likelihood of government actions to benefit them in "What Futures for the People of the Tropical Forests?" *World Development* 27, no. 5 (1999): 789–805.

Rural Development: Putting the Last First, by Robert Chambers (New York: Longman Scientific and Technical, 1983), is a classic plea for local community empowerment as a means of bringing about more equitable societies in developing countries. Although Chambers devotes greater attention to farms than to forests, his pioneering analysis has stood up well. A more targeted work, by Chambers, with N. C. Saxena and Tushaan Shah as co-authors, is *To the Hands of the Poor: Water and Trees* (Boulder: Westview Press, 1989).

There is no more eloquent a general treatise on the qualities and importance of sustainable development than *For the Common Good* (Boston: Beacon Press, 1989, 1994), written by environmental economist Herman E. Daly and theologian John B. Cobb Jr. Key in the authors' thinking is the need to redefine economics, in large measure for the sake of advancing communities, and communities of communities.

Our Africa chapter relies heavily on the insights of James Fairhead and Melissa Leach about misguided colonial and post-colonial forest management efforts in several countries. In addition to her co-authorship of the benchmark work *Misreading the African Landscape*, Leach co-edited (with Robin Mearns) a volume of essays published by the International African Institute in London in

1996. Its title—*The Lie of the Land: Challenging Received Wisdom on the African Environment*—needs no amplification.

Robert J. Fisher and Donald A. Gilmour's "Putting the Community at the Center of Community Forestry Research" was prepared for the seminar "Research Policy for Community Forestry" at the Bangkok Regional Community Forestry Training Centre, Kasetsart University, Bangkok, Thailand, July 1990. The authors find that the major obstacles to the successful implementation of community forestry are social (specifically institutional and organizational) rather than technical. Fisher and Gilmour argue that research should focus on implementation of community forestry and attempt to resolve those social—that is, human—problems. Community forestry calls for village users to be the forest managers and to be at the center of all research activities including problem identification, research action, on-site adaptation of solutions, and evaluation. They point out that this sort of research requires genuine interdisciplinary cooperation between specialists and a revamping of current research methodology.

Louise Fortmann and John W. Bruce edited the well-known *Whose Trees? Proprietary Dimensions of Forestry* (Boulder: Westview Press, 1988). This volume was derived from work at the Land Tenure Center (University of Wisconsin, Madison) and ICRAF (Nairobi, Kenya) to identify, review, and annotate the literature on rights to trees and land with trees and the impact of those rights on planting and conservation of trees. The book begins with an essay on why tree and land tenure matter and concludes with a discussion of the "daily struggle" for tree rights. In chapters 2 through 8, the authors provide excerpts and whole works from thirty-nine sources worldwide; each piece begins with a short annotation. The topics are tree tenure, tree and tenure interactions, communities and trees, tenure and deforestation, tenure and afforestation, the gender division of tenure, and the state and the forest. A more recent work by Bruce, *Legal Bases for the Management of Forest Resources as Common Property*, was published in 1997 by the Forests, Trees, and People program of the Food and Agriculture Organization of the United Nations. Also of interest is *Common Forest Resource Management: Annotated Bibliography of Asia, Africa, and Latin America*, a volume of essays edited by D. Messerschmidt (Rome: U.N. Food and Agriculture Organization, 1993).

Another useful analysis of property issues is the essay by C. J. N. Gibbs and

D. W. Bromley, "Institutional Arrangements for Sustainable Management of Rural Resources: Common Property Regimes and Conservation," in *Common Property Resources: Ecology and Community-Based Sustainable Development*, edited by Fikret Birkes (London: Belhaven Press, 1986). The authors first define *resources* and *property*, then discuss the characteristics, functions, and performance of common property regimes. They argue that understanding and respecting customary rules and conventions for the management of resources as common property must increase. These arrangements are of special interest to conservationists because they have provided access to resources equitably and sustainably at reasonable cost. The essay concludes by relating institutional arrangements to the depletion of renewable resources and arguing for institutional innovation for the future without losing sight of the past.

In "The Tragedy of the Commons," published in *Science* 162 (1968): 1243–1248, Garrett Hardin sets forth a scenario based on a nineteenth-century model of overgrazing in a common pastureland whereby a pervasive free-rider mentality leads to privatizing the lands as the only rational solution. This misleading narrative has become codified in the dogma of free-market economics as demonstrating the implausibility of developing successful systems for managing common property. Nonetheless, this story remains prominent in the literature as a warning that access to common property requires governance.

No one thought more sensitively about the talents and deprivations of indigenous and forest-dwelling communities and their relationship to the broader society than the French anthropologist Claude Lévi-Strauss. *Tristes Tropiques*, the author's masterful tale of his journey into the heart of Brazil, should be a prerequisite for any study in the field. First published in Paris in 1955, the book's English language version was published by Athenaeum Publishers in 1974. The paperback edition was issued by Penguin Books in 1992.

Owen Lynch and Kirk Talbott have provided an excellent summary of the problem in Asia and the Pacific of overlapping legal rights in *Balancing Acts: Community-Based Forest Management and National Law in Asia and the Pacific* (Washington, D.C.: World Resources Institute, 1995). The book offers key insights into policy solutions for the recognition of customary property rights of indigenous and tribal peoples and assesses the legal complexities more succinctly than does any other book on the topic. The authors' work was drawn from extensive fieldwork and contacts in the region. Lynch's lengthy experience in the Philippines and Talbott's experience in Nepal make them uniquely suited to craft a well-honed document. The book is in many ways the result of much collaboration with local partners.

In *The Question of Commons: The Culture and Ecology of Communal Resources* (Tucson: University of Arizona Press, 1990), editors B. I. McCay and J. M. Acheson assembled writings that succinctly summarize Garrett Hardin's argument: "According to the theory popularized by Hardin, all resources owned in common are, or eventually will be, overexploited. When resources such as trees are 'free' or open to everyone, costs arising from their use and abuse can be passed on to others. The rational individual has the incentive to take as much as possible before someone else does. No one is motivated to take responsibility for the resources. Because they belong to everyone, no one protects them. The causes of overpopulation, environmental degradation, resource depletion may be found in freedom and equality." The book's authors go on to deflate Hardin with overwhelming contrary evidence that resources can be and are managed communally in many places. Fellow students in Louise Fortmann's common property seminar at the University of California, Berkeley, referred to this edited volume as the "yellow pages" of common property. A powerful set of edited contributions help to clarify the complexity and sophistication of common property management systems of many different kinds of resources.

In *Governing the Commons: The Evolution of Institutions for Collective Action* (Cambridge: Cambridge University Press, 1990), Elinor Ostrom analyzes three influential and widely used models: the tragedy of the commons, the prisoner's dilemma game, and the logic of collective action. The author shows that these models, although pervasive, are dangerous because they are assumed to be fixed unless external authorities change them: "As long as individuals are viewed as prisoners, policy prescription will address this metaphor." Ostrom's main point is that empirically reality, particularly with regard to common property resources, is fluid and dynamic and that models must address multiple levels of analysis to be effective. The author offers a framework for analysis of common property resources (CPRs). This book has revolutionized the way that CPRs are discussed because the author so successfully translates the CPR concepts into the language of the models in order to refute them with specific concrete realities. Ostrom's design principles have become an essential feature of analyzing institutional change in relation to CPRs.

Nancy Peluso analyzes the dilemma of Indonesia's densely populated Java, where overlapping customary and state claims on forest land have frequently resulted in violent conflicts, in *Rich Forests Poor People: Resource Control and Resistance in Java* (Berkeley: University of California Press, 1995). The author provides a combination of field-based ethnography and historical analysis to develop insights into the understanding of forest-based conflicts. Peluso's excellent study theorizes this familiar problem of conflict over resources in creative new ways, offering an explanation of power and the Indonesian state while also developing a sophisticated picture of the everyday social practices and political economy of forest resource management. Moreover, the study offers a broader understanding of the processes of ecological deterioration and social change by contextualizing the problems in hierarchical levels of analysis. Peluso forged a new direction in political ecology with this work. She also opened a way to use field-based studies to provide policy direction and recommendations. Implicit in this work is the author's brilliant grasp of the complexities of tenure and property relations.

A Forest Journey: The Role of Wood in the Development of Civilizations (Cambridge, Mass.: Harvard University Press, 1989), by John Perlin, is an enlightening and highly readable romp across time and space.

For more than a quarter of a century Mark Poffenberger has been advocating the advancement of community forestry in Asia in his myriad roles as foundation program officer, social scientist, networker, and policy gadfly. The many publications issued by his Asia Forest Network detail strategies and accomplishments in individual nations in the region. A summary of the trend toward community empowerment and its importance is presented in "Hidden Faces in the Forest: A Twenty First Century Challenge for Tropical Asia," *SAIS Review* 26, no. 1 (1996), co-authored by Poffenberger and Roger D. Stone. Most frequently cited of Poffenberger's works is *Keepers of the Forest: Land Management Alternatives in Southeast Asia*, co-written with Betsy McGean (West Hartford, Conn.: Kumarian Press, 1989).

From her base in London Gill Shepherd has for many years studied the evolution of social and community forestry endeavors in Africa, debunking many icons of conventional wisdom. Among Shepherd's many works is *Forest Policies, Forest Politics* (London: Overseas Development Institute, 1992), a volume of essays that she edited. The book concludes with her essay, "The Reality of the Commons," which offers strong counter to Hardin's famous essay. "The real tragedy," she writes, "comes when the commons are thrown open and unrestricted exploitation allowed" (p. 74).

Several chapters in *Natural Connections: Perspectives in Community-based Conservation* (Washington, D.C.: Island Press, 1994), edited by David Western and R. Michael Wright, highlight forest management issues. Although this book focuses more on biodiversity conservation than on human development, it is widely cited and praised. Within the book are contributions from several prominent analysts including Frances Seymour, John G. Robinson, Kent G. Redford, and Fabio Feldmann.

In addition to these contributions from individuals, we should finally note the consistent output from several concerned institutions.

The analysts working for the World Resources Institute (WRI) in Washington, D.C., published a steady flow of useful long essays in the 1990s. Among these are *Breaking the Logjam* (1994), about forest policy reform in the United States and Indonesia; *Lessons from the Ground Up* (1995), about African development that works; *Back to the Wall in Suriname* (1995), about forest policy there; *Profit Without Plunder* (1996), about how Guyana might best profit from its rich forest resources; and *The Last Frontier Forests* (1997), about alarming rates of forest shrinkage in remote places. Newer publications, many issued under the auspices of WRI's Global Forest Watch program, review forest policy and practice in Venezuela, Gabon, and Cameroon and at the World Bank. A full listing of WRI publications is available at the organization's website, www.wri.org.

The Switzerland-based World Conservation Union's Working Group on Community Involvement in Forest Management has also published a number of useful studies, beginning with its 1996 overview, *Communities and Forest Management*. Since then it has issued a lengthening list of handsomely produced regional studies covering Southeast Asia, Africa, and other principal tropical forest locations. The organization's website is www.iucn.org.

Although not known for its concentration on international environmental issues, the Council on Foreign Relations recently conducted two initiatives that bear on the question of forests. One of these, organized in partnership with the World Wildlife Fund and the World Bank, sought to define a "vision" for the world's forests as of the year 2050, especially the emerging role of plantation forestry. A council study group convened for 1999–2000 sought also to define technology solutions to global warming. David Victor, science and technology senior fellow, played key roles in both these efforts. The organization's website is www.cfr.org

For all the criticism that has been leveled at it, and for all its continuing shortcomings, the World Bank has also continued to produce an inexhaustible flow of information about itself and its projects. A trip to its website, www.worldbank.org, can be lengthy and absorbing.

A principal research effort at the International Institute for Environment and Development in London has sought to identify policy that works for forests and people. At last count, this program listed thirteen country studies and other pertinent publications. The organization's website is www.iied.org.

We end by reiterating our admiration for the continuing work of the Regional Community Forestry Training Center at Kasetsart University in Bangkok, another indefatigable supplier of important documentation whose efforts in Asia, as we say in our text, merit replication elsewhere. The organization's website is www.recoftc.org.

INDEX

Page numbers in italic refer to illustrations.

Tribals (non-Hindu Indians) *(continued)*
separate compounds of, 110; with
village bank, 98–99
Troeng, Sebastian, 217
Tropical Forest Action Plan, 48
Tropical forests: Africa's traditional
protection of, 157–58, 164, 178; biological diversity of, 27–28; commodity view of, 41–43; deforestation statistics on, 15; enforcement problems
in, 45; logging operations in, 35–36,
37–40; nutrient system of, 24–25;
populations dependent on, 1, 29–31,
32, 33, 198; projected demands on,
264–65, 266; road access to, 41. *See
also* Deforestation
Turtles (Tortuguero, Costa Rica), 215–
17, 219–22
Tzotzil (Oaxaca and Chiapas), 36–37

Uganda, 177
Uhl, Christian, 193–94
Ullsten, Ola, 239
U.N. Commission on Sustainable De-
velopment, 49
U.N. Development Program, 258
U.N. Environment Program, 258
U.N. Food and Agriculture Organi-
zation (FAO), 4, 48, 65, 161, 255,
256
U.N. Intergovernmental Forum on
Forests, 4–5, 237
United States: foreign aid policy of,
250; on global forests convention,
49, 237–38; NGOs from, 257–58;
Philippine logging operations of, 64–
65, 66
U.S. Agency for International De-
velopment (USAID), 75, 250–51,
257
Upper Nan Watershed Irrigation Proj-
ect, 53–54
Uraivan Tam-Kim-Yong, 54–55
Urban populations, 32, 271–72

USAID (U.S. Agency for International
Development), 75, 250–51, 257
Uttar Pradesh (Himalayas), 84

Várzea fertile zone, 189
Vasundhara Institute (Orissa), 100, 108–
9
Venezuelan National Guard, 36
Visayas (Philippines), 65–66

Wa-Iraqw tribe (Tanzania), 31–32
WALHI (Indonesian Environmental
Forum), 121, 268
Wallace, Alfred Russel, 206
Wallace Global Fund, 288n28
Walpole, Peter, 67, 76, 78; and
D'Andrea in Bendum, 62–63, 71–72;
background of, 61–62; and Bendum
project, 69, 70–71
W. Alton Jones Foundation, 288n28
Wangchuck, Tashi, 267
WARSI (Jambi, Sumatra), 130
Water goddess (Bajarkot village), 111
Water supplies: in Africa, 154, 155; and
siltation, 23–24
Wawan, Pak, 131–33
WCED (World Commission on Envi-
ronment and Development), 33–34,
85, 239
WCFSD. *See* World Commission on
Forests and Sustainable Develop-
ment
WCMC (World Conservation Moni-
toring Centre), 162
Wells, Michael, 168–69
West Africa, 7–8, 158, 162–64, 177
West Bengal, 84
Western, David, 178, 272
Westoby, Jack, 65
Weyerhaeuser, 66
Whitaker, Jennifer, 160
Wildlands and Human Needs, 207, 257
Wildlife, 27–28, 165–66, 169–70
Wilson, Edward O., 28

Cartographer: Bill Nelson
Indexer: Patricia Deminna
Compositor: Binghamton Valley Composition, LLC
Text: Janson 10/15
Display: Janson
Printer and binder: Maple-Vail Manufacturing Group